EXPLORING URBAN YOUTH CULTURE OUTSIDE OF THE GANG PARADIGM

Critical Questions of Youth, Gender and Race On-Road

Edited by
Jade Levell, Tara Young and Rod Earle

With a Foreword by
Claudia Bernard

First published in Great Britain in 2025 by

Bristol University Press
University of Bristol
1-9 Old Park Hill
Bristol
BS2 8BB
UK
t: +44 (0)117 374 6645
e: bup-info@bristol.ac.uk

Details of international sales and distribution partners are available at bristoluniversitypress.co.uk

© Bristol University Press 2025

British Library Cataloguing in Publication Data
A catalogue record for this book is available from the British Library

ISBN 978-1-5292-2557-0 hardcover
ISBN 978-1-5292-2558-7 paperback
ISBN 978-1-5292-2559-4 ePub
ISBN 978-1-5292-2560-0 ePdf

The right of Jade Levell, Tara Young and Rod Earle to be identified as editors of this work has been asserted by them in accordance with the Copyright, Designs and Patents Act 1988.

All rights reserved: no part of this publication may be reproduced, stored in a retrieval system, or transmitted in any form or by any means, electronic, mechanical, photocopying, recording, or otherwise without the prior permission of Bristol University Press.

Every reasonable effort has been made to obtain permission to reproduce copyrighted material. If, however, anyone knows of an oversight, please contact the publisher.

The statements and opinions contained within this publication are solely those of the editors and contributors and not of the University of Bristol or Bristol University Press. The University of Bristol and Bristol University Press disclaim responsibility for any injury to persons or property resulting from any material published in this publication.

Bristol University Press works to counter discrimination on grounds of gender, race, disability, age and sexuality.

Cover design: Andrew Corbett
Front cover image: Getty/ beastfromeast

Contents

Notes on Contributors		v
Foreword		viii
Claudia Bernard		
Preface		xi
Jade Levell, Tara Young and Rod Earle		
1	Introduction: Youth and On-Road – Making Gender and Race Matter	1
	Jade Levell, Tara Young and Rod Earle	
2	Black, British Young Women On-Road: Intersections of Gender, Race and Youth in British Interwar Youth Penal Reform	20
	Esmorie Miller	
3	Tainted Love: Intimate Relationships and Gendered Violence On-Road	39
	Yusef Bakkali and Ezimma Chigbo	
4	(The) Trouble with Friends: Narrative Stories of Friendship and Violence On-Road	59
	Tara Young	
5	The Sexual Politics of Masculinity and Vulnerability On-Road: Gender, Race and Male Victimisation	81
	Jade Levell	
6	The Road, in Court: How UK Drill Music Became a Criminal Offence	100
	Lambros Fatsis	
7	On-Road Inside: Music as a Site of Carceral Convergence	115
	Chris Waller	
8	*Jeta e Rrugës*: Translocal On-Road Hustle, Within and from Albania	134
	Jade Levell and Stephanie Schwandner-Sievers	

9	'He's shown me the road': Role Model and Roadman *Peter Harris*	155
10	Diary of an On-Road Criminologist: An Auto-Ethnographic Reflection *Martin Glynn*	170
11	Conclusions, Compromises and Continuing Conversations *Jade Levell, Tara Young and Rod Earle*	186

| Index | 201 |

Notes on Contributors

Yusef Bakkali is a Legacy In Action Fellow at the Stephen Lawrence Research Centre, De Montfort University. Growing up in Brixton, South London, Dr Bakkali became aware of injustice and inequality operating in society. As he traversed education, and later academia, Yusef found sociology could equip him with a language to diagnose and challenge social problems affecting himself and the community. Consequently, Dr Bakkali has developed a research and teaching praxis focused on social justice and change. He hopes to encourage students to develop critical skills, developing fresh perspectives to aid them in tackling the challenges, both of today and the future.

Ezimma Chigbo is a writer and creative facilitator with a background in youth work. She specialises in working with young women involved in the criminal justice system using drama, discussion and creative writing to explore difficult topics. Her main interests are race, gender and serious youth violence which she explores through poetry, prose and articles. Ezimma delivers anti-racism, collective care and wellbeing trainings to third sector organisations. She is the co-host of *The Echo Chamber* podcast and has written on a range of topics that serve as love letters of exploration, celebrating upbringing, culture and identity.

Rod Earle is Senior Lecturer in Youth Justice in the School of Health, Wellbeing and Social Care at The Open University. He has worked as a printer and a youth social worker. He writes mostly about convict criminology, race and racism. He is one of the founding members of British Convict Criminology and has published a monograph on this topic in 2016; *Convict Criminology: Inside and Out*. He has also co-edited *Degrees of Freedom: Prison Education at The Open University* (with James Mehigan, 2019) as well as co-edited handbooks, including *The Palgrave Handbook of Prison Ethnography* (2015) and the *Youth Justice Handbook: Theory, Policy and Practice* (2009).

Lambros Fatsis is Senior Lecturer in Criminology at the University of Brighton. His main research interests revolve around police racism and the criminalisation of Black music subcultures fusing Cultural Criminology with Black radical thought. He has published books including *Policing the Pandemic* (co-authored with Melayna Lamb, 2021) and *The Public and Their Platforms* (co-authored with Mark Carrigan, 2021). When he doesn't teach or write, he continues to exist as a never-recovering vinyl junkie and purveyor of Afro-Caribbean music and UK soundsystem culture.

Martin Glynn is Lecturer in Criminology at Birmingham City University. Dr Martin Glynn is a criminologist and Winston Churchill Fellow with over 35 years' experience of working in criminal justice, public health, and educational settings. He a researcher-writer in residence at the National Justice Museum. Published works include: *Black Men, Invisibility, and Desistance from Crime: Towards a Critical Race Theory from Crime* (2014), *Speaking Data and Telling Stories: Data Verbalization for Researchers* (2019), *Reimagining Black Art and Criminology: A New Criminological Imagination* (2021) and *Invisible Voices: The Black Presence in Crime and Punishment in the UK, 1750–1900* (2023).

Peter Harris is Senior Lecturer and Course Coordinator for Criminology at Newman University, Birmingham. Dr Harris spent 18 years as a youth worker and then as a senior manager for a children's charity before entering higher education in 2010. In 2012 he co-led a multinational research project examining youth work responses to youth violence, the findings of which became a book entitled *Responding to Youth Violence through Youth Work* (2016). He has presented at the British and European Societies for Criminology and Outreach Youth Work conferences in the UK and Scandinavia on youth violence and has published in the area of youth work and youth crime.

Jade Levell is Senior Lecturer in Social & Public Policy (Criminology & Gender Violence) at the University of Bristol. Her research interests include adverse childhood experiences, childhood domestic violence, life on-road for marginalised youth, serious youth violence, masculinity theory, domestic violence and abuse perpetrators, and feminist praxis. Her monograph, *Boys, Childhood Domestic Abuse, and Gang Involvement: Violence at Home, Violence On-Road*, was published in 2022. She has expertise in music elicitation as both a research tool and an innovative way of hearing and connecting with people. Prior to research Jade worked for over a decade in front-line charities supporting survivors of gender-based violence.

Esmorie Miller is an early career Lecturer in Criminology at Lancaster University. She holds a PhD in Political Theory from Queen's University Belfast, where her doctoral research explored restorative justice as a more appropriate logic than retribution, in both principle and practice, for dealing with the racialised youth who have become the normalised subjects of state scrutiny.

Stephanie Schwandner-Sievers is Associate Professor in Applied Anthropology at Bournemouth University. At Bournemouth University she co-directs the university's research centre for 'Seldom Heard Voices: Marginalisation and Societal Integration'. Her ethnographic research and academic consultancy practice among, about and with Albanians in post-socialist Albania, post-conflict Kosovo, and as migrants in translocal contexts, has led to numerous publications focusing on questions such as identity constructions in recourse to contested pasts. More recent publications focus critically on topics such as transitional justice, epistemic justice, policing, and international interventions, corresponding with several participatory arts-based research projects.

Chris Waller is Lecturer in Criminology at London South Bank University. His research looks at the role of music in the daily life of prisoners and his doctoral study involved a quasi-ethnographic study of a men's local prison in the south of England. He is interested material culture, carceral geography and the intersection of the prison with urban culture/space.

Tara Young is Senior Lecturer in Criminal Justice and Criminology at the University of Kent. She focuses on serious violence as it relates to collective offending by young people identified as 'gang associated'. Her research critically examines the manifestation of gangs in England and Wales and criminal justice responses to violent crimes involving young people as victims and perpetrators. Recently Dr Young has examined the disproportionate use of joint enterprise law to prosecute young Black and minoritised men. She is currently critically examining how social media content, in particular music videos and lyrics, is used as evidence by prosecuting counsel, and how friendship, violence and legal awareness relate to collective violence among young people.

Foreword

Claudia Bernard
Goldsmiths, University of London

In *Exploring Urban Youth Culture Outside of the Gang Paradigm: Critical Questions of Youth, Gender and Race On-Road*, editors Levell, Young and Earle usefully offer a deep analysis of the embeddedness of deficit narratives censuring the on-road subculture that frames the everyday lives of racialised and working-class young people. The contributors take a deep dive into the ways in which the marginalised are constructed in youth culture rhetoric and public policy discourses, and question the societal and environmental factors that create and sustain racism and disadvantage. As such, they decipher the cascading effect of structural inequalities to provide a critical analysis of how racially minoritised youths are treated in education and youth services. Indeed, they argue that because racism is so entrenched in our society, inequality and disadvantage play a pivotal role in the growth and development of marginalised youth. In other words, structural and institutional racism, which is endemic to British society and within education, child welfare and youth justice systems, plays a significant role in the problems that bring racially minoritised children to the attention of child welfare and youth justice services and contributes to the significant overrepresentation of Black children in the care system.

I think it is worth considering that by virtue of their disadvantaged racial and socioeconomic backgrounds, Black children and young people are typically under-served, under-supported, intensely surveilled and over-policed (Bernard and Carlile, 2021; Bernard and Harris, 2019). As Johnston and Akay (2022) observe, racially minoritised young people are often criminalised based on their friendship groups, as well as for the music they listen to and where their habits and behaviours are seen as deviant. It is important to restate that assumptions of deviance are habitually made, and that Black children are often perceived as less innocent than White children and somehow less deserving of support and protection (Bernard, 2019). Yet, the realities of racism mean that Black children often experience adultification, and other subtle and unconscious societal and race-based biases that negatively affects the ways they are treated in the child welfare and youth sector (Bernard, 2019). The most shining example to illustrate a growing recognition of the ways adultification manifest in the safeguarding arena is in the case of Child Q, a 15-year-old Black girl with multiple inequalities, who was strip-searched by police officers in her school (UK Parliament, 2022). In short, the key safeguarding partners, namely the police and her school, did her a terrible disservice. We need to recognise and acknowledge how Child Q experienced violence to the spirit and body. To be abundantly clear, it is not surprising that young Black people are deeply mistrustful of those in authority. A more nuanced understanding of the various textures of raced, classed and gendered experiences of racially minoritised children and young people is therefore crucial to make sense of the complex pattern of inequalities, which is why this book is so timely.

With theoretical frameworks grounded in intersectional feminist thinking, critical race inquiry and social constructionism, *Exploring Urban Youth Culture Outside of the Gang Paradigm: Critical Questions of Youth, Gender and Race On-Road* allows a diverse group of established and emerging scholars and practitioners from different disciplines and backgrounds to bring their particular expertise to bear to introduce new theoretical conceptualisations of on-road. Here the authors address a range of critical themes, including locational disadvantage, the racialisation of crime, sexual politics, the criminalisation of drill and grime music, experiences of harm, youth justice, and the commonly accepted racist discourse about Black male masculinity, to engage with issues of extra-familial harms, neighbourhood violence, peer-on-peer violence, and criminal and sexual exploitation. Together, the authors situate racially minoritised young people at the intersectional of gender, race and class and therefore offer insights of on-road to illuminate their lived realities and perspectives. In so doing, they contribute greatly to our understandings of the attitudinal and navigational barriers that compromise the wellbeing of this population of young people, and the importance of using a social harm lens. Importantly, this book platforms issues that bring to the fore the voices and experiences of racially minoritised young people, thus allowing us to understand the compounding effects on young people's resilience, and more specifically, how they resist and circumnavigate the obstacles they have to overcome. Importantly, their analysis of the layered forms of oppression powerfully reminds us that youth support services are presently at a critical point, because of austerity measures and the legacy of the COVID-19 pandemic which has disproportionately impacted Black and minority ethnic communities. Simply stated, there is a tendency to push back on anti-racist thinking and values, and the contributors to this book spell out the issues clearly and do not shy away from difficult questions.

With regards to my own work on young people's voices, as I have argued elsewhere, research that interrogates the impact of trauma as a result of entrenched racism permits us to understand and portray the lived experiences of multiply marginalised young people (Bernard and Carlile, 2021). I posit that probing the sociocultural locations of young people's experiences is a necessary task for research that troubles the waters of youth studies. Therefore, this book is to be welcomed because it disrupts the prevalent perception that racially minoritised young people's lives are not valuable or worthy. Namely, it pays attention to the uncomfortable questions which bring us face-to-face with the ways in which systems of oppression make young people victims of the circumstances of their lives. Indeed, the book engages very well with consideration of risks and vulnerabilities to understand the needs, aspirations and unique struggles of racialised youths. The chapters in this book therefore grab readers' attention and fill a critical gap of knowledge for innovative, reflective interventions and diversionary activities to keep young Black people safe. To be sure, this insightful volume will be required reading for anyone working in the field of youth studies who wants to understand the underlying factors that are necessary to safeguard young people who sit at the crossroads of multiple categories of social difference. The authors should be commended for advancing scholarship that exposes and challenges the habitually pathologising discourse that frames debates of multiply marginalised young people.

References

Bernard, C. (2019) Using an intersectional lens to examine the child sexual exploitation of black adolescents. In J. Pearce (ed) *Child Sexual Exploitation: Why Theory Matters*. Bristol: Policy Press, pp 193–209.

Bernard, C. and Carlile, A. (2021) Black girls navigate the physical and emotional landscape of the neighbourhood: Normalized violence and strategic agency. *Qualitative Social Work*, 20(3): 866–883.

Bernard, C. and Harris, P. (2019) Serious case reviews: The lived experience of black children. *Child & Family Social Work*, 24 (2): 256–263.

Johnston, A. and Akay, L. (2022) *Radical Safeguarding: A Social Justice Workbook for Safeguarding Practitioners*. London: Maslaha.

UK Parliament (2022) Child Q and the law on strip search. *House of Commons Library*, 14 April. Available at: https://commonslibrary.parliament.uk/child-q-and-the-law-on-strip-search/

Preface

Jade Levell, Tara Young and Rod Earle

As this is a book which at the heart is about intersectionality (Crenshaw, 1991), it is impossible not to comment on the process of editing the collection. An edited collections can be viewed as both a process of collaboration gatekeeping, inclusion and exclusion. It is inevitable that a boundary will be drawn between those people approached to contribute and others who were not. In this regard, as editors, we would like to provide readers with a brief explanation of who we approached to collaborate with us on this collection. Further, we will also discuss how feminist praxis guided our thinking. Criminology has long been critiqued for being *malestream* (Bernard, 2013), in that it is androcentric both in its traditional focus on men's lives, and also that masculine patterns are reproduced in the scholars who are deemed to be at the top of the academic scene. Historically this is the academic norm, and it remains true that, despite gains made, 'the highest positions in our professional association are held by men, particularly by White men' (Chesney-Lind, 2020: 407). Although Chesney-Lind writes from experience principally in the US, it is undoubtedly the case that a similar profile exists and there is also a double penalty for women scholars; work by men is given a higher valuation by peers, but also those who publish explicitly feminist work. There have been many studies which have shown that White men are more often ranked higher than women and those from minoritised communities (Chesney-Lind, 2020).

Academic citation practices have also been heavily critiqued by critical race scholars as they can firmly reproduce the niche inner circles of academia and its pervasive Whiteness (Mills, 1997; Anderson, 2022). In the ground-breaking commentary, the *Imperial Scholar* (Delgado, 1984), it was noted the work of many Black scholars fades into insignificance and is not cited by the inner circle: 'It does not matter where one enters this universe; one comes to the same result: an inner circle of about a dozen white, male writers who comment on, take polite issue with, extol, criticize, and expand on each other's ideas. It is something like an elaborate minuet' (Delgado, 1984: 563). Research by Kim and Hawkins (2013: 411) reviewed

20 years of journal data and found that White men were more often ranked as top-cited criminologists (77.1 per cent of the time), which was in stark comparison to White women (12.4 per cent), minority men (1.3 per cent) and minority women (0.7 per cent). These findings highlight the fact that citation and publication is an intersectional issue. Black women are even less often cited, which has led to the ongoing 'Cite Black Women' campaign and collective[1] whose goal it is to '"interrupt" academic conference spaces by pushing people to think reflexively and dialogically about their citational practices'. Friends cite friends, and so it goes on, but those who are more likely to become known as experts in the field and liked is not a neutral process innocent of race and gender dynamics.

In studies that compare women and men's citation scores, it was found that women's work is cited less often, and that is partly due to the fact that women write less (Aksnes et al, 2011). Wold and Wenneras (1997: 342) found that women need to be 'on average 2.5 times as good' to receive a positive review on their work in comparison to their male peers. This is in general, although during the writing of this book the COVID-19 pandemic hit. This was a disaster for many female scholars who were loaded with home-schooling young children and trying to keep up with teaching their students online. Working mothers often had to work increasing hours in order to meet the demands of childcare and the workplace during the lockdown phase of the COVID-19 pandemic (Jessen and Waights, 2020). This could suggest there was a reduction in time available for women and carers to devote to career-advancing activities as core work was prioritised (Augustus, 2021). One study which looked at publication rates between men and women during the pandemic found that the output for women was 17 per cent lower than men's in 2019, and 24 per cent lower in 2020 (Madsen et al, 2022). Significantly, it also took an additional toll on scholars working in the field of violence and abuse, who had to manage the challenges of working with intense subject matter during a global increase in gender-based violence, called the 'shadow pandemic' by the United Nations (UN Women, 2020).

Attempting to create an inclusive collection with women and racially minoritised scholars, who are often less heard in criminology, presented us with some challenges. Our intention was to push back against the tendencies towards an oppressive and exploitative form of social reproduction which repeatedly plays out as part of the status quo in academia. As Debbi Kilroy, Tabitha Lean and Angela Y. Davis (2023) ask, 'What is the use of talking about decolonial scholarship if we do not, in fact, employ, honour and practice it?'. Feminist praxis requires us to apply our principles in action (Ahmed, 2017). This project represents our attempt to honour the practice of decolonial scholarship by producing a book that includes the work of academics from minoritised communities whose research does not emanate from the exclusive (and exclusionary) inner circles. We wanted to produce a collection of work that emphasised the lived experience of marginalised young people and spoke truth to power regardless of the consequences. To do this we carried out a process of reflection, constantly checking back on ourselves and each other to acknowledge our privilege, marginalisation or lack thereof, in an exercise of inclusivity. At points in the process we realised we had overlooked some scholars and tried to rectify the omissions by digging deeper in the field to draw out new and exciting scholarship from a more diverse group. At other times, our attempts to include work by key scholars in the field failed because of a lack of availability.

In order to bring about this edited collection, we felt the need to extend beyond the academy of White scholarship to foreground voices that are less 'malestream', less White, less heard. This involved wrestling with our ingrained tendencies to drift, or be drawn, towards the more well-known names as we realised over time our lists were 'Whitening' and becoming more masculine. As we know, scholarship is still dominated by White men. This is a legacy of traditional university structures and practices which have historically excluded the contributions to literature by women and people from minoritised communities. Our decision not to include some key scholars was not an exercise in neglect, far from it. We admire and respect the research of a great many male and White scholars whose work does not feature in this book. Where they have not directly contributed to the chapters, we have done our best to recognise their contribution to the field by citing their work.

By sharing our thoughts in this preface we wanted to present our explicit recognition of the issue of academic gatekeeping and our reflections on our role within this process. In doing so we wanted to open up a space to explore what is really meant by the pursuit of anti-sexist, anti-racist decolonising academic practice when we edit collections, make boundaries and gatekeep the discipline. To ask ourselves these questions and work on them is an integral part of feminist praxis and a conversation we aim to continue throughout our scholarly careers, no matter how hard or uncomfortable. Thus, we have tried hard to bring together the work of a group of scholars – who write about how gender, race and exclusion intersect in the lives of young people – that are eclectic and ethnically diverse. We are writing this with an uncertainty of the extent to which we achieved our aims. Indeed to see this as a project which can ever be completed would be naive and potentially tokenistic, but rather we see engendering an openness important in the pursuit of greater equality and representation.

Note
[1] https://www.citeblackwomencollective.org

References
Ahmed, S. (2017) *Living a Feminist Life*. Durham, NC: Duke University Press.

Aksnes, D.W., Rorstad, K., Piro, F. and Sivertsen, G. (2011) Are female researchers less cited? A large-scale study of Norwegian scientists. *Journal of the American Society for Information Science and Technology*, 62(4): 628–636.

Anderson, E. (2022) *Black in White Space*. Chicago: University of Chicago Press.

Augustus, J. (2021) The impact of the COVID-19 pandemic on women working in higher education. *Frontiers in Education*, 6(May): 1–4.

Bernard, A. (2013) The intersectional alternative: Explaining female criminality. *Feminist Criminology*, 8(1): 3–19.

Chesney-Lind, M. (2020) Feminist criminology in an era of misogyny. *Criminology*, 58(3): 407–422.

Crenshaw, K.W. (1991) Mapping the margins: Intersectionality, identity politics, and violence against women of colour. *Stanford Law Review*, 43(6): 1241–1299.

Delgado, R. (1984) The imperial scholar: Reflections on a review of civil rights literature. *University of Pennsylvania Law Review*, 132(3): 561–578.

Jessen, J. and Waights, S. (2020) *Effects of COVID-19 Day Care Centre Closures on Parental Time Use: Evidence from Germany*. Available at: https://voxeu.org/article/covid-19-day-care-centre-closures-and-parental-time-use

Kilroy, D., Lean, T. and Davis, A.Y. (2023) Abolition as a decolonial project. In C. Cunneen, A. Deckert, A. Porter, J. Tauri and R. Webb (eds) *The Routledge International Handbook on Decolonizing Justice*. Abingdon: Routledge.

Kim, B. and Hawkins, P.M. (2013) Who's getting cited: Representation of women and non-white scholars in major American criminology and criminal justice journals between 1986–2005. *International Journal of Criminology and Sociology*, 2(0): 306–321.

Madsen, E.B., Nielsen, M.W., Bjørnholm, J., Jagsi, R. and Andersen, J.P. (2022) Author-level data confirm the widening gender gap in publishing rates during COVID-19. *ELife*, 11: 1–15.

Mills, C. (1997) *The Racial Contract*. New York: Cornell University Press.

UN Women (2020) *The Shadow Pandemic: Violence against Women during COVID-19*. Available at: https://www.unwomen.org/en/news/in-focus/in-focus-gender-equality-in-covid-19-response/violence-against-women-during-covid-19

Wold, A. and Wenneras, C. (1997) Nepotism and sexism in peer review. *Nature*, 387: 341–343.

1

Introduction: Youth and On-Road – Making Gender and Race Matter

Jade Levell, Tara Young and Rod Earle

If you've lived or worked in any of England's major cities over the last 25 years and had any contact with young people, you will probably have heard them use the phrase 'on-road' to refer to their experiences. Each of the editors has encountered this phrase and appreciated the uncertain urgencies of its meaning to young people (Earle, 2011; Hallsworth and Young, 2011; Levell, 2019). Our concern has been to listen more closely and explore the meanings evoked in the term 'on-road'. As young people appropriate language to express new meanings they shine a light on the limitations of our existing conceptual lexicon and this book hopes to expand it by attending to what they are feeling and experiencing. 'On-road' tells us of a travelling vitality by invoking familiar and implicit sociological tropes of youthful 'street culture'. It is a creative phrase which accommodates the complexity and fluidity of youthful urban life but, as we argue in this book, even as its use has become widespread among young people, as a concept it has largely escaped sociological scrutiny. In this collection, we gather diverse research on experiences of life on-road that reflects part of the vibrant urban diversity of young working-class people in Britain's multicultural cities. Part of our objective is to disrupt criminological assumptions that stereotype young people's lives as violent, or criminalise or racialise routine aspects of their everyday life, particularly when they are not White. The vernacular use of 'on-road' has become a popular shorthand that refers to the myriad ways that some young people move into and out of home life, school life and income-generating activity of various kinds. It encompasses streets and clubs, pavements and takeaways, social and work life, worklessness, recreation, leisure, boredom, and random ways of making a living.

'On-road' creatively evokes open vistas of a life propelled, going somewhere out there, but in a way that is uncontained; a direction without a destination. Being 'on-road' or, for some young men, becoming a 'roadman', is not the same as being in a gang, or becoming gang affiliated, but each of these conditions are relevant to it by reference or proximate reality. Being 'on-road' is both a state of mind and a way of life. It refers to aspects of the physical reality of a particular street-based subculture and a general way of being. It refers to ontology as well as social practice. For a young person being 'on-road' may encompass gang involvement, or it may not.

Being 'on-road' is a catch-all part of young people's vernacular culture that reflects use of the street as a social space as well as various transactional features of the low-level drug economy and, often, its associated violence. If these aspects of 'on-road' have come to attention our objective is to go further and deeper and include some of what has been left out, such as the way young people find love or fail to, tend intimacies or make music, grow or regress, seek trouble or make peace, lose themselves or find refuges.

It is common for young people to coin their own words and phrases to capture and communicate their reality when adults' words fail to convey the complexities of their lived experiences. Take, for example, the word 'sick'. In adult minds it is associated with being 'under the weather' or unwell, yet when young people use the word 'sick' they convert it into an adjective that means 'great', someone 'fabulous' or 'impressive'. Perhaps the most widely popularised and internationalised inversion is the word 'bad' to signify 'good'. The youthful appropriation and invention of words is an assertion of power, making a point about language and what it can do. Lyrical language is developed on-road as both a way to signify a cool aesthetic and separate from the hegemonic norms. Many slang words on-road in London are developed from Jamaican Patois (Gunter, 2008; Ilan, 2012). This nods to the Caribbean connection between London and the Caribbean established prior to and since the Windrush generation and also is a vernacular reference to the Black roots of life on-road.

Perhaps the retirement of the reference to life *on-road* for young people is likely soon, as 'roadman' is now embraced in the *Cambridge English Dictionary*, which defines it as 'Someone, usually a young man, who spends a lot of time on the streets and may use or sell drugs, or cause trouble' (*The Cambridge English Dictionary*, 2022). In this narrow and flat definition of a 'roadman' there is a clear association with gender [*male*], space [*streets*] and criminality [*drugs/trouble*]. In this collection we wanted to bring together scholars who go deeper into understanding the dynamics of life on-road outside the confines of stereotypes and narrow definitions. The aim is to understand the nuances and complexities of lives lived on-road and what this means to the young people involved. The urgent need for depth and nuanced analysis has been propelled by the way in which on-road subculture has become subsumed into mainstream fashion, music and television dramas in a process that could be defined as akin to the cultural accommodation of the illicit (Parker et al, 2002), especially when 'road life' intersects with drug dealing. A search online will find numerous articles paying attention to the 'roadman' aesthetic, with fashionistas advising on how to present in 'roadman style' for middle-class consumers of drill music. This trend has become more prominent with the mainstream success of UK rap, drill and grime rap genres, which have catapulted the concept of life on-road from an edgy niche concept into the mainstream.

The profound significance of 'on-road' to contemporary British culture can be appreciated by its relevance to, and presence in, grime and drill music, the BBC/Netflix TV series *Top Boy* and the film *Blue Story*. Directed by Andrew Onwubolu, *Blue Story* was temporarily banned from British cinemas on its release out of fears it would provoke disorder. British rap artist Dave's album, *Psychodrama*, being awarded 'Album of the Year' at the 2019 Brit Awards offers additional recognition of the power of its narrations and atmospheres. The increased attention directed at life on-road has both advantages and disadvantages. The artistic and creative skill of otherwise overlooked on-road musicians has been a breath of fresh air in wider UK society. In 2019 Stormzy, a grime rapper who has broken into mainstream music, became the first Black solo artist to headline Glastonbury Festival. It was a cultural watershed moment, pushing back against spurious associations with youth criminality and racial marginalisation within the mainstream UK music and the Whiteness of festival scenes. The contrasting poles of on-road hypervisibility either as festival headliners or splashed across the front pages of newspapers in some ways reflects the wider extremes of the visibility of Black men. As Gunter (2010: 31) noted, Black male youth are either portrayed as 'sexy and creative cultural innovators or as deviant and aggressive individuals beset by social disadvantage and alienation'.

The tension that has arisen with the popularity of on-road subculture for young people is that part of its allure is the proximity or claim of a gangster aesthetic and cool (Ilan, 2015). The word 'gang' enjoys wide use in film, music and other forms of popular culture as well as in general conversation. It means a lot of different things to different people. When some adults use the noun 'gang', particularly professionals working with the criminal justice system, it is used with reference to street-based groups that are:

> A relatively durable, predominantly street-based group of young people who (1) see themselves (and are seen by others) as a discernible group, (2) engage in a range of criminal activity and violence, (3) identify with or lay claim over territory, (4) have some form of identifying structural feature, and (5) are in conflict with other, similar, gangs. (The Centre for Social Justice, 2009: 21)

Since the early 2000s, law enforcement agencies, policy makers and some academics have argued that such groups have infiltrated the social fabric of Britain's cities causing rates of serious and violent crime to substantially increase (Pitts, 2008). The popular conception of gangs is based on the notion that they are large, organised collectives with a structured hierarchy and complex divisions of labour. Accordingly, the UK is seemingly home to 'super articulated gangs' (Pitts, 2008), 'corporate style' gangs (Toy, 2008) and gangs that use rape as a weapon of choice (Firmin, 2011) and wield 'dangerous dogs' to patrol and enforce control over demarcated residential or drug dealing territory (Harding, 2010). Most recently, gangs are linked to expanding the drugs market through 'county lines', peddling crack cocaine and heroin from large metropolitan areas such as London, Birmingham, Liverpool and Manchester to small towns and coastal areas (National Crime Agency, 2016). They are linked to the exploitation of children and vulnerable people (Children's Society, 2019). Controversially, the gang, as a concept, has been disproportionately applied to the anti-social and offending behaviour of young Black and brown people, fuelling a racialising discourse about gang groups (Hallsworth and Young, 2004, 2008; Smithson et al, 2013) that has exacerbated the over-policing of minoritised youth in many communities (Williams, 2015; Williams and Clarke, 2018). Interpretations of certain aspects of on-road youth subculture such as drill and grime rap music have been interpreted as being inherently connected to gangs based on 'street-illiterate' understandings of forms of youth expression, rooted in racist stereotypes (Ilan, 2020). The result is increasingly punitive sentencing for people of colour and the disproportionate incarceration of Black and mixed-race young men.

In this edited collection we have sought to dig beneath the institutional focus on gangs, as well as the subcultural surface of street culture, and instead home in on the origin story and lived experiences of life on-road from an intersectional perspective. Intersectionality was conceptualised by Kimberlé Crenshaw (1991) to understand the ways in which interlocking axes of oppression, particularly around race and racism, can further marginalise individuals. The key premise is that experiences of exclusion and marginalisation are not simply additive, but fundamentally interactive and co-constitutive, combining to change the lives of individuals and structure social processes. This is pertinent when considering life on-road for young people, who are often battling with multidimensional experiences of exclusion and oppression that arise from racism, class hierarchy and the gender order. The contributions gathered here reflect a commitment to intersectional approaches which foreground analysis of the racialised and racialising dynamics of young people's lives 'on-road'. The young people for whom life 'on-road' is most central and influential are often from the UK's minoritised ethnic communities. Black, brown and mixed-heritage or mixed-race, their social collectives and personal identities often reflect complex multicultural conviviality and tensions that pulse through Britain's cities (Gilroy, 2004). This is not to say that young White people are not part of this scene, they are, and their presence is also reflected in the research gathered for this collection.

The social exclusion of certain young people on-road also runs on different axes of difference, including those who have insecure immigration status. The report commissioned by the Mayor of London (Jolly et al, 2020) highlighted that an estimated 107,000 children in London alone are undocumented, with a further 26,000 in the 18–24 age group. Albanian unaccompanied children asylum seekers have been squarely in the focus of both the UK government and UK media across 2022, with them being labelled as potential gang members both inside and outside parliament (ITV News, 2022). When the 'gang' label is used, its function is to transform the subjects from vulnerable child asylum seekers to potential criminal threats. The discursive shifts lead to their adultification, which is often a process that is both gendered and racialised (Davis and Marsh, 2020). The implications of this are that these undocumented and unaccompanied migrants, many of whom are Albanian, end up on the 'translocal road' (as discussed in Chapter 8). The complexities and shifting realities of race and racism are central to the theorisation we seek to develop with this collection. We push back and against tendencies in academic analysis to invisibilise Whiteness and instead look at the axis of inclusion and exclusion across intersectional lines.

In discussing 'on-road' life, the contributors to this collection acknowledge it as a social continuum that encapsulates, on the one hand, a space where marginalised young people socialise with each other and where a few engage in the hustle of low-level criminality found within the urban street space. And, on the other hand, as an alienating environment where young people, excluded by disadvantage and marginalisation, develop a deep, somewhat enduring discontentment with their lives and social relationships. As Young and Hallsworth's research highlights, 'on-road' is:

> The 'hood' or the 'ghetto' where young people, worn down by marginalisation and exclusion, struggled to survive in a society they believed did not care or cater for their needs. At its most extreme, the hood – and by extension 'the road' – was a place where young people adopted a 'hood mentality', a fatalistic attitude to life that held 'no dreams, no ambition, no drive; no nothing'. (Young and Hallsworth, 2011: 3)

It is important to note in the context of this bleak definition that young people themselves use the term 'on-road' to refer to a catch-all of behaviours which can include gang involvement but are not predicated on it. Life on-road is as much about the mundane struggles as the 'spectacular' (Gunter, 2008, 2010, 2017). Indeed, Bakkali has coined the concept of the 'munpain' as a way to articulate the routine, quotidian turbulence and torpor that gathers into a 'mundane pain' that young people experience on-road, inflected with the structural violence that shapes their lives. Bakkali notes the way in which marginalised young people are 'locked in an existential struggle against a sense of malaise permeating many of their everyday experiences' (Bakkali, 2019: 1).

The connection between existential vulnerability and life on-road has come more to the forefront of on-road scholarship in recent years (Levell, 2020, 2022a), aided by an increased policy focus on Adverse Childhood Experiences, highlighting the complexities of children's lives who may find themselves in youth offending services by mid-adolescence. Billingham and Irwin-Rogers focused on the 'terrifying abyss of insignificance' that young people who engage in serious youth violence on-road can feel. They posit that the core concern of life on-road is the ways in which young people look for ways to 'matter' to each other and wider society, in order to address the 'adolescent ontological insecurity' that defines their (lack of) self-esteem (Billingham and Irwin-Rogers, 2021: 1225). Whilst the explicit focus on UK gangs within policy and academia may have peaked with the London riots of 2011, since then there has been a policy shift to focus on 'Serious Youth Violence' (Home Office UK, 2018; Densley et al, 2020; Home Office, 2021). This has drawn attention to the physicality of on-road life being in the public forum of the streets, indeed the UK Serious Violence Duty explicitly focuses on 'public space youth violence' (Home Office, 2021). Viewing adolescents' experiences of violence in spatial ways can enable a deeper understanding of the opportunities the road affords for young people, by the streets being a refuge for young people living in unsafe conditions and seeking alternative places to inhabit, or to matter (Levell, 2022b). Without doubt, the research of Billingham and Irwin-Rogers and others, as well as studies contained in this collection, offer the conceptual space within which to discuss 'on-road' in a multidimensional way.

Roads of history, paths of patriarchy: the endless excess of youth terminated?

The cultural critic Frederic Jameson's injunction to 'always historicise' has never been more important. The triumphant resurgence of nationalism and racism in the last decade has created a kind of timelessness in which the future simply disappears in favour of an empty, nostalgic populism (Nilges, 2020). These dehistoricising pressures bear heavily on youth cultures and young people because youth have, historically, always represented both the future and fears of the future. Young people are often cast as the angels and devils (Warner, 1994) that haunt the social imagination but as modernity's colonial engine stalls they are increasingly simply abandoned in the UK. With the horizon ahead dissolving into a series of impending ecological and economic catastrophes, the cultural critic Slavoj Žižek (2011) warns that we now live in 'End Times'. This is a terminal crisis in the social relations of racial capitalism which now includes the real possibility of the 'End' of everything once taken for granted by the richer, Whiter countries of the world. In this context, it becomes easier and more comforting to neglect the future and its coming generations in favour of a selective focus on the comforts of an imagined past. While social theorists disagree about whether capitalism is indeed ending or transforming into something worse, what is less contentious is that an explosive cocktail of climate change, violent nationalism, police brutality and a deadly pandemic has at least 'made dystopia great again' (Morozov, 2022: 89). The arguments centre on a growing consensus that a new global regime is emerging that resembles something closer to the dark ages than the Enlightenment. Whether this is called 'neo-feudalism' or 'techno-feudalism' the changes are driven by prolonged economic stagnation, politically driven upward redistribution of wealth, staggeringly ostentatious consumption by super-rich elites and the increasingly blatant immiseration of vast numbers of the world's population.

Conventional models of modern, social democratic and public statecraft are at risk of being superseded by private powers of patronage emanating from enormous personal wealth. As in feudal times, any person living beyond the protection of this arbitrary private power has little or no protection from a state being hollowed out to its martial limits. Pre-modern forms of pauperisation and radically restructured wealth hint at a kind neo-medievalism emerging from the imploding contradictions of neoliberalism (Morozov, 2022). Comforting images of the past may fuel conservative agendas for short-term (electoral) gain, but in the pursuit of electoral success politicians refuse to learn its lessons. Consistent within sociological and criminological research, one omnipresent lesson is that alienation arises in the face of external social constraints and subcultural groupings of young people on-road – such as 'gangs' that are often associated with anti-social behaviour and violence – form when social institutions fail to provide the basic requirements necessary to live a dignified and meaningful life. Young people, especially young men, who are denied the opportunity to cultivate the material wealth, respect and cultural status required – and associated with successful masculinities in patriarchal societies – are overwhelmingly the inhabitants of life on-road and the perpetrators (and victims) of harmful acts including interpersonal violence.

Historical studies of gender and masculinity (Tosh, 2005) convincingly argue that patriarchal ideology is messy, muddled and contradictory but also a structuring feature of men's lives. Patriarchy as a 'gender regime' (Walby, 2020) remains a useful category of analysis for accounting for the distribution of power and status that create or sustain gendered hierarchies. While the term patriarchy suggests a monolithic system of men's domination of women, the reality is of a perpetually contested and shifting set of social relations in which older men tend to dominate both women and younger men (Connell, 1987). They are relations that change over time so that the patriarchal relations that characterised the 16th century may correspond in various ways with those of the 19th or 20th century but will also vary considerably in their specifics and contexts. As Beier (1987) notes, for men at the social margins of society in early modern England, the prospects narrowed into varieties of itinerant precarity – they took to the roads, such as they were. They were seen by the emerging urban elites of the new and growing cities of mercantile capitalism as 'a menace to the social order because they broke with the accepted norms of family life. If the ideal was the patriarchal household, they had no place in it, and for that reason they were considered pariahs' (Beier, 1987: 51).

Being 'on-road' or becoming a 'roadman' in contemporary England is not so many miles from this medieval pariah status. Longitudinal studies of childhood and youth indicate the centrality of mobility to the 'material and symbolic practices through which young people move from the status of children to that of adults' (Thomson and Taylor, 2005: 328). For bourgeois, often White, cosmopolitans, the 'kinetic elite' for whom movement within nations is as easy as movement between nations, being fixed to local boundaries and neighbourhoods is increasingly unlikely. By contrast, for many young men in the kinetic underclass whose mobile horizons are more constrained and more fiercely local, going 'on-road' with its 'live fast, die young/get rich quick or die trying' mottos, offers them at least the armour of an identity in a world where the state, the formal economy and family life can find no place for them. In this respect they bear a striking resemblance to Beier's (1987) description of 'masterless men', the vagrants, vagabonds and brigands of medieval society. Shepard's (2003: 94) meticulous account of 'youthful excess and fraternal bonding' among young men in the affluent university town of 16th-century Cambridge includes resonant descriptions of 'nightwalking'. Shepard goes so far as to suggest that 'the boldest resistance to patriarchal concepts of order was performed by young men, many of whom espoused potent inversions of normative meanings of manhood ... and subverted patriarchal imperatives of order, thrift and self-control' (2003: 93). Then, as now, the role of men in groups and loose forms of collective affinity were central to youthful exploits and disruptive assertions of masculine presence. Shepard (2003: 95) notes, as do contributors to this volume, that while the disruptive, violent and accumulative behaviour of young men validated their claims to manliness, it was also an important but largely unacknowledged 'source of intimacy during this most homosocial phase of the life course'.

Young women's lives on-road

As with gang scholarship, on-road scholarship focuses on the adolescent male experience and is usually analysed through the gaze of the academic male (Letherby, 2003). Although there is a growing body of pivotal research – written by women academics – that focus on the existential experiences of young women who purport to be 'on-road' or associate with groups, including gangs, that exist therein (see Young, 2009; Choak, 2018; Dziewanski, 2020), the lack of visibility of young women's lives on-road was a key concern in the bringing together of this collection. One of the objectives of this collection is to create a space for reflections on the distinctive meanings of 'on-road' for young men *and* young women. Historically, girls and young women are often perceived as peripheral to life 'on-road', however research undertaken by Choak and others clearly illustrate that young women are not always side-lined, as participants on-road they draw their own 'bad ass' femininity to combat the patriarchal oppression they inevitably experience (Young and Trickett, 2017) to stave off victimisation and engage in forms of criminality, like street robbery, drug supply and violence that is usually the proclivity of men (Choak, 2018). In this collection we present perspectives that are sensitive to the way gendered power is threaded through life 'on-road' for both young women and young men. This approach builds from research that explores on-road and gang masculinities by two of the editors (Levell and Young). This work (Young and Trickett, 2017; Levell, 2019, 2020) focuses on the connections between experience of domestic violence and young men's lives on-road and challenges the way young women's lives have been rendered peripheral by academic neglect. Moreover, Bakkali and Chigbo (Chapter 3, this volume) further add to our knowledge of young women's experience via their analysis of the concept of love as it manifests on-road. Such critical reflections of young people's experiences of relationships are crucial, enabling a deeper understanding of the ways that young women and men create viable lives. Using a lens attuned to dynamics of gender, heteronormativity and homophobia aids a deeper understanding of youth relationality.

Outline of the collection

The intersectional nature of the contributions to this edited collection presents a multifaceted portrait of life on-road within the axis of lives which are also gendered, racialised and classed. Young people are impacted not only by the exterior gaze of state systems which were set up for surveillance and punishment, but also by their interior worlds which can reproduce values of inequality.

Reflecting our concern to include an historical perspective, Chapter 2 by Esmorie Miller focuses on the historical antecedents of being on 'the road'. The chapter explores 'the road' as a gendered space with hitherto neglected historical antecedents. It explores the intersection of race and gender politics in the interwar period in Britain, examining how they informed early youth penal reform. To achieve this, the analysis draws on documentary research from the Liverpool University Archives, including the Fletcher Report (1930) and the digitised catalogue of the *Eugenics Review*, a populist journal spanning 1909 to 1968. While documents like the Fletcher Report introduced racialised youth to Britain as a problematic cohort, the pseudo-science promulgated in the *Eugenics Review* supported the racial politics positioning these youth outside the redemptive scope of early penal reform efforts. Miller's distinctive contribution here emphasises the relevance of eugenicist discourse in the formation of ideas about intervention in young people's lives and how their discredited categorisations disappeared from view but not from effect. Fletcher (1930: 26) concluded that: 'These families have a low standard of life, morally and economically, and there appears to be little future for the children.' Miller's conclusion stands as antithetical to the institutional narrative supporting rehabilitation for White, working-class youth. Despite the rich body of research on the role of class in early youth penal reform, race remains both largely invisible and distorted within this history. According to Miller, the concept of being on 'the road' offers a unique lens to give gendered relevance to this history. If, for instance, 'the road' signifies resistance against exclusion, a space co-opted by youth to carve out resources and opportunities, girls' participation historically exposed them to particular stigma and penalty. Remarking on racialised girls, Fletcher's report argued that their pursuits 'lead to grave moral results, particularly in the case of the girls' (Fletcher, 1930: 38). Miller argues that girls' and young women's search for opportunities (their 'road' pursuits), became linked to sexualisation, and this actualised an enduring association between race and sexual deviance. In historicising and gendering 'the road' in this way, Miller's chapter expands understandings of racialised youth's contested positioning and affords greater appreciation of their agency. Historicising and gendering the logic of 'the road' enables exploration of racialised youth's circumstances as part of a historic exclusion from the resources and opportunities associated with early modern justice reform.

In Chapter 3, Yusef Bakkali and Ezimma Chigbo discuss love, intimacy and desire on-road. They focus on the emotional lives of men and women who have lived in proximity to road life. Building on the work of Bakkali (2019), they draw on narrative interviews in order to examine the central importance of love and self-awareness of their marginality for those at the margins. This involves an unusual and welcome critical engagement with analytical literature around love, relationships and gender dynamics in street settings (Anderson, 2000; Miller, 2002, 2008; Bourgois, 2003; Young, 2009; Trickett, 2015). Adopting a situated approach (Bakkali, 2019), Bakkali and Chigbo examine accounts of how both young men and women became involved in road life, arguing that while the roads are a gendered space, both groups' involvement included a level of proximity and long-standing spatial/cultural/familial proximity to the roads as a relational space (Bakkali, 2019). Their work reveals how proximity ties gendered relations in these contexts to a situated set of needs and networks. In particular, they engage with the narratives of two female and two male participants, noting how differential vocabularies and priorities emerge around relationships, intimacy and domestic life, where gaps and silences in the accounts of men become significant and telling. They note how the dissonance in narratives is of analytical importance, highlighting the ways in which pockets of silent vulnerability around intimacy and desire are active features of men's lives, in search of love, negotiated with hesitancy and difficulty as they surface through the inevitabilities of physical proximity. In the context of what can be an often unpredictable, trauma-laden and sometimes hostile street environments, these gendered struggles take place across a society organised around the principle of White supremacist capitalist patriarchy (hooks, 1994). The results can be, at times, damaging and traumatic, involving instances of domestic violence and controlling behaviours (Stark, 2007; Levell, 2022a). Bakkali and Chigbo draw on deep wells of experience and research to generate an invaluable account of how these gendered struggles around intimacy on-road amalgamate into the everyday hardships of the munpain. They are stories of tainted love, abuse and deep emotional turmoil but they also reveal agency and resistance among young women navigating an antagonistic, male-dominated environment.

Extending our concern to bring intimacy into analytical perspective, Tara Young, in Chapter 4, discusses friendship on-road. Young's empirical research draws on the narrative stories told by young men convicted of serious violent offences. Drawing on philosophical scholarship, she highlights the universality of friendship and demonstrates how young people on-road want what humans have desired for millennia; good, loyal and trustworthy friends who care about them. However, her data show on-road friendships to be fragile, dependent upon the sociocultural mores of street life that dictate who is considered 'good', and how loyalty and trustworthiness are expressed. Young suggests that in the pursuit of the ideal friendship, some young people on-road misinterpret the intentions of those with whom they forge relationships, resulting in pressure, internal and external, to engage in acts that end in serious or lethal violence, which they may not have intended, but for which, nonetheless, they have been incarcerated.

Maintaining the central focus on gender relations, in Chapter 5 Levell explores some of the lesser told stories of sexual relations on-road. Levell is concerned to show how feminist and gender theorists have long argued that sex is inherently political; summed up in the slogan the 'personal is political'. The premise was that how individuals and couples related in their intimate relationships was as important as the broader societal picture; connecting the micro and macro levels (Millett, 1970). In this chapter, Levell deploys Raewyn Connell's masculinity theory to analyse young men's experiences on-road with a specific focus on the ways the racialisation and sexualisation of Black young men's bodies operate within a heteronormative context. Levell examines how this dynamic has limited Black men on-road from finding a space and/or being offered a voice to talk about their own non-consensual, exploitative, abusive or transactional sexual experiences. These hitherto neglected aspects of their lives on-road are brought into view to extend a critical appreciation of the way men make sense of their lives and account for their experiences.

In Chapter 6, Lambros Fatsis brings an encyclopaedic knowledge of contemporary musical forms to bear on a critical discussion of the way criminal law has, again, become a controversial feature of musical and cultural production. In recent years, UK drill music has become an almost routine feature in the nation's courtrooms. It is frequently presented as *prima facie* evidence of wrongdoing if you are young and Black and formally associated with young people 'on-road'. Fatsis considers the way the genre's graphic lyrical and video imagery has been harvested by police and prosecution agencies to produce a dangerous 'rush to judgment' that will be all too familiar to anyone well-versed in the repetitive demonisation of Black cultural forms. While such a response may seem justified to some due to a number of fatal incidents in which drill music has been identified as an operative feature of the convicted person's cultural repertoire, it remains difficult to prove a direct link between drill lyrics or videos and the evidential facts of criminal offences. Fatsis warns that relying on drill music to bring criminal charges against individuals not only turns music-making into a criminal offence, it also involves prosecutorial tactics that fail to uphold high standards of evidence, thereby endangering the civil rights of all and everyone. As in the past, this opportunistic evidential shortcut can only be accomplished through the reproduction of racist stereotypes about Black music genres and 'criminality'. In this chapter, Fatsis is able to combine his activist involvement as an expert defence witness challenging court cases that translate drill lyrics and videos into incriminating evidence with deep immersion in critical cultural studies. This chapter contributes to a growing body of literature that challenges the admissibility of drill music as evidence to prove guilt (see Owsusu-Bempah, 2022; Schwarze and Fatsis, 2022) and argues that putting drill on trial in this way conflates the literary and the literal, risking prejudicial assumptions about an art form, its producers and audiences.

Continuing the exploration of the way being 'on-road' can frequent mesh with being 'on trial' or being under various forms of judicial supervision, in Chapter 7 Chris Waller focuses on the cultural continuum, nay pipeline, between road and prison. Waller explores the ways in which the production and consumption of music builds cultural spaces of continuity between road culture and prison. By drawing on his research looking at music consumption in a local prison in Greater London, Waller considers the ways in which on-road culture is both adapted and imported into the prison. Drawing on the cultural geography of the prison, he examines the ways in which music provides both connections to the outside as well as a situated form of problem-solving and identity construction. Throughout the chapter, Waller provides examples of how road and prison cultures intersect in rap music, how artists often incorporate recordings of telephone calls to prison into their work. He develops an argument that music represents a means of working through complex ideas of self, identity, authenticity and, importantly, trajectory for young people.

In Chapter 8, Jade Levell and Stephanie Schwandner-Sievers analyse findings from music elicitation interviews with men involved with the Albanian criminal justice system, both those who are incarcerated and those in the community. The primary focus of their research was to hear the narratives of men previously identified as being 'at risk' or actually involved in serious and organised crime. The chapter notes the way in which hip-hop culture and rap music have been focused on as evidence of the 'problem' of Albanian illegal migration and crime in UK media moral panics. However, using music elicitation as a co-listening tool revealed a more tender and nuanced picture of childhood adversity and young people trying to survive and respond to masculine pressures on the translocal road. In this chapter, Levell and Schwandner-Sievers note the parallels between how the young Albanians spoke about their experiences and the UK concept of life 'on-road'. Here, they point out that like 'on-road' in the British context, the neighbourhoods of Albania, both locally and in the transnational context, provided solidarity and belonging among the boys on-road beyond conventional kinship ties, as well as a relatively intelligible structure of behavioural rules (street codes). The authors illustrate how 'on-road' involves the interplay between homosocial peer groups, street violence, criminality, and the desire for financial independence and family independence. In their study, Levell and Schwandner-Sievers focus on the way young men articulated their experiences through various musical forms, removing the need to explain these through cliched labels such as 'gang' and 'traditional Albanian culture' that are easily attached to research of this kind. By employing a creative methods technique the conformed to an anthropological, social constructivist epistemology that not only recognises stereotypical representations of 'gangs', 'offenders' or 'Albanian criminals', but allows for greater appreciation of the ways in which these obscure more complex social and historical realities. Music elicitation offered ways of excavating experiences, emotions and subjective interpretations of the lives lived on-road, locally and transnationally, that facilitate a deeper understanding of life choices, motives and rationale of young Albanian men in conflict with law.

Issues of professional practice are also the subject of Peter Harris's chapter. There has been some support in the UK political arena for the inclusion of older Black men as role models to resolve rising rates of youth violence and knife crime. In Chapter 9, Harris discusses men's work in youth work with young people 'on-road'. Here, he takes a case study approach, interrogating the older male as role model for the young 'roadman' through a psychosocial lens. Harris critically examines the validity of this trope via a single case study of a young Black man and his older, White, male youth worker, arguing that racial symmetry between the role model and young person appears to be a self-evident solution for crime and youth violence in Black communities, but it masks important intersectional factors that can emerge in professional working relationships between people who are ethnically diverse. Academic analysis of road life, suggests Harris, may not be keeping pace with the construction of youthful masculinities such as the 'roadman', and he highlights some implications for our understanding of relationships between male youth work professionals and the young men they work with living 'on-road'. According to Harris, policy making and professional training regimes should be more aware of the intertwined psychic and social dimensions of these complex relationships.

The final chapter, Chapter 10, is written by Martin Glynn, who rounds off the collection with an autobiographical account of his own 'road' experience as a practitioner and academic. It is a reflexive narrative of someone who has operated professionally in both prisons and his neighbourhood for over four decades. For Glynn, becoming an 'on-road' criminologist means gaining acceptance, approval and permission from sections of the community who occupy the world of the 'streets' (on-road). It means having to curate access to young men and women who some criminologists cannot access, or will not approach. As an ethnographic 'on-road' criminologist, Glynn, does not operate via focus group in comfortable academic constructs and spaces but immerses himself in the sociocultural environment of his constituents? His strategy of enquiry is not exercised from a distance, via the dissemination of questionnaires in the relative safety of a classroom or the recording of an interview from the comfort of a warm office. 'On-road' research is gritty and embedded in the real world. It takes place, says Glynn, in shopping centres, on pavements, outside barbershops, in betting shops, fast-food takeaways, car parks, street corners, and other locations that tend to elude the academic or the practitioner. In this chapter, Glynn evocatively recalls his experiences through reflection, verse and rhyme and posits a personal manifesto couched in the appeals of and for a 'political Blackness' in research practice.

The collection of chapters here cannot map 'road life', but by providing the first serious attempt to engage with its complexities and possibilities we hope to build better understanding of what being 'on-road' means for young people and to the older people who work with them. As the field develops, the omissions and inadequacies that are inevitable in any 'first attempt' can be addressed. Our collection has not gathered or included the diverse experience of young migrants for whom the questions of being 'on-road' is particularly heavily loaded. The experiences of Asian-heritage youth in the UK is also notable by its absence from our collection. There is a vibrant research literature engaging with the complexities of cultural identities and social practice among such young people (Kalra, 2009; Alam, 2020). As Alexander (2004) notes, some of this literature was propelled by familiar agitation among powerful White constituencies in policy and academic communities for whom the gang vernacular was as inevitable as it was indispensable. Alexander (2004: 535) challenges the way 'Asian young men [who] were previously largely invisible – certainly in academic discourse – the assumed heirs of patriarchal privilege and "community", are now the hyper-visible embodiments of a racialized dysfunctionality'. The return to invisibility in this collection is our failing and one that seeks remedy in future work. Such work may be guided by Amin's (2002: 10) cautionary remarks: 'There is a complexity to the cultural identity of the Asian youths that cannot be reduced to the stereotype of traditional Muslim, Hindu, Sikh lives, to the bad masculinities of gang life … to the all too frequently repeated idea of their entrapment between two cultures'. Yunis Alam's (2020) invigorating and inspired ethnography of car culture among Bradford's young Muslim men is an example of what can be achieved.

The uniqueness of this collection lies in its concentration on 'on-road' as a distinctive concept rather than the ubiquitous focus on 'gangs', 'gang-association', 'gang-related offending', 'county lines' or any other moniker used by some academics and practitioners to analyse the social life of Black, poor or minoritised communities. Some authors herein recognise 'gangs' as part of the landscape of 'on-road', but do not reduce a complex social system to it; not least because the (sub)culture of the road, as perceived by the young people who inhabit the physical space or adopt a 'road mindset', do not necessarily use these terms to describe their experiences. In this collection we hope to open up a conversation about what matters to them. This collection is not a definitive guide to 'road life'. We acknowledge the gaps that need to be filled (for example, more experiences of girls and young women, transgender young people, and the inclusion of international perspectives), but it is a start. In producing this collection, we aim to provide the first serious attempt to engage with its complexities and possibilities and to build better understanding of what being 'on-road' means for young people and to the older people who work with them. So, for more on-road read on.

References

Alam, Y. (2020) *Cars: Race, Taste and Class*. Bristol: Policy Press.

Alexander, C. (2004) Imagining the Asian gang: Ethnicity, masculinity and youth after 'the riots'. *Critical Social Policy*, 24(4): 526–549.

Amin, A. (2002) Ethnicity and the multicultural city: Living with diversity. *Environment and Planning A*, 34(6): 959–980.

Anderson, E. (1999) *Code of the Street: Decency, Violence and the Moral Life of the Inner City*. New York: W.W. Norton and Company.

Bakkali, Y. (2019) Dying to live: Youth violence and the munpain. *The Sociological Review*, 67(6): 1317–1332.

Beier, A. (1987) *Masterless Men: The Vagrancy Problem in England, 1560–1640*. North Yorkshire: Methuen.

Billingham, L. and Irwin-Rogers, K. (2021) The terrifying abyss of insignificance: Marginalisation, mattering and violence between young people. *Onati Socio-Legal Series*, 11(5): 1222–1249.

Bourgois, P. (2003) *Selling Crack in El Barrio* (2nd Ed). New York: Cambridge University Press.

The Cambridge English Dictionary (2022) Roadman. Available at: https://dictionary.cambridge.org/dictionary/english/roadman

The Centre for Social Justice (2009) *Dying to Belong: An In-Depth Review of Street Gangs in Britain* [Report]. Available at: https://www.centreforsocialjustice.org.uk/library/dying-to-belong-an-in-depth-review-of-street-gangs-in-britain

Children's Society (2019) *Counting Lives: Responding to Children Who Are Criminally Exploited*. The Children's Society. https://doi.org/10.1016/0376-6349(78)90015-9

Choak, C. (2018) *Young Women On Road: Feminities, Race and Gangs in London*. PhD Thesis, University of East London. https://doi.org/10.1051/matecconf/201712107005

Connell, R.W. (1987) *Gender and Power*. Stanford: Stanford University Press.

Crenshaw, K. (1991) Mapping the margins: Intersectionality, identity politics, and violence against women of color. *Stanford Law Review*, 43(6): 1241–1299.

Davis, J. and Marsh, N. (2020) Boys to men: The cost of 'adultification' in safeguarding responses to Black boys. *Critical and Radical Social Work*, 8(2): 255–259.

Densley, J., Deuchar, R. and Harding, S. (2020) An introduction to gangs and serious youth violence in the United Kingdom. *Youth Justice*, 20(1–2): 3–10.

Dziewanski, D. (2020) Femme fatales: Girl gangsters and violent street culture in Cape Town. *Feminist Criminology*, 15(4): 438–463.

Earle, R. (2011) Boys' zone stories: Perspectives from a young men's prison. *Criminology & Criminal Justice*, 11(2): 129–143.

Firmin, C. (2011) *Female Voice in Violence. Final Report on the Impact of Serious Youth Violence and Criminal Gangs on Women and Girls Across the Country*. Race on the Agenda. Available at: https://barrowcadbury.org.uk/wp-content/uploads/2012/01/ROTA_Female-Voice-in-Violence-report.pdf

Fletcher, M.E. (1930) *Investigation into the Colour Problem in Liverpool and Other Ports*. Liverpool Association for the Welfare of Half-Caste Children. Original from, the University of Wisconsin: Madison.

Gilroy, P. (2004) *After Empire: Melancholia or Convivial Culture?* London: Routledge.

Gunter, A. (2008) Growing up bad: Black youth, 'road' culture and badness in an East London neighbourhood. *Crime, Media, Culture*, 4(3): 349–366.

Gunter, A. (2010) *Growing Up Bad: Black Youth, Road Culture and Badness in an East London Neighbourhood*. London: The Tufnell Press.

Gunter, A. (2017) *Race, Gangs and Youth Violence*. Bristol: Policy Press.

Hallsworth, S. and Young, T. (2011) Young people, gangs and street-based violence. In C. Barter and D. Berridge (eds) *Children Behaving Badly? Peer Violence Between Children and Young People*. Oxford: Wiley-Blackwell. Chapter 5.

Hallsworth, S. and Young, T. (2008) Gang talk and gang talkers: A critique. *Crime, Media, Culture*, 4(2): 175–195.

Harding, S. (2010) Status dogs and gangs. *Safer Communities*, 9(1): 30–35.

Home Office (2021) *Serious Violence Duty: Preventing and Reducing Serious Violence. Draft Guidance for Responsible Authorities*. May. Available at: https://www.gov.uk/government/publications/police-crime-sentencing-and-courts-bill-2021-draft-guidance/serious-violence-duty-draft-guidance-for-responsible-authorities-accessible-version

Home Office UK (2018) *Serious Violence Strategy*. April. Available at: https://www.gov.uk/government/publications/serious-violence-strategy

hooks, b. (1994) *Teaching to Transgress*. New York: Routledge.

Ilan, J. (2012) 'The industry's the new road': Crime, commodification and street cultural tropes in UK urban music. *Crime, Media, Culture*, 8(1): 39–55.

Ilan, J. (2015) *Understanding Street Culture: Poverty, Crime, Youth and Cool*. London: Palgrave Macmillan.

Ilan, J. (2020) Digital street culture decoded: Why criminalizing drill music is street illiterate and counterproductive. *British Journal of Criminology*, 60(4): 994–1013.

ITV News (2022) Suella Braverman faces criticism for Channel migrant 'invasion' claim, 1 November. Available at: https://www.itv.com/news/2022-10-31/braverman-deflects-blame-for-manston-migrant-saga-as-she-denies-blocking-hotels

Jolly, A., Thomas, S. and Stanyer, J. (2020) London's children and young people who are not British citizens: A profile [Report]. Mayor of London. https://doi.org/10.13140/RG.2.2.13839.12964

Kalra, V.S. (2009) Between emasculation and hypermasculinity: Theorizing British South Asian masculinities. *South Asian Popular Culture*, 7(2): 113–125.

Letherby, G. (2003) *Feminist Research in Theory and Practice*. Maidenhead: Open University Press.

Levell, J. (2019) 'Those songs were the ones that made me, nobody asked me this question before': Music elicitation with ex-gang involved men about their experiences of childhood domestic violence and abuse. *International Journal of Qualitative Methods*, 18: 1–10.

Levell, J. (2020) Using Connell's masculinity theory to understand the way in which ex-gang-involved men coped with childhood domestic violence. *Journal of Gender Based Violence*, 4(2): 207–221.

Levell, J. (2022a) *Boys, Childhood Domestic Abuse and Gang Involvement: Violence at Home, Violence On-road*. Bristol: Policy Press.

Levell, J. (2022b) Internal homelessness and hiraeth: Boys' spatial journeys between childhood domestic abuse and on-road. In H. Bows and B. Fileborn (eds) *Geographies of Gender-based Violence: A Multi-disciplinary Perspective*. Bristol: Policy Press, pp 50–62.

Miller, J. (2001) *One of the Guys: Girls, Gangs and Gender*. New York: Oxford University Press.

Miller, J. (2008) *Getting Played: African American Girls, Urban Equality and Gendered Violence*. New York: New York University Press.

Millett, K. (1970) *Sexual Politics*. Champaign: University of Illinois Press.

Morozov, E. (2022) Critique of techno-feudal reason. *New Left Review*, January/April. Available at: https://newleftreview.org/issues/ii133/articles/evgeny-morozov-critique-of-techno-feudal-reason

National Crime Agency (2016) *County Lines Gang Violence, Exploitation & Drug Supply 2016: 0346-CAD National Briefing Report*. Available at: https://www.nationalcrimeagency.gov.uk/who-we-are/publications/15-county-lines-gang-violence-exploitation-and-drug-supply-2016/file

Nilges, M. (2020) *Right-Wing Culture in Contempoary Capitalism: Regression and Hope in a Time Without Future*. London: Bloomsbury.

Owusu-Bempah, A. (2022) The irrelevance of rap. *Criminal Law Review*, 2: 130–151.

Parker, H., Williams, L. and Aldridge, J. (2002) The normalization of 'sensible' recreational drug use: Further evidence from the North West England longitudinal study. *Sociology*, 36(4): 941–964.

Pitts, J. (2008) *Reluctant Gangsters: The Changing Face of Youth Crime*. Cullompton: Willan Publishing.

Schwarze, T. and Fatsis, L. (2022) Copping the blame: The role of YouTube videos in the criminalisation of UK drill music. *Popular Music*, 41(4): 463–480.

Shepard, A. (2003) *Meaning of Manhood in Early Modern England*. Oxford: Oxford University Press.

Smithson, H., Ralphs, R. and Williams, P. (2013) Used and abused: The problematic usage of gang terminology in the United Kingdom and its implications for ethnic minority youth. *British Journal of Criminology*, 53(1): 113–128.

Stark, E. (2007) *Coercive Control: How Men Entrap Women in Personal Life*. Oxford: Oxford University Press.

Thomson, R. and Taylor, R. (2005) Between cosmopolitanism and the locals. *Young*, 13(4): 327–342.

Tosh, J. (2005) *Manliness and Masculinities in Nineteenth-Century Britain: Essays on Gender, Family and Empire*. Abingdon: Routledge.

Toy, J. (2008) *Die Another Day: A Practitioner's Review with Recommendations for Preventing Gang and Weapon Violence in London in 2008*. Available at: https:/resources/forum/218/dieanotherday.pdf.

Trickett, L. (2015) 'Birds and Sluts': Views on young women from boys in the gang. *International Review of Victimology*, 22(1): 25–44.

Walby, S. (2020) Varieties of gender regimes. *Social Politics*, 27(3): 414–431.

Warner, M. (1994) *Managing Monsters: Six Myths of Our Time – The 1994 Reith Lectures*. New York: Vintage.

Williams, P. (2015) Criminalising the other: Challenging the race-gang nexus. *Race and Class*, 56(3): 18–35.

Williams, P. and Clarke, B. (2018) The black criminal other as an object of social control. *Social Sciences*, 7: 1–14.

Young, T. (2009) Girls and gangs: 'Shemale' gangsters in the UK? *Youth Justice*, 9(3): 224–238.

Young, T. and Hallsworth, S. (2011) Young people, gangs and street-based violence. In D. Berridge and C. Barter (eds) *Children Behaving Badly? Exploring Peer Violence Between Children and Young People*. Hoboken: Wiley-Blackwell, pp 73–83.

Young, T. and Trickett, L. (2017) Gang girls: Agency, sexual identity and victimisation 'on road'. In K. Gildart, A. Gough-Yates, S. Lincoln, B. Osgerby, L. Robinson, J. Street, P. Webb and M. Worley (eds) *Youth Culture and Social Change*. London: Palgrave Macmillan, pp 231–259.

Žižek, S. (2011) *Living in the End Times*. London and New York: Verso Books.

2

Black, British Young Women On-Road: Intersections of Gender, Race and Youth in British Interwar Youth Penal Reform

Esmorie Miller

Introduction

This chapter develops from the analytical logic of being 'on-road'. Used by racialised, urban male youth, the logic of 'on-road' characterises the contemporary street as a space for both discrete individual transformation and wider social participation (Honneth, 1995). Being 'on-road' references activity constituted by youth's co-option of the road, a 'disenfranchised social milieu' distinguished from 'engagement in conventional society' (Young, 2016: 35). The street represents an irregular space, in this regard, supporting youth's performance of 'a physical reality and, or a general way of being' (Young, 2016: 11). Hallsworth and Silverstone (2009), for instance, emphasise the prevailing exclusion characteristic of youth's disenfranchisement, denoting their relegation from conventional resources and opportunity structures (Merton, 2019 [1995]). While violence delineates the road as a disenfranchised space for social participation, disqualification is constituted by the broader 'consumption logic of consumer capitalism' (Hallsworth and Silverstone, 2009: 361), shaping social exclusion from conventional resources and opportunities (Young, 2007). In this way, the urban street exposes contradictions wrought by modernity's undertaking of greater social progress, by emphasising the social disaffection, alienation and social strain tenaciously normalising itself into the efforts of the many, consequently (Merton, 1938, 1968).

Building on this logic, the chapter historicises 'on-road', exploring an intersection between youth, race and gender. Specifically, it explores an intersection of racialised, gendered politics informing interwar British youth penal reform. Historicising the intersection between youth, gender and race expands 'on-road' to give a unique insight into entrenched social exclusion experienced by racialised young women, in the historic British Metropole. The 'on-road' logic, for instance, contributes a unique racially specific gendered relevance to rich critical gendered histories of this period (see Lawless, 1995; Cox, 2003; Bland, 2005; Christian, 2008; Cox and Shore, 2018). If, for instance, 'on-road' signifies contemporary racialised, urban boys' resistance against exclusion, a space co-opted to carve out both material and moral resources and opportunities, this chapter places racialised young women within this longer historic trajectory. This corresponds with Black, feminist epistemologies both condemning and exhorting the invisibility of historic race, gender concerns (Hill Collins, 2000; Young, 2016; Battle, 2019; Choak, 2020; Hill Collins and Bilge, 2020). While much formative Black, feminist research of race, gender intersections is influenced by African American forerunners (Crenshaw, 1989, 1991, 2013; Miller, 2008; Jones, 2010; Ness, 2010; Kendall, 2021), the 'on-road' logic structures insight within the British context (Young, 2016; Young and Trinkett, 2017; Choak, 2018, 2020). Arguably, these works represent the emergence and expansion of a British contribution to calls for a Black feminist criminology. The urban focus contributes a particular British orientation, given the relegation of racialised demographics to cities in this context, situating them at the mercy of law and order.

Against this backdrop, the analysis adopts and adapts critical race theory (CRT) scholar Kimberlé Crenshaw's intersectional logic, including the CRT emphasis on the need to look to history to assess contemporary concerns with race and exclusion, more appropriately. According to Crenshaw, race and gender intersect, overlap and heighten racialised women's experiences of exclusion from wellbeing-enhancing resources and opportunities. Applied within the distinctive rationalities of treatment, care and control informing interwar British youth penal reform, Crenshaw's intersectional logic contributes needed gendered specificity to CRT's concern with racialised peoples' exclusion from expanding modern rights. For youth, exclusion from rationalities of treatment, care and control is argued in this chapter to be a positioning synonymous with exclusion from resources necessary for their transformation into adulthood (Miller, 2020, 2022). According to the working thesis, historically, racialised youth were outside the imaginings of British interwar youth penal reform objectives, with racialised, female youth occupying its own remarkably adverse positioning (Miller, 2022). Thus, the chapter proposes that being 'on-road' signifies racialised girls' positioning against a backdrop of normative struggles, denoting evolving wider socio-political caprices outside their control. Ultimately, this is a situation experienced punitively and which is historically contingent.

The chapter is structured in two parts. Part I takes emerging contemporary scholarship about young women's experience 'on-road' as a starting point for historicising the intersection between race and gender, in the context of interwar Britain's youth penal reform. Extant literature defines racialised young women's contemporary experiences as a situation comprised by a series of deficits. Relying on Crenshaw's intersectional logic, young, racialised women's experiences are defined as a positioning constituted by ongoing normative conflicts (Merton, 1938, 1968; Cohen, 1972; Young, 2007), operating to undermine the processes characteristic of both discrete individual and social development. The interruption of young women's access to prosocial participation by external forces in the contemporary is situated as a historic version of this. Here, the notion of a normative conflict reflects the ideological divides between competing groups, who are acting to ensure that their way of life is recognised and preserved (Miller, 2015). The greater aim is to challenge the hypervisible representation of young women, moving beyond their normalised deficit representation as risky to demonstrate their entrenched vulnerability. Part II develops young, racialised women's experiences within interwar British youth penal reform as the formative seeds of these intersecting legacies of vulnerability. This historic illustration responds to concerns within contemporary criminology about race, youth and penalty (Chigwada-Bailey, 2003; Young and Choudary, 2014; Gelsthorpe and Sharpe, 2015; Phillips et al, 2019). It, for instance, demonstrates contemporary race concerns to be constituted by a longer historic trajectory. Interwar Britain reflects a diachronic space within which experiences intersecting at youth, race and gender remain hidden in the historic criminological canon. Notably, the wider aim is to contextualise contemporary concerns as historically contingent, encouraging a reorientation of the normalised hypervisible representations of racialised, young women from risky to vulnerable. Life 'on-road', according to this, signifies racialised young women's exclusion as indicative of their historic placement against a backdrop of ideological struggles.

Methodology

The analysis in this chapter draws on documentary research from the Liverpool University Archives, including the Fletcher Report (1930) and the digitised catalogue of the *Eugenics Review*, a populist journal spanning 1909 to 1968. While documents like the Fletcher Report introduced racialised youth to Britain, as a problematic cohort, the pseudo-science promulgated in the *Review* supported the racial politics positioning these youth outside the redemptive scope of early penal reform efforts. Fletcher (1930: 26) concluded that '[t]hese families have a low standard of life, morally and economically, and there appears to be little future for the children'. This conclusion stands counter to narratives supporting rehabilitation for White, working-class youth, especially during the interwar period (Miller, 2022). As already noted, the concept of being 'on-road' offers a unique lens to give gendered relevance to this history. For example, during this time, young women's search for opportunities met with resistance at both the societal and institutional levels. In this regard, Crenshaw's intersectional logic attends to the important intersections of race, gender and youth, giving critical currency to the wider implications of this exclusion. Historicising and gendering 'on-road' in this way, the chapter emphasises the importance of conceptual approaches expanding the explanatory scope about racialised youth's contemporary contested positioning, beyond the customary suturing to crime and punishment. Historicising and gendering 'on-road' enables exploration of racialised youth's circumstances as part of a historic exclusion from the resources and opportunities associated with modern progress.

Part I

The contemporary Black, British urban girl on-road: the contentious preconditions shaping girls' individual and social development

> Law and order is a social service. Crime and the fear which the threat of crime induces can paralyse whole communities, keep lonely and vulnerable elderly people shut up in their homes, scar young lives and raise to cult status the swaggering violent bully who achieves predatory control over the streets. I suspect that there would be more support and less criticism than today's political leaders imagine for a large shift of resources from social services to law and order—as long as rhetoric about getting tough on crime was matched by practice. (Thatcher, 2011 [1995]: 558–559)

The aim to historicise an intersectional conception of Black, British young women 'on-road' begins with an understanding of their contemporary positioning, elucidated here as one construed by a hypervisibility paradox (Crenshaw, 1991, 2013; Phillips and Griffin, 2015). According to the paradox, girls are rendered simultaneously distorted and invisible: they are maligned for purportedly risky dalliances with interpersonal violence (Bernard and Carlile, 2021), and deviant alliances contributing to their exploitation (Harding, 2014); all the while, they are rendered invisible as credible subjects whose vulnerabilities are heightened by wider social preconditions, outside their control. The 'on-road' logic allows that girls' participation aligns with the normative processes of identity formation, but processes occurring in institutional and wider social contexts sustaining a historic exclusion from authorship of the authoritative narratives positioning them as risky instead of vulnerable. An identified paucity of research on Black, British young women demands more expanded explanatory scope (Chigwada-Bailey, 2003; Young and Choudary, 2014; Gelsthorpe and Sharpe, 2015; Choak, 2020; Bernard and Carlile, 2021) consistent with the multitude of scholarship on their Black, male counterparts.

The chapter's analysis corresponds with these emergent concerns, within British criminology, problematising and seeking to rectify the research paucity (Chigwada-Bailey, 2003; Hallsworth and Young, 2008; Young and Choudary, 2014; Gelsthorpe and Sharpe, 2015; Choak, 2020; Bernard and Carlile, 2021). A developing scholarship demonstrates that Black young women's life-worlds – like those of their male counterparts – are heavily mediated by a deepening series of vulnerabilities, including sexual exploitation, interpersonal violence, mounting state surveillance and penalty (Beckett et al, 2013; Young, 2016; Young and Trinkett, 2017; Andell and Pitts, 2018; Havard et al, 2021). The wider impetus to understand more about these young women is informed by the noted series of vulnerabilities, characterising racialised youth's experiences, within a British, urban context marked by amplified racialisation of crime and punishment (Hall et al, 1978; Hallsworth and Young, 2008). Various policy reviews, for instance, adducing race and youth in Britain, emphasise the normalisation of racialised youth as subjects of policing surveillance, disproportionate contact and punishment (Mullen, 2014; Lammy, 2017; Graham et al, 2019).

The 'on-road' logic contributes necessary critical currency to extant analyses of Black young women's experiences, situating their attitudes and actions as part and parcel of what philosophers (Honneth, 1995) remark upon as the normative effort to self-actualise – the self-realisation constituted by both a discrete individuality and a social character. This perspective allows for an understanding of young women's 'on-road' experiences as part of a wider normative conflict, distorting the quality of their efforts towards self-realisation. An illustration of something corresponding with a normative conflict is captured in the opening quotation by former British Prime Minister Margaret Thatcher. In her invocation, Thatcher rationalises the seeds by which the normalisation of law and order as a social service, in racialised, working-class communities, were nurtured. Extant scholarship situates such invocations as indicative of shrinking state welfarism and expanding correctionalism (Garland, 2001; Jones, 2010). As Rose (1990) notes, this shift must not be treated simply as a dispute between the political right and the left. Indeed, it is best understood as part of the collapse of an entire normative system and the rise of another – from rehabilitation, care and treatment to the rationalisation of punishment, zero tolerance and individual responsibility.

Formative scholarship like that of Hall and colleagues (1978: 276) gave racial specificity to the correctionalist advent, demonstrating that the race question became key to the rationalisation of correctionalism. This was helmed by a series of 'discordant themes' – from immigration woes regarding the enemy at the gate (and within), to anxieties about a fledgling economy – collapsed together to inspire the sort of moral panic (Cohen, 1972) justifying law and order. Black, British young women's 'on-road' experiences, therefore, are situated in this chapter as coterminous with individuals seeking to actualise their transformation into adulthood and citizenship, against wider historic caprices. Ultimately, it is argued that efforts at identity formation, on the part of these young women, have historically unfolded against a backdrop of contentious social preconditions, rendering them paradoxically 'over-policed but under-protected' (Gelsthorpe and Sharpe, 2015: 51).

Margaret Thatcher's logic in the opening quotation captures the productive practice of surveillance and penalty characterising the contemporary spaces (like the road) shaping Black, young women's experiences. This is a thinking characterising life 'on-road' as a situation steeped in crisis, demarcated in the prioritisation of law and order in response to entrenched social exclusion (Hall et al, 1978; Maynard, 2017). While Hall's seminal study represents formative insight into the detriments of policing disadvantage, more recent research (Pitts, 2008) contextualises Thatcher's sentiments as an evolution of this, accentuating a wider context where socioeconomic decline positions the most vulnerable at the mercy of the most dangerous. Extant literature correspondingly reflects on tough on crime justifications and the concomitant rise of individual responsibility, in tandem with the decline in statutory positive rights obligations, inevitably impacting the most socially marginal (Lea, 2002; Young et al, 2006; Pitts, 2008). This is problematically bookended by an unabashed rationalisation of zero tolerance (Garland, 2001; Muncie, 2001).

The contentious preconditions wrought by rationalising law and order as a social service contributes an equivocality defaming Black young women's pursuits, in correspondence with a dark side of female liberation narrative (Cunningham, 2008; Jones, 2010; Ness, 2010; Miller, 2022). Scholarship exposes narratives of a 'shemale gangster' (Young, 2009) and jihadi girl (Cunningham, 2008), superseded only by those implicating girls as architects in their peculiar vulnerabilities due to their associations, particularly with deviant groups typically populated by men (Firmin, 2011; Beckett et al, 2013; Harding, 2014; Andell and Pitts, 2016; Havard et al, 2021). Young and Trickett (2017) emphasise the role of feminist scholarship in offering necessary critical insights into young women's worlds. These formative works expose how meta-anxieties contribute to young women's occlusion from normative considerations. In the American context, such accounts are united by the explorations of the entrenched structural gauntlets of gendered violence young women must navigate, where an absence of protection pervades life from classroom to sidewalk, as Ness (2010: 2) and Jones (2010) found, in their distinct ethnographies of girls' experiences of interpersonal violence, in two impoverished, urban American neighbourhoods. Ness's question, 'Why do female adolescent youths in impoverished urban neighbourhoods so readily engage in street fights and other forms of physical violence?', unifies the broader concerns with social insecurity underpinning both research aims. Both portray interpersonal violence among girls. Yet, interpersonal violence is identified as a microcosm of the ferocious wider state surveillance mechanisms suturing girls' lives to the shadow of state policing scrutiny. Indeed, Jones describes a scene at a neighbourhood high school, of a young woman whose daily efforts to attend school comes short of a strip search by uniformed guards, as part of the securitised requirements for attendance. The scene Jones paints is not one of state protection, but of scrutiny and control. Jones (2010: 207) notes that 'institutional protection is inadequate – they [girls] are aware that they may become targets in school or on the street and they too feel pressure to develop strategies that will help them successfully navigate their neighbourhoods'.

Against a similar backdrop, scholarship from the British context remarks on the instrumental role of female aggression, denoting consistency with Messerschmidt's analysis of male violence as a resource (Levell, 2020; Bernard and Carlile, 2021). Like their male counterparts, females draw upon violence to overcome exclusion from normative resources and opportunities – including security. In this chapter's attempt to forward an understanding of these girls within the 'on-road' logic, such a positioning is analysed as exclusion from the prosocial resources customarily relied upon to enable individual efforts towards self-realisation. Black, British young women's positioning, therefore, indicates the absence of accountability mechanisms for which the endeavours contributing to their categorisation as risky instead of vulnerable, represents a compensatory resource.

In summary, Black, British young women's contemporary experiences have been customarily organised and deployed in a manner problematising their choices as risky, a categorisation integral to their exposure to institutional and social scrutiny. However, this chapter uses the logic of 'on-road' to organise young women's experiences more appropriately as part and parcel of wider normative conflicts, outside their control. These are caprices which undermine their efforts at discrete individual and social development crucial to their transformation into adulthood. Ultimately, such conflicts and such outcomes are argued to be steeped in a historic, gendered, racial intersection of exclusion and penalty.

Black, British young women on-road: intersections of a historic gendered, racial marginality

Crenshaw's (1989, 1991, 2013) intersectional logic offers an opportunity for contextualising the hypervisibility occluding Black, British young women from consideration as individuals, seeking self-actualisation against a backdrop of conflicts outside their control. Crenshaw reveals a marginal positioning, uniquely steeped in intersections of a historic gendered, racial discrimination. Her original case study was the plight of Black American women whose ontological disadvantage reflected a unique marginal race, gender overlap central to her exposition. The disadvantage reflected in how race and gender overlap and compounds the marginality of Black American women is a useful starting point for demonstrating how this applies to Black, British young women, adapted in this chapter as life 'on-road'.

According to Crenshaw, Black women have distinct negative experiences that neither mainstream 'feminist theory' nor 'antiracist policy' can address, without rethinking and recasting. This is because 'Black women's experiences are much broader than the general categories that discrimination discourses provides' (Crenshaw, 1989: 149). Recasting and rethinking require consideration of how each social identity overlaps, with the overlap focused on the historic deficit positioning of exclusion characterising both gender and race – and necessarily compounding. Attendance to the historic element is rooted in the CRT tradition from which Crenshaw's intersectionality derives. According to CRT, continuities of historic racial discrimination remain relevant to the contemporary experiences of racialised peoples.

In taking Crenshaw's intersection of gender and race, I also include youth as an important social intersection. Including youth is a crucial distinction for situating exclusion as something synonymous with punitiveness, experienced trans-institutionally, inter-related across structural and institutional settings. For youth, this is quite relevant, as the systems on which they rely, including the justice system, the education system, as well as their access to recreation and employment, hold within them continuities of exclusionary principles and practices (Bell, 1980, 1992, 2000). Youth itself represents an important life stage where levels of responsibility, agency and personal autonomy are examined by institutions who use these features to determine insiders and outsiders (Becker, 1973). This corresponds with the revelations associated with the deviance invention tradition which has contributed a great deal to our knowledge of the intersections between youth, gender and class (Platt, 1969; Shore, 2011; Ward, 2012). The chapter contributes racial specificity to these concerns, including the possibility for interrogating the true character of racialised female youth's over-policed and under-protected positioning.

Understood against the logics of racialised young women's positioning 'on-road', this intersection of gender, race and youth is most appropriately understood as historically contingent. This allows that the normative conflicts which shape racialised young women's contemporary experiences are indicative of a longer history of exclusion. Notions of a normative conflict have established lineages in criminology. Scholarship adducing concerns with social strain (Merton, 1938, 1968), moral panics (Cohen,

1972) and vertigo (Young, 2007) are bound up with concerns about wider social fears regarding social stability, particularly whose value system defines it, which value systems raise panics about challenges to this stability, and ultimately pinpoints insiders and outsiders. Cohen (1972: 203), for instance, emphasises how young people were transformed into 'active agents of social change' and therefore became targets for wider social anxieties. Merton's theory of strain shows how the emphasis on wealth accumulation can lead to non-conformity and deviance (Merton, 1938). Young et al (2006), with their proposal for left realist criminology, argue that Merton's thesis can be the basis for a more critical account of the normative conflicts specifically constituted within modern capitalist arrangements. Participation 'on-road', according to the left realist perspective, is not to be romanticised as forms of resistance. Street crime, for instance, including the interpersonal violence, gang membership and exploitation which shape racialised young women's life-worlds, has devastating outcomes. Here, the conflict which left realists pinpoint rationalises the integration of law and order into social life, making room for penality as a legitimate response to the identifiable disconnections between culturally induced goals – prioritising wealth accumulation as a signifier of individual responsibility – and the means to achieve this definition of stability and responsibility.

Adapting these logics according to Crenshaw's CRT-informed analysis allows for what Merton (2019 [1995]) described as a concrete application of a more generalisable set of ideas about social arrangements, as defined by modernity's differentiated undertaking of social progress. In a retrospective on his legacy, Merton cites the wide-ranging application of his strain theory as representative of the multitudinous ways his more general paradigm of social exclusion can be interpreted and applied to specific social attitudes, behaviours and contexts. For instance, scholarship chronicling racialised young women's experiences emphasise their underclass status, suggesting that their categorisation as over-policed and under-protected aligns with wider efforts to contain threats to social stability. Here, young women's underclass status represents the antithesis to wealth accumulation and prosperity and can thus be read as a signifier of failure, from which social stability must be protected. The policing of underclass communities, while situated by left realists as a legitimate effort to countermand underclass residents' idiosyncratic positioning among the most dangerous, is one way to explain young women's exposure to policing. Crucially, the CRT perspective takes this a step farther, indicating young women's categorisation as under-protected, particularly in the face of law and order scrutiny, to be read as part of the paradox of racialised peoples' historic marginalisation from universal rights (Bell, 1980, 1992, 2000). In this way, CRT produces a firmly relational account of marginalisation, beyond traditional criminological references to individual rational choice or inherent evil character, situating marginalisation as exclusion and (crucially) experienced punitively.

Thus far, Part I of the chapter takes emerging contemporary scholarship about young women's experience 'on-road' as a starting point for historicising the intersection between race and gender, in the context of interwar Britain's youth penal reform logics. Relying on Crenshaw's intersectional logic, young, racialised women's experiences are defined as a positioning constituted by ongoing normative conflicts, operating to undermine the processes characteristic of both discrete individual and social development. The notion of a normative conflict reflects the ideological divides between competing groups, who are acting to ensure that their way of life is recognised and preserved. In this context, racialised young women's experiences 'on-road' speak to an entrenched historic exclusion from opportunities and resources crucial to their discrete individual and social development, key to the transformation into adulthood. The wider challenge has been with the normalisation of these young women's participation as risks to social stability; this is a hypervisible obviation of the consequential vulnerabilities imposed upon them by the conflictual social preconditions against which they are forced to perform the important developmental goals constitutive of their transformation into adulthood. Part II offers a case study which demonstrates young women's 'on-road' participation to be historic, a formative seed embedded within interwar institutional British youth penal reform.

Part II

On-road: forged in modernity's fury of racialised, gendered exclusion

This final section of the chapter begins with reference to Thatcher's quotation (see p 23). The normalisation of law enforcement in contemporary underclass communities reflects a continuity in a more historic rationalisation of institutional surveillance in the lives of the poor working classes. As Thatcher notes, such scrutiny is intended to safeguard individuals within communities who are exposed to threats from dangerous others; for instance, the curtailment of the swaggering bully is key to securing the more vulnerable, including the young and the elderly. The claim in this chapter is that the rationalisation of such scrutiny is a continuity of a more entrenched historic rationalisation of surveillance, customarily imposed into the lives of the socioeconomically marginalised. In essence, surveillance is a modern instrument used to maintain purportedly benign, yet more dispersed, forms of discipline (Foucault, 1975).

Foucault's (1975) perspective on the intersection between discipline and punishment is a commentary on the malignance defined and rationalised into the everyday experiences of demographics regarded as a threat to modern ideals and practices of progress. Foucault's discussion on the disappearance of punishment as a public spectacle sets up his discussion on the imposition of techniques of power on the self. He contends that the imposition of pain onto the body (characteristic of premodern times) was replaced by something more subtle, but something terrifyingly potent. Aligning with Foucault, Taylor contends that it is modern techniques of power that mark particular individuals and communities as objects (or subjects) of surveillance and control (Taylor, 1986: 78).

As noted previously, one way to observe the place of discipline, or its cognates (penalty, punishment, exclusion), is to consider the role it plays in the modern struggles for conformity. Within these struggles the logic of 'on-road' expands consideration for those excluded from the normative processes, including the opportunities and resources, availed to those aligned with conformist induced goals. Therefore, while being 'on-road' references activity constituted by youth's co-option of the road, as 'disenfranchised social milieu' distinguished from 'engagement in conventional society' (Young, 2016: 35), this disentrancement is bound up with the inner workings of modernity's failure to curtail exclusion. Indeed, 'on-road' represents the utilitarian induced outcome, when control of those marginalised from conventional participation is prioritised ahead of contending with the processes contributing to marginalisation. In this regard, those like Merton implicate modern institutions in the plight of those marginalised from conventional participation. This is key to Merton's identification of the deficiency in institutional means (for example, poor access to education) as key to undermining conventional participation (Merton, 1938: 676).

Crenshaw's intersectional logic allows observation of a racial, gendered specificity, against the backdrop of these more general theorisations. Meanwhile, the 'on-road' logic allows observation on the historic intersection of racialised young women's experiences with exclusion from convention. Indeed, as noted earlier, this is exclusion forged in modernity's furious advanced towards greater societal progress. What follows next is a case study of this historic racial, gendered exclusion. It implicates interwar youth penal reform efforts, emphasising the role of modern institutions in rationalising the seeds of the intersectional exclusion to which Crenshaw draws attention. Importantly, the discussion adapts Young's thesis about the disequilibrium imposed by late modernity and argues that the vertigo of which he speaks is indicative of a trajectory forged in modernity itself. Adapted as such, Young's thesis usefully emphasises modern institutions as billboards for exclusion. The aim is to situate racialised young women's exclusion from convention – emphasised in their adaptation to life 'on-road' – as exclusion paradoxically established within modernity itself.

On-road: race and gender in interwar British youth penal reform

In her work titled *Report on an Investigation into the Coloured Problem in Liverpool*, author Muriel Fletcher spoke of something called *An Experimental Training*

Scheme and its Results (Fletcher, 1930: 35). The experiment aimed to see if training racialised girls in forms of creative craft could help mitigate their marginalisation from paid employment. Fletcher explained that over 50 per cent of employers refused to hire racialised young people, upon their leaving school, for a variety of reasons linked to their skin colour. Employers argued either that White employees would object to having a racialised colleague or that customers would object, similarly. In this chapter the reasons necessitating the scheme is prioritised over the exposition of the scheme's content. Yet, this is a useful starting point. Five young, mixed-race women (deemed Anglo-Negroid, White mother, Black father) were chosen to attend a class for one hour, twice a week, for six months, where they would learn to embroider (Fletcher, 1930). Though unpaid, the girls were promised five shillings for those with perfect attendance at the end of the scheme. Ultimately, only two of the five completed the experiment, each of whom were deemed 'most unpunctual' (Fletcher, 1930: 37). Fletcher goes on to admit that compensation for work, in future schemes, might prove a greater incentive than the unpaid arrangement.

The Report was a product of interwar British youth penal reform. This was a context following from the 1908 separation of youth justice from the adult penal system. Fletcher, a social worker and ethnographer, was part of the wider effort to concretise the principles and practices coterminous with the role the new institution would play. Key features were the implementation of knowledges defining the working-class youth, and eventually the working-class racialised youth, as objects for interventions. This included marking out the principles about how they should be managed. This is the context within which punishment was repudiated and ideas prophesising the healing effects of rehabilitation, treatment and care formed the basis of intervention. The rehabilitation account of youth justice, therefore, was marked by an approach to deviance which 'emphasised four features: the psychology of adolescence as a distinct developmental stage of life, the indiscipline and character deficiencies of large sections of working-class youth, the malign influence of bad urban environments, and the lack of recreational facilities' (Hendrick, 1994: 163). The work of psychologist Cyril Burt, particularly his definitive study *The Young Delinquent* (1925), was an important influence in the development of these ideas. Reformers and practitioners fused environmental considerations like poverty with an education and mental health agenda. Robinson and Crow (2009: 17) argue that rehabilitative accounts on the management of deviance can be understood as a move from a corporal to a carceral rationale, consistent with Foucault's thesis on the distinction between the brutality of punishment and the purportedly benign character of modern disciplinary measures marked out by carceral/environmental control. In a previous work I categorised these beliefs as an effort to capitalise on youth as a transformative phase, denoting their malleability to (positive) change (Miller, 2022).

The Fletcher Report marks an example of how ideas guiding the new youth institution were shaped and imposed. Extant literature commenting on the Report allows for deeper critical commentary on the stigmatisation coterminous with works like these, specifically for the racialised cohort on whom it focused. Bland (2005) talks about the wider context of anti-Black racist exclusion in which the Report was written. Youth were deemed to be 'handicapped' by their race, for instance, instead of the racist attitudes imposed on them (Fletcher, 1930: 5). Their family lives, particularly the union of parents, were maligned as antithetical to the stability and success the progressive modern machinery sought to establish for British society. Consider, also, the title of the Report, whose title assigns blame to race instead of racism. This is the seat of the exclusion which occasioned the experiment discussed earlier. Racialised girls were particularly exposed to this, as the experiment attests. Others, like Lawless (1995) and Christian (2008), emphasised that the Report itself was not an autonomous piece of work, but part of a larger machinery disseminating derogatory ideas about the racialised demographics within the population and stirring up racial hatred (Miller, 2022). The 1919 riots – which raged across British port cities between the White and racialised population – also occurred in Liverpool and stand as an exemplar of the racism permeating interwar reform efforts.

The role of eugenics pseudo-science, in this racism, cannot be overstated (Peel, 1997). The rise of eugenics as a tool coincided with the rise of other formative ideas about modern progress, including those shaping the management of youth earmarked for intervention. This movement, for instance, in furthering ideas asked and answered the question of how societies should progress. Key figures, like Francis Galton (1822–1911), promoted the links between economic development, political stability and social engineering (Mudge, 1920). In this link, concerns about heredity and malleability were bound up with the rationalisation of interventions in the lives of families regarded as struggling to meet their socialisation function (Miller, 2022). However, the control legitimised by eugenics also contributed to the stigmatisation and exclusion of those deemed antithetical to social stability (Jones, 1998). Concerns with progress of the British nation, therefore, centred around the purported impurity occasioned by miscegenation, denoting racial mixing (Fleming, 1930). Far apart from the racism levelled against their Black fathers and the sexism levelled against their White mothers, the progeny of miscegenation were deemed especially antithetical to notions of modern progress and stability. Indeed, they were deemed to embody the worst traits of both parents – bestial, uncivilised fathers and mothers deemed deficient for their choice of partners (Bland, 2005). Crucially, Galton's influence was ubiquitous, attested by his relationships with institutional actors, including academia and government

(Jones, 1998). Indeed, the Galton society still exists in contemporary Britain (as the Adelphi Genetics Forum), despite the delegitimisation of eugenics.

Young's thesis casting late modernity as a period of vertigo, particularly for racialised peoples, usefully adjourns this analysis. This notion of vertigo captures appropriately Crenshaw's concern with how social deficits intersect and compound to shape marginalisation can be accessed according to Young's notion of disequilibrium. Contrary to Young's placement of this within the late modern period, the argument in this chapter is that disequilibrium was a factor earlier, for the racialised. Indeed, I argue that Young's discussion of institutions as concrete sites of exclusion is rooted in this period, particularly with the mistreatment of youth. The youth justice system, the media, employers and the philanthropic movement were each important institutional frameworks espousing this paradox. On the one hand, institutions originated to further an idea of progress; on the other hand, their idea of progress was one marked by class, gender and racial differentiation. These differentiates, it is argued, contributed to strains to which those like Young and Merton alluded.

As with the contemporary setting, the understanding of racialised young women as over-policed and under-protected is seen in this early period. For instance, their position among the poor working classes rationalised interventions into their homes and daily lives. What is remarkable is that interventions and the scrutiny to which they contributed did not appear to offer the caring ethos guiding reform efforts. That young women and their families were reported on as a 'Problem', to the wider public, attests to this over-policed and under-protected status. That these events unfold amidst young women's efforts at identity formation speaks to the proposal that these youth's development processes historically occurred against the backdrop of normative struggles, outside their control. Consider, for instance, that as they each carried on with their daily lives all around them debates unfolded, rationalising their exclusion from normative participation. Employers were excused for denying these youth access to opportunities; experts marked them as unlikely to contribute to social stability; and, as Fletcher noted, they had no future in British society.

Conclusion

In this chapter, I developed the analytical logic of being 'on-road'. The chapter historicises 'on-road', exploring an intersection between youth, race and gender, specifically, the intersection of racialised, gendered politics informing interwar British youth penal reform. I argue that while being 'on-road' is used by racialised, urban male youth to characterise their contemporary disenfranchisement from conventional participation, the concept also relates to racialised young women whose experiences are similarly set against the backdrop of racial differentiation. The focus on racialised young women, during the interwar period, allows that the disenfranchisement is historically entrenched, coinciding with the paradoxical denial of universal rights to racialised peoples. Crenshaw's intersectional logic contributes needed gendered specificity to CRT's concern with racialised peoples' exclusion from expanding modern rights. In taking Crenshaw as the primary analytical device, I adapt this to speak more specifically about youth, as a response to two key concerns about race in contemporary criminology. The first is with the paucity of research on racialised, British young women. This is problematic since what is known about them contributes to a hypervisible representation which at once distorts and renders them invisible: on the one hand, their vulnerabilities are distorted as risks, casting them as threats to social stability; on the other hand, they are rendered invisible as credible subjects whose vulnerabilities are heightened by wider social preconditions, outside their control. The second criminological concern to which this chapter responds is with the dehistoricisation of contemporary race matters. The historical account presented here allows for a more expanded thinking about the normalised intersection between race, youth and penalty in contemporary society. The chapter considers that this intersection is a continuity of racialised youth's formative exclusion from modern rights, emphasised in their marginalisation from the care agenda grounded the interwar period. It is argued that racialised young women's 'on-road' participation can be understood as their response to the normative struggles which positions racialised peoples as threats to social stability. In this way, 'on-road' exposes contradictions wrought by modernity's undertaking of greater social progress, emphasising the social disaffection, alienation and social strain normalising in the lives of racialised peoples, in general, and racialised youth, in particular.

References

Andell, P. and Pitts, J. (2016) The end of the line? The impact of county lines drug distribution on youth crime in a target destination. *Youth & Policy*. Available at: https://www.youthandpolicy.org/articles/the-end-of-the-line/

Battle, N.T. (2019) *Black Girlhood, Punishment, and Resistance: Reimagining Justice for Black Girls in Virginia*. London: Routledge.

Becker, H. (1973) *Outsiders: Studies in the Sociology of Deviance*. New York: The Free Press.

Beckett, H., with Brodie, I., Factor, F., Melrose, M., Pearce, J., Pitts, J., Shuker, L. and Warrington, C. (2013) *'It's wrong – but you get used to it': A Qualitative Study of Gang-associated Sexual Violence towards, and Exploitation of, Young People in England*. London: The Office of the Children's Commissioner/University of Bedfordshire.

Bell, D. (2000) *Race, Racism, and American Law (Casebook S.)*. Boston: Apsen Publishers.

Bell, D.A. (1980) Brown v. Board of education and the interest convergence dilemma. *Harvard Law Review*, 93(3): 518–533.

Bell, D.A. (1992) Racial realism. *Connecticut Law Review*, 24(2): 363–379.

Bernard, C. and Carlile, A. (2021) Black girls navigate the physical and emotional landscape of the neighbourhood: Normalized violence and strategic agency. *Qualitative Social Work*, 20(3): 866–883.

Bland, L. (2005) White women and men of colour: Miscegenation fears in Britain after the great war. *Gender & History*, 17(1): 29–61.

Burt, C. (1925) *The Young Delinquent*. London: University of London Press.

Chigwada-Bailey, R. (2003) *Black Women's Experiences of Criminal Justice: Race, Gender and Class: A Discourse on Disadvantage*. Hook: Waterside Press.

Chigwada-Bailey, R. (2004) Black women and the criminal justice system. In G. McIvor (ed) *Women who Offend*. London: Jessica Kingsley Publishers, pp 183–208.

Choak, C. (2018) *Young Women On Road: Femininities, Race and Gangs in London*. Doctoral dissertation, University of East London.

Choak, C. (2020) British criminological amnesia: Making the case for a Black and postcolonial feminist criminology. *Decolonization of Criminology and Justice*, 2(1): 37–58.

Christian, M. (2008) The Fletcher Report 1930: A historical case study of contested black mixed heritage Britishness. *Journal of Historical Sociology*, 21(2–3): 213–241.

Cohen, S. (1972) *Folk Devils and Moral Panics: The Creation of the Mods and Rockers*. London: Routledge.

Cox, P. (2003) *Gender, Justice and Welfare in Britain, 1900–1950: Bad Girls in Britain, 1900–1950*. Hampshire: Palgrave Macmillan.

Cox, P. and Shore, H. (eds) (2018) *Becoming Delinquent: British and European Youth, 1650–1950*. London: Routledge.

Crenshaw, K. (1989) Demarginalizing the intersection of race and sex. *Feminist Legal Theory*, 1: 57–80.

Crenshaw, K.W. (1991) Mapping the margins: Intersectionality, identity politics, and violence against women of color. *Stanford Law Review*, 43(6): 1241–1299.

Crenshaw, K.W. (2013) From private violence to mass incarceration: Thinking intersectionality about women, race, and social control. *University California Los Angeles Legal Review*, 59: 20–50.

Cunningham, K. (2008) The evolving participation of Muslim women in Palestine, Chechnya, and the global jihadi movement. In C.D. Ness (ed) *Female Terrorism and Militancy: Agency, Utility, and Organization*. London: Routledge, pp 85–98.

Firmin, C. (2011) This is it. This is my life: Female voice in violence final report London. *Race on the Agenda*. Available at: https://www.rota.org.uk/content/rota-march-2011-female-voice-violence-project-final-report-it-my-life

Fleming, R.M. (1930) Human hybrids. *Eugenics Review*, 21(4): 257–263.

Fletcher, M.E. (1930) *Report on an Investigation into the Colour Problem in Liverpool and Other Ports*. Liverpool: Liverpool Association for the Welfare of Half-Caste Children.

Foucault, M. (1975) *Discipline and Punish: The Birth of the Prison*. London: Penguin.

Garland, D. (2001) *The Culture of Control: Crime and Social Order in Contemporary Society*. Oxford: Clarendon Press.

Gelsthorpe, L. and Sharpe, G. (2015) Women and sentencing: Challenges and choices. In J.V. Roberts (ed) *Exploring Sentencing Practice in England and Wales*. London: Palgrave Macmillan, pp 118–136.

Graham, B., White, C., Edwards, A., Potter, S., Street, C. and Hinds, D. (2019) *Timpson Review of School Exclusion: Consultation Outcome*. London: UK Parliament.

Hall, S., Critcher, C., Jefferson, T., Clarke, J. and Roberts, B. (1978) *Policing the Crisis: Mugging, The State, and Law and Order*. Hong Kong: Macmillan.

Hallsworth, S. and Young, T. (2008) Gang talk and gang talkers: A critique. *Crime, Media, Culture*, 4(2): 175–195.

Hallsworth, S. and Silverstone, D. (2009) 'That's life innit': A British perspective on guns, crime and social order. *Criminology & Criminal Justice*, 9(3): 359–377.

Harding, S. (2014) *The Street Casino: Survival in Violent Street Gangs*. Bristol: Policy Press.

Havard, T.E., Densley, J.A., Whittaker, A. and Wills, J. (2021) Street gangs and coercive control: The gendered exploitation of young women and girls in county lines. *Criminology & Criminal Justice*. https://doi.org/10.1177/17488958211051513

Hendrick, H. (1994) *Child Welfare: England 1872–1989*. London: Routledge.

Hill Collins, P. (2000) *Black Feminist Thought*. New York: Routledge.

Hill Collins, P. and Bilge, S. (2020) *Intersectionality*, 2nd edn. Hoboken: Wiley.

Honneth, A. (1995) *The Struggle for Recognition: The Moral Grammar of Social Conflict*. Cambridge, MA: MIT Press.

Jones, G. (1998) Theoretical foundations of eugenics. In R.A. Peel (ed) *Essays in the History of Eugenics*. London: Galton Institute, pp 1–19.

Jones, N. (2010) *Between Good and Ghetto*. New Brunswick: Rutgers University Press.

Kendall, M. (2021) *Hood Feminism: Notes from the Women that a Movement Forgot*. London: Penguin.

Lammy, D. (2017) *The Lammy Review: An Independent Review into the Treatment of, and Outcomes for, Black, Asian and Minority Ethnic Individuals in the Criminal Justice System*. London: Ministry of Justice.

Lawless, R. (1995) *From Ta'izz to Tyneside: An Arab Community in the North-East of England During the Early Twentieth Century*. Exeter: University of Exeter Press.

Lea, J. (2002) *Crime and Modernity*. London: SAGE.

Levell, J. (2020) Using Connell's masculinity theory to understand the way in which ex-gang-involved men coped with childhood domestic violence. *Journal of Gender-Based Violence*, 4(2): 207–221.

Maynard, R. (2017) *Policing Black Lives: State Violence in Canada from Slavery to the Present*. Halifax: Fernwood Publishing.

Merton, R. (1938) Social structure and anomie. *American Sociological Review*, 3(5): 672–682.

Merton, R. (1968) *Social Theory and Social Structure*. New York: Free Press.

Merton, R. (2019 [1995]) Opportunity structures: The emergence, diffusion, and differentiation of a sociological concept, 1930s–1950s. In F. Adler and W.S. Laufer (ed) *The Legacy of Anomie Theory*. London: Routledge, pp 3–78.

Miller, E. (2015) *Recognition, Retribution and Restoration: Youth Penal Justice and the Issue of Youth Gangs and Crime in Canada and England*. Unpublished PhD Thesis, Queen's University Belfast.

Miller, E. (2020) Moving beyond crime and punishment narratives and analyses: Critical race theory and racial specificity in youth justice. *British Society of Criminology Newsletters*, 85. Available at: www.britsoccrim.org/wp-content/uploads/2020/08/BSCN85-Miller.pdf

Miller, E. (2022) *Race, Recognition and Retribution in Contemporary Youth Justice: The Intractability Malleability Thesis*. London: Routledge.

Miller, J. (2008) *Getting Played: African American Girls, Urban Inequality, and Gendered Violence*. New York: New York University Press.

Mudge, G.P. (1920) The menace to the English race and to its traditions of present-day immigration and emigration. *The Eugenics Review*, 11(4): 202–211.

Mullen, J. (2014) *Improving Outcomes for Young Black and/or Muslim Men in the Criminal Justice System*. London. Available at: https://www.prisonpolicy.org/scans/young_review/improving_outcomes.pdf

Muncie, J. (2001) Policy transfer and what works: Some reflection on comparative youth justice. *Youth Justice*, 1(3): 27–35.

Ness, C.D. (2010) *Why Girls Fight*. New York: New York University Press.

Peel, R.A. (ed) (1997) *Essays in the History of Eugenics*. London: Galton Institute.

Phillips, C., Earle, R., Parmar, A. and Smith, D. (2019) Dear British criminology: Where has all the race and racism gone? *Theoretical Criminology*, 24(3): 427–446.

Phillips, J.D. and Griffin, R.A. (2015) Crystal Mangum as hypervisible object and invisible subject: Black feminist thought, sexual violence, and the pedagogical repercussions of the Duke lacrosse rape case. *Women's Studies in Communication*, 38(1): 36–56.

Pitts, J. (2008) *Reluctant Gangsters: The Changing Face of Youth Crime*. Uffculme: Willan Publishing.

Platt, A. (1969) *The Child Savers: The Invention of Delinquency*. Chicago: University of Chicago Press.

Robinson, G. and Crow, I. (2009) *Offender Rehabilitation: Theory, Research and Practice*. London: SAGE.

Rose, N. (1990) *Governing the Soul: The Shaping of the Private Self*. London: Routledge.

Shore, H. (2011) Inventing and reinventing the juvenile delinquent in British history. *Memoria Y Civilizatión*, 14 : 105–132.

Taylor, C. (1986) Foucault on freedom and truth. In T.C. Hoy (ed) *Foucault: A Critical Reader*. Oxford: Basil Blackwell, pp 69–102.

Thatcher, M. (2011 [1995]) *The Path to Power*. Glasgow: HarperCollins.

Ward, G.K. (2012) *The Black Child-Savers: Racial Democracy and Juvenile Justice*. Chicago: University of Chicago Press.

Young, T. (2009) Girls and gangs: 'Shemale' gangsters in the UK? *Youth Justice*, 9(3): 224–238.

Young, T. (2016) *Risky Youth or Gang Members? A Contextual Critique of the (Re)Discovery of Gangs in Britain*. Doctoral dissertation, London Metropolitan University.

Young, T. and Choudary, N. (2014) *The Sexual Abuse and Exploitation of Females by Gang-Affiliated Youth in Enfield*. Enfield Community Safety Unit.

Young, T. and Trickett, L. (2017) Gang girls: Agency, sexual identity and victimisation 'on road'. In K. Gildart, A. Gough-Yates, S. Lincoln, B. Osgerby, L. Robinson, J. Street, P. Webb and M. Worley (eds) *Youth Culture and Social Change*. London: Palgrave Macmillan, pp 231–259.

Young, J. (2007) *The Vertigo of Late Modernity*. London: SAGE.

Young, J., Lea, J., Mathews, R. and Kinsey, R. (2006) *Left Realism: The SAGE Dictionary of Criminology*. London: SAGE.

3

Tainted Love: Intimate Relationships and Gendered Violence On-Road

Yusef Bakkali and Ezimma Chigbo

Introduction

Early in Kahlil Gibran's *The Prophet* there is an exchange between Almeetra, a wise woman, a seeress, of the city Almustafa is visiting. The people of the city have asked Almustafa to share his wisdom with them 'to tell us all that has been shown you of that which is between birth and death'. The prophet says he can only tell them 'what is moving within their souls', prompting Almitra to say 'Speak to us of Love'. The prophet responds:

> When love beckons to you, follow him,
> Though his ways are hard and steep.
> And when his wings enfold you yield to him,
> Though the sword hidden among his pinions may wound you.
> And when he speaks to you believe in him,
> Though his voice may shatter your dreams as the north wind lays waste the garden.
> For even as love crowns you so shall he crucify you.
> Even as he is for your growth so is he for your pruning. (Gibran, 1926/1991: 12–14)

Kahlil Gibran's prose reminds us of the breadth of love's potential. It seems love, in Gibran's sense, carries almost simultaneous possibilities for both joy and destruction. This chapter seeks to foreground the reflections and experiences on intimate life among young people with experience of road life. We will be introducing the concept of 'tainted love'; one which seeks to validate the possibilities of love persisting in marginalised spaces, but which reflects the ways it can be *tainted* by complex histories and processes of structural violence. Often its hue is shared with wider societal issues, but in marginalised spaces may at times become more acute – exacerbated by issues such as ontological, economic and existential insecurities.

What the data in this chapter will present is the micro social process in which love is informed by the structural manifestations of race, class and gender. In this way, and although the voices we situate are from both cisgender men and women, weaved throughout is our own and the participants' reinterpretation of love within the very specific terrain of road life. These specificities are intensified by the patriarchal social reproductions which we explore through the varied experiences of our participants.

Road life, a variant form of street culture, is often constructed as virulently violent. This chapter considers how patriarchal violence might look in this context, but also the ways in which histories of racialisation and other connected forms of oppression and exploitation actively texture life in such spaces. Effort is made to understand ways in which young men find themselves in binds of hypermasculine performativity, as self-objectification is regarded as a pathway to realising subjecthood, as some tread the perilous sword's-edge between classed/racialised anxieties and exoticised desires. This feeds into processes of homosocial struggle, among/between men and male-dominated institutions like the police, which shape heterosexual relations as well as drawing on them as an organising and adorning factor. We see processes emerge where street performativity causes young people to burn hot, like supernovae, in order to cultivate desire and increase the possibilities of wearing love's radiant crown, though this process is an ephemeral one, often precipitating an implosion, one which lays waste to intimate lives.

Women are both implicated in and affected by these processes, as they display deep investment in heterosexist-desire, while having to navigate the minefield of love and selfhood on the hard-edge of the White supremacist capitalist patriarchy (hooks, 1994). Experiences of domestic abuse against female participants are explored, highlighting an acute manifestation of the wider structural violence of patriarchy, one which impresses upon intimate life. One of the 'bubbling pressures' (Bakkali, 2019) under the façade of impenetrable masculinity – the desperate need to be loved – surfaces, exacerbated by the lack of male capacity to love and disproportionate need for women to heal this anguish – creating a crushing heaviness, weighing down on the possibilities of experiencing enriching loving relationships.

The chapter will begin by outlining a brief account of how road life might be understood. This will be followed by two subsequent sections which focus around the racialised and gendered aspects of road culture, these in particular provide some context for the kinds of structural impressions bearing on intimate life in the later data sections. The chapter will then foray into a discussion about love, and how it has been differently understood/conceptualised, outlining the ways in which romantic love specifically has always had associations with joy and suffering. A short methodological section will precede the data section, where interview data will be presented and connections made illustrating how 'tainted love' unfolds in intimate life on-road. Finally, we will offer some closing reflections on grounded understandings of intimate life and possible futures.

Road and racial ambiguity

Road culture (Gunter, 2008, 2010) is a UK-based variation on 'street culture' strongly associated with symbols of Black Atlantic popular culture (Gilroy, 1993) embodied in fashion, speech and musical tastes. Criminological studies have tended to view road life in fairly 'narrow' (Gunter, 2010) terms, capturing snapshots of the roads while investigating subjects such as gun crime (Hallsworth and Silverstone, 2009), incarceration (Earle, 2011; Glynn, 2013), the drug economy (Reid, 2023) and gangs. Gunter (2010) regards road as more of a hybrid social milieu, co-produced by the multiethnic communities occupying the housing estates of England's major urban centres. Definitively defining road culture is difficult, as it can often contain multiple, and often complex and contradictory, modes of being (Ilan, 2015). Gunter and Watt (2009: 520) warn against conceptualising road culture in *exclusively* racial or gendered terms, though this should be appropriately nuanced.

Many of the cultural signifiers associated with road life are commonly applied to and also mobilised by Black youth to variegated extents. However, these are also implicated in stereotypical connections between Black youth and criminality. Tropes associated with the 'roadman' follow trajectories of popular Western racialisation, which include depictions like the 'bad buck' (Hall, 1997), the 'gangsta/rapper' (hooks, 1994) and the 'mugger' (Hall et al, 2013); something which can have destructive consequences. Amnesty International (2018) highlighted the ways in which the police and other services often drew on musical tastes, activities and fashion choices as indicators for gang involvement, illustrating the articulations (Hall, 2021) between these sets of meanings in action.

The other edge of the blade of racialisation is its relationship to desire. Ove Sernhede (2007) drew on elements of psychoanalysis to argue that in Western societies a collective consciousness of racism can be observed, coalescing with capitalist cultures of consumption. He argues that the essentialising qualities fixed onto Black communities in order to legitimise unjust systems of differentiation (racism), represent repressed, yet deeply desired, elements in Western consciousness. This relationship between marginality, desire and commodification is something also borne out in street culture research (Ilan, 2015). Later it becomes apparent that similar tropes cross into intimate life, where young men discuss how cultivating these dispositions are part of what makes them desirable.

One must be attentive to the ways in which racialisation of Black communities is crucial in understanding the panacea of road cultural representations, but also be mobile enough to consider how different actors, of differential ethnic, cultural, classed, sexually oriented, gendered dispositions, might 'slide' (Hall, 2017) into contact with different dimensions of structural influence via their social *situatedness* (Bakkali, 2022). This presents possible conditions for exploitation and violence, but also possibility for cultural opportunity among marginalised youth on-road. These issues and ambiguities around race also intersect with ambiguities around gender on-road.

Road life, patriarchy and gender

The roads are generally cast as a masculine space (Hallsworth and Silverstone, 2009; Earle, 2011; Glynn, 2013), commonly interpreted as valorising particular kinds of (hyper)masculinities and organised along, at times brutal, patriarchal logics. In the United States studies have examined intimate relationships in street settings at length. Liebow (1968) wrote extensively on the intimate lives of a street-oriented African American community. Dominant expectations of marriage and fatherhood could be a site of failure for men without the resources to perform to the patriarchal canon. Attention was also paid to the ways care, tenderness and violence intersect in complicated ways. However, Leibow's rich descriptions formed part of a myopia which led him to struggle to identify the structural racism and patriarchy shaping the lives of participants.

Anderson (2000), acknowledging the influence of urban decay and racism, also found that the expectations of hegemonic masculinity weighed heavy on the shoulders of street-oriented men. He, too, found intimate spaces represented sites of failure for young men who, at some level, aspired to more conventionally sanctioned modes of masculinity. Limited educational and employment opportunities combined with the destructive force of the drug economy, worked to wreck familial structures, luring marginalised young men with the promise of fast money, as well as shattering lives through the evils of addiction and mass incarceration. In the absence of the possibility of being a legitimate provider, men tried to realise a sense of autonomy through 'playing' women and found self-worth in sexual conquest. Bourgois (2003) highlighted a similar process whereby the Puerto Rican men in New York struggled to actualise the working-class masculine ideals of rural Puerto Rico in the wake of deindustrialisation in the city. As their earning potential and job security became increasingly precarious, and the drug economy took hold, violence and coercion became the last remaining currency left to cash in to the patriarchal dividend.

Miller (2008) highlighted the ways in which street spaces tended to be unsafe for young women, who typically remained in close proximity to the homes of family or friends. Young women tended to depend on men for physical security, though the violent dispositions necessary for 'safety' put women at risk from those assigned to protect them. Volatile relationships were common, with the patriarchal advantage of young men leading male-perpetrated violence to have a debilitating impact on young women's lives.

In the UK, explorations of intimate life tend to focus on exploitation of women by male gang members. Young and Trickett (2017) highlight the risks of physical and sexual victimisation for gang-involved women. Heteronormative identities were found to be crucial; young women were expected to perform sexual purity, while young men were socially rewarded for promiscuity. Both were at risk of receiving social stigma if word spread of them contravening sanctioned sex roles. In response to these pressures, 'deflecting' behaviours were observed where participants would engage in the 'negative labelling of others helps to shift the attention from oneself' (Young and Trickett, 2017: 251).

Clare Choak (2021: 63) argues young women on-road are able to adopt 'hegemonic masculinity' (Connell, 1987) via forms of badness, though despite this, young women's sexualities are still policed to maintain 'respectability'. Gunter (2010) described how 'linking' (dating) was a leisure activity that both young men and women engaged in, also pointing to the fact that young women tended to spend more time indoors than young men, highlighting their involvement in 'bedroom culture'. Bakkali (2018) found that women with more mediated involvement in the world of 'badness' still have to navigate acute manifestations of patriarchy in street spaces. Given the conceptual focus of the chapter, we will proceed to think more carefully about our use of the word love in relation to intimate life and the breadth of its usage in emotional and intellectual life.

Theorising love

In this section we will consider the ways in which love has been understood as having the potential to both liberate and devastate. In the Western canon love has been roughly categorised into four (though sometimes more) variations: *philia*, *storge*, *agape* and *eros*. *Philia* is commonly thought of as enduring 'friendship love' (Cherry, 2019). *Storge* tends to be considered as familial love, carrying connotations akin to tenderness (Tagirov, 2018). *Agape* is neighbourly love, signifying a recognition of a 'common humanity' (de Sousa, 2015). Finally, *eros* is understood as romantic love, sexual attraction and passion, the type of love which most corresponds to the focus of this chapter.

De Sousa (2015: 3) drew on Tennov's (1979) term limerence, to articulate the most virulent manifestation of *eros*, one he argues 'hogs most of love's press'. According to Wilmott and Bentley (2015: 20), '[l]imerence is an unexpected, overwhelming and debilitating experience that relates to the feeling of "being in love"'. De Sousa (2015) caveats his assertion by saying that not all aspects of erotic love can be captured by limerence, though *eros* has strong links to destructive forms of human emotion; selfishness, jealousy, obsession and rage. Similarly, Freud (2006: 243) commented that there is a 'compulsive character that is to a certain degree a part of passionate love'.

Rather than being an emotional state itself love might be understood as a complex gearing together of the emotions, whereby a person becomes sensitised to the joys and sorrows of another, as well as to their behaviours, like withdrawal or rejection (Baier, 1991). This is echoed by de Sousa (2015: 3–4), who advises us to 'think of love as a condition that shapes and governs thoughts, desires, emotions, and behaviours around the focal person who is the beloved'. This heightened emotional sensitivity makes love *unsafe* (Baier, 1991). In the process of loving, one is risking the possibility of suffering, indeed Baier (1991) commented that love has historically been less safe for women than for others, however, she states that in contemporary times these disproportionate risks have abated: 'Love is now as risky to the health for all of us as it has always been for women. Now, all is fairly fair in love and war, no more special exemptions' (Baier, 1991: 447).

Firestone (1970) considered love to be central to gendered exploitation, whereby dominant male culture sought to expropriate emotional labour from women. Love, to Firestone, is about a 'mutual exchange', whereby lovers become 'wide open' and emotionally vulnerable to one another. Within the context of patriarchy men are conditioned not to be able to reciprocally perform love, often taking unquestioningly without giving. For these reasons, emotionally harmful experiences of love are widespread and pragmatic resignation exists towards relationships which offer social and economic security (Firestone, 1970).

bell hooks' (2001) perspective on love does not fit neatly into the previously outlined varieties. For hooks, love is commonly (mis)understood as a noun, a word describing a feeling or emotion, whereas she conceptualises love as a *verb*, something which is performed in action and intention. Fromm (2000), who inspired some of hooks' thinking on love, claims that *giving* freely is the true *action* of love and behaviours driven by emotions, like jealousy and greed, are passive as they are dominated by passion. He argued that there are four common elements in all forms of love; these are *care*, *responsibility*, *respect* and *knowledge* (Fromm, 2000), definitions that hooks herself shared.

hooks wrote extensively about the ways in which patriarchy and racism imprint themselves on people's intimate lives and relationships (for example, see hooks 2001, 2004) but also fought to establish a clear definition which sought to equip marginalised groups to transcend the limitations of structural oppression through loving practices (hooks, 2001). One of the important ways in which she sought to develop this was by making clear distinctions between love and other processes/emotions like care and 'cathexis' (hooks, 2001). According to hooks, unloving behaviours often co-exist in relationships where actors also experience attachment or engage in acts of care and compassion, meaning in her thinking many relationships lack love.

It seems love has both liberatory possibilities and unequally distributed risks. What dictates this level of risk largely seems to be influenced by the *situatedness* (Bakkali, 2022) of the individual within the social structure. Eva Illouz (2012) approaches love from a sociological standpoint, arguing that structural influences have a bearing over how and why we love, as well as the many forms of distress and anxiety which emerge from it. We suggest social location and structural violence are factors which situate and impact on the possibilities for someone to give, receive and experience love. Use of the term *tainted* hopes to demonstrate recognition of love's perseverance and liberatory potential as well as a 'willingness to accept that none of us can find our way out unsullied from living within the pathology of imperialist, white supremacist, capitalist, heteropatriarchy' (Palmer, 2021). We will proceed, after outlining our methodology, to draw on data exploring the intimate lives of both men and women to help to further elucidate and analyse this concept.

Methodology

The data in this chapter originates from a project involving 12 in-depth narrative interviews with young people involved with life on-road. A purposeful intensity sampling approach (Patton, 1990) was taken, with rich cases selected from across the road cultural continuum (Gunter, 2010) in order to capture a multiplicity of experiences of life on-road. Recruitment of participants relied heavily on personal friendship networks, though these stretched across London and the Midlands, the lead author's youth spent in Brixton, south London was crucial to this. This led to 'varying degrees of insiderness' (Contreras, 2015) across each interview encounter, with unique histories and relationships existing between researcher and participants.

These encounters produced rich and lengthy data, as the closeness allowed for frank, but also tactile, conversations exploring 'the meanings … [participants] place in their worlds' (Heyl, 2001: 369). The degrees of difference between encounters produced a kind of reflexive dynamism as the project developed in an inductive fashion. Sensitising concepts (Blumer, 1954) were developed as data emerged, helping to incubate and further interrogate emerging findings as the interview process went on. Such an approach is influenced heavily by grounded theory (Corbin and Strauss, 1990), drawing 'interpretive devices' in order to anchor them, allowing them to gain a 'deep understanding of social phenomena' (Bowen, 2006: 20). It also avoids working from a hypothesis, instead following the threads emerging from the interview data.

The themes present in this chapter emerged in the initial study, but have subsequently been developed further through critical discussion between the authors, both of whom have long-standing proximate relationships to road life, along with years of practitioner experience. The feeling that having both male and female voices in the text was crucial, both authorial and in the data. The concepts in this chapter developed with this in mind, attempting to give language to sensitive and complex issues like masculine fragility and domestic violence in a way which might further our understanding. We will now proceed to dive into the data and allow these conversations to come forth.

Fixity, desire and heterosexist eroticism

Men in the study were reluctant to talk about intimacy, with bravado sometimes mobilised to deflect the conversation. There were various exchanges throughout the interviews in which men cast negative aspersions about the character of women in relationships with men on-road. However, while this strategy is certainly apparent, we will see in the following section that this façade drops at times, with deeper dynamics revealed:

T: Most people on-road, on-road actively aren't in a relationship … it's not gonna last init, if you're like you're just active on the road, you know it's not gonna last at all … there's just too many girls, on the road and stuff, and too many distractions for a relationship … if you're like on-road actively and you're an active drug dealer, what type of girl is gonna want to support you anyway and be with you …

Yusef: So, you think active road guys get the least girls yeah?

T: Yeah, I think the active ones, they get the least wives, but get the most, ah how can I put it, loose women. … There's not really a lot of women on-road, it just they come to the area, you know? Every woman has their, like um sexual needs and stuff so they come to the area you know. But nah they don't go and commit offences with the lads … they just have a nice time with them, like get drunk and sex that's it. … I think it's part of that as well that just gets the police more angry … because they see that people actually do like us and we're not just like outcasts, people do like us.

There are spectres of the men in Anderson's and Leibow's ethnographies beginning to surface, alluding to the ephemeral nature of life at the margins.

Concerns about the capacity of men on-road to effectively engage in 'lasting' intimate relationships surface. T is reflecting on the value of outlaw street masculinities in contemporary society, and the ways in which this is tied to sex and desire, something which is counterposed with the abjectifying (Tyler, 2013) gaze of the state and authorities. In the context of recent narratives around the exploitation of women in street space it is interesting that T exaggeratedly mentions the willingness of young women with romantic aspirations to be spending time with 'the lads'. T is asserting the value and desirability of young men in his community despite the view of the police and other authorities, lifting the lid on the ways 'heterosexual desire here masks interracial homosocial fear and desire' (Bergner, 1995: 80). Here we see Fanonesque social processes whereby racialised and marginalised youth struggle for personhood and 'social authority' (Bergner, 1995: 80), with those representing the strong arm of the White supremacist capitalist patriarchy (hooks, 2004) – a struggle which is 'played out on sexual terrain' (Bergner, 1995: 80). In addition to this, T is suggesting that women whom he would consider desirable outside of the pursuit of sex or physical intimacy are unlikely to see men on-road as desirable partners. Further, this presents a dynamic in which there is a discursive precedent that women are expected to perform a gendered version of respectability which transcends road culture.

However, the comportment and behaviours underpinning this desire are also restrictive and harmful to these young men. This could be regarded as inversion of the same set of fears, described in relation to the police, into an 'aesthetic idealization of racial[ised] Otherness that merely inverts and reverses the binary axis of the repressed fears and anxieties that are projected onto the Other in ... psychic representations' (Mercer, 1991: 187). Both positions – fear and desire – channel stereotypes in order to 'fix' the subject, subsequently reproducing meanings rooted in 'colonial fantasy' (Mercer, 1991: 187).

In the lives of young men on-road, there seems to be some acute awareness of this bind between value and exclusion, fear and desire. In many instances young men described feelings of low mood and self-worth (Bakkali, 2019), and clearly sought care, value and inclusion (Bakkali, 2022). The realm of intimate life seemed to be an important space where these feelings played out, with young men describing situations where themselves or others would be willing to mobilise street tropes and the underground economy to tap into feminine desire and fetishisation, as Stephen describes here:

Yusef: Why do you think image is so important?
Stephen: Its girls man, its girls that drive it man.
Yusef: Do you think a lot of road man are just doing it for the girls?
Stephen: *Of course!! I know man ain't dressing up for men, that's – trust me. ... I know its girls man, they're like yeah girls like this.*

> And I've seen girls say all that talk, I like my boys that wear blah blah blah.

While Stephen's choice of language signifies cultural commitments to heteronormativity and patriarchy, he also speaks to a sense of positioning of the male subject. Stephen's comments carry connotations of a connectedness to the underground economy, as within marginalised contexts the possibilities of affording such high-end luxury goods are limited, these then become signifiers of certain kinds of value connected to successful street masculinities. In the next quote, Moussa, similarly to T earlier, also observes the attraction to 'bad boys', interestingly in the context of a discussion about the content of rap music, where he observed the same aesthetics which draw people to street narratives in music, also cross over into intimate life:

> 'Cause if I started rapping, even if I started rapping today, you're gonna start rapping about street shit 'cause it's gonna be rapping about beef and that … whereas if I said something like I'm going to work and I ain't got no problems or something like that, I don't know if it would come across the same as, I think when there's danger involved it just sounds better anyway bruv, girls love bad boys anyway, it's 'cause the whole world, I think it's a human being thing to go against the grain init.' (Moussa)

A deep investment exists in 'heterosexist-eroticism' (hooks, 1994: 131), which leads men unable or unwilling to 'talk tough and get rough' (hooks, 1994: 129) to 'feel like losers' (hooks, 1994: 130), making it a hinge upon which heterosexual identities turn. This is a kernel at the heart of certain street performativities and should be understood as a deeply sensitive factor in the development of the selfhood of people of all genders in these spaces. Indeed, young women's accounts also reflected a commitment to heterosexist-eroticism, valuing provider masculinities, with 'hood rich' lifestyles highly sought after in a partner. In the following, Alicia describes how the possibility of subverting the malign boredom of urban poverty was something which attracted her to her child's father:

> Alicia: He did sell stuff. And live quite a flamboyant life, that's kinda what attracted me to him … at the time we kind of attracted each other, because we both had the money, we lived that flamboyant life and you know it was, yeah it was like, two, young people, two hood rich young people [laughs].
> Yusef: What's hood rich?
> Alicia: Hood rich … basically not being wealthy, we're just hood rich, it's not … most people when you're in the hood you

don't really have money, people in the hood are poor … and most people, you know, in the hood, don't have nice cars, you know, struggle, probably on benefits. We didn't, we could do whatever we wanted at the time, because we had the funds, so that's what I mean hood rich. Well I drove an alright car at the time, he drove a good car as well, we could party, we could travel, *we could do whatever basically*, and that's what attracted us, I believe that you attract what you radiate, what you give out, yeah and that's what I was giving off.

At this time Alicia herself was working as an adult entertainer, and had her own income, though her new partner demanded she stopped that line of work later, making her more financially dependent on him for a time, highlighting the ways in which female sexualities might also be desired and policed. There was also a sense that the outlaw masculinities of young men on-road provided a sense of excitement for some women in the study, the two extracts from Cassie that follow describe periods in her own life and her sister's in which their proximity to road life varied, but her sense of desire both in terms of her choice of partner and surrounding lifestyle drew her back. As she puts it, "I love it":

'I moved, got a job, went and did my A-levels, had a boyfriend who had a job but he used to *bore* me. And I spoke to my brother about it. I was like he *bores me* and me and my brother was like "*He's not road enough for ya*". … But at the same time me and my sister, we were around basically exactly the same people at exactly the same time, in exactly the same place and she turned out completely different so. … She went to the same school was me, she was two years above me … we had basically all the same friends in school and out of school … but, one day, her friend got like stabbed really bad and he nearly died and she was just like I hate this town and moved … and never came back … but I was just like *I love it!!* [laughs] … I stuck around.' (Cassie)

Cassie's dialogue demonstrates awareness of her agency when choosing to date men on-road in contrast to her sister who chooses to date from a different cohort of men. Dating men on-road provides Cassie with a sense of security and excitement. This micro-social process presents as a broader exemplification of the differing manifestations of patriarchy. Proximity to a version of masculinity that presents a pseudo sense of self-worth for women is a multi-classed phenomena; however the risks for women on-road exist within a very particular and (working) classed precarity.

We can see here the beginning of a kind of social situatedness both young men and women on-road find themselves in. The need to feel desired and valued, along with desire for feelings which transcend the mundanity of life in 'the hood' form a central element. Young men seem to be motivated to take risks by embodying tropes in their dispositions which, while the focus of desire and fetishism, are also the site of state fears and personal risk. In this way the search for love is not only connected to histories of power, colonialism and domination, even among marginalised men, but also connected to the possibilities of life and death. To be loved is life-affirming, but becoming a subject worth loving is laden with the risk of falling into a state of objectification and this is the case for all genders. Across the stories of intimate life, the frustrations expressed often centred around the temporality of transcendent experiences, like love and joy, in street spaces. The risks involved in love and desire, as outlined earlier, for various reasons seemed to cause relationships to fall apart over time, as Stephen highlights:

> '[G]irls are gonna like roadmen because if they're seeing a man with Ferragamo belt and shoes and he's driving a 63 plate Kompressor, they're gonna be like "*Wow, look at what he's doing, imagine what he can do for me*" so they're thinking about stability and gains, it's only until shit starts getting real, like his door starts getting boomed, he's on an operation, they're finding arresting her, they're saying you're a part of it that's when they're like hold on I don't want, you feel me.' (Stephen)

Stephen captures a sense of frustration at the limited resources and risks taken in the pursuit of desire. This kind of insecurity in the intimate lives of young people led to the notion of the 'street supernovae', ephemeral situations where young people burn hot in order to 'radiate' the value required to become the subject of desire as well as survive on-road. Both the activity required to establish the state of street supernova, and the common implosion which occurs, can be deeply damaging to both men and women on-road. The performativity young men engage in also seems to alienate them from their own essential need for love, compassion and care. At this juncture it is important to reflect on the expressions of the 'munpain' (Bakkali, 2019) and borrow an extract which appeared in that paper, in order to further reflect on what we can understand about intimate life:

> Yusef: So you think on the roads it can be emotionally draining?
> Stephen: Yeah 'cause there's a lot of people that … there might be nobody they can talk to. … They might tell their bredrin like "Yo man, listen man, I'm going through something" and their bredrin might be like "*man toughen up man, stop crying, it's not that deep man, just bitching*" you feel me? You can't go to your friend and be like "Brudda man I'm going through suttim kinda mad" they'll just be like "[kisses teeth]

> listen man stop crying, toughen up man, stop moving like a *punk*" like or a bitch, do you know what I mean? You just laugh like haha, *then you just go home and it's like, it's like who you gonna go to?* … that's why I know a lot of men confide in women and that, they just doing all that … 'cause they're hurting and they think the woman's gonna help it to heal.

Stephen opens up here about the limited capacity of other men to offer emotional support in times of desperate need. What was poignant was Stephen's observation of the feminine capacity to care in the context of road life, that men were/are seeking women to help to ease or 'heal' emotional anguish. This is reminiscent of Firestone's observation that 'love is the weak spot in every man. … Women have always known how men need love, and how they deny this need … they can see their men are posturing in the outside world' (Firestone, 1978: 248). What Stephen's assertions omit is the assumption that women know and are more rehearsed in the art of loving. Often, women in these environments are from loveless backgrounds grounded in the confines of normative hetrosexual patriarchal conditions. In this way, women perform a version of love in an attempt to secure stability and loyalty in return.

The street is a patriarchal space, where impenetrable masculinities and male interests seem to dominate, but underneath that there is a desire/need to love and be loved, to be supported and cared for. The dispositions some young men in these spaces cultivate, in order to become objects of desire, limit their capacities to care for themselves and others, which also exposes them to the possibilities of harm. Ultimately, in its most acute manifestations this is a crippling bind, which can have deeply harmful and at times violent outcomes, as we will go on to further examine.

Implosion and gendered violence

It was mostly in the accounts of young women where intimate life came through as a central theme, and in particular the pains of loving men involved in life on-road. While loving in the state of supernovae brought passion and excitement, it often precipitated a later collapse in intimate lives on-road. In the first extract in this section, Alicia describes how her relationship with the father of her child began to encounter difficulties, in her words "falling apart", as the realities of family life set in. The activities, attitudes and dispositions which made him successful and desirable on-road created barriers to successfully adjusting to domestic life, interestingly even as he moved away from road in terms of how he earned his income, the patriarchal values carried over also:

> '[I]t's rare to find families that are married on the roads … personally I have had problems with my daughter's dad because of his lifestyle …

that's partly our issues ... because they have to be on the road so much, in order to be successful and that takes time away from the family and that is a very big issues of ours, I mean he's *never around*, I'm the main carer for my daughter and it has been difficult because I've never been a mum and you know ... I dunno what to do with a child sometimes. ... You know and he doesn't understand, he sees it as a woman's role to look after the kids while he goes out and makes money but it is, you know... we are losing a lot ... that is why we've had issues and our relationship is falling apart basically because of the roads as well, so it's a good thing and a bad thing. ... Well mainly, mostly a bad thing ... but then ... you know, the roads do provide that stability.' (Alicia)

Words like stability and care are important in Alicia's account, while perhaps material concerns are not at the fore, there seems to be a lack of ability to offer care for both her and their daughter. Perhaps we are seeing here the ways in which passion struggles to actualise into more unconditional forms of love like *philia* or *storge*. The investment in patriarchy also seems to be a limiting factor as men on-road are socialised into becoming 'bent on proving [their] virility in that large male world of "travel and adventure"' (Firestone, 1978: 248), and they might struggle to manifest masculinities where care and empathy are central practices. Alicia's account represents the tip of a metaphorical iceberg, and while her and her former partner have their differences, love can take people to more harmful places, as we will continue to explore. In a patriarchal street space, men can be critically aware of how women can be differentially vulnerable, and the presence of other men mitigates these vulnerabilities. The following exchange is thus worth quoting at length:

Cassie: I have lots of ex boyfriends and stuff that have hard feelings towards me. So, I like to be with somebody that can look after me. ... Because if I don't have a boyfriend to look after me, who's looking after me? My brothers, so then who's going to end up in prison when they kill somebody? *My brothers.* ... When I was younger, like I think I was about 17 ... my ex-boyfriend, phoned me ... and said "I'm bringing arms to your dad's house ... right now". And it was like two in the morning and I didn't know what to do. ... I phoned my cousin, and he came ... that just scares me because ... I know this guy and I know he has guns ... I know he's crazy and I know he hasn't got a lot to lose ... it is scary, it is a real ... worry ... sometimes I hear ... these guys go to prison ... and I actually feel so happy like I feel safer ... there was this guy and he was my friend but ... he wanted to have sex with me and I didn't wanna have sex with him and he just

	hated me ... when everyone used to ask him why do you hate Cassie so much he used to say she told me to suck my mum, and that boy is so crazy like I would ever tell him that, like I don't have a death wish ... he used to phone me and he'd be like "If I ever see you, I'm gonna beat the life out of ya" ... I used to be so scared and then, I was with Anton [a later partner] walking through town and I saw him and my heart was racing, I thought "Oh my god this guy is gonna kill me". ... He said safe to Anton and I was like "Oh, so I'm okay now". ... And that's why, that's why I pick these guys.
Yusef:	So do you think fear is a big part of relationships on-road?
Cassie:	*Yeaaahh.* Probably more so in other relationships than mine. ... I have lots of friends that don't have big brothers or cousins and stuff that will look after them. And they don't they don't leave their boyfriends 'cause they're scared. Scared in a lot of ways, like scared that he'll smash up their house ... or, scared that he'll beat them up ... scared for their kids' safety and scared about their financial future.

Cassie's account here is revelatory in a lot of ways. It demonstrates the ways in which women rely on a gendered version of road social capital (Bakkali, 2022), drawing on their networks to help to keep them safe. It is not clear here how this plays out in physical space, but across social networks, where they are known to one another on-road, it seems these networks inform the levels of risk and violence young women might be exposed to. A homosocial nature of male-perpetrated violence in this space emerges, whereby a kind of competition and mutual recognition plays out between men, organised around networks and capacity to do violence. Perhaps at a deeper level we can see a connectedness between love, care and violence. In a world where the winner takes all, the capacity for violence seems at times a necessity to hold the space for love, however violence is fluid and not easily contained or directed. The partners who were once the protectors in Cassie's account, themselves potentially can also become the perpetrators, when their love is spurned.

Jade LB (2021), author of *Keisha the Sket*, a viral sensation in the 2000s and subsequent landmark print publication, opens up about the ways in which life in the 'endz' imprinted on the content of her life and writing. At the time she began writing Keisha's story she was only in her early teens, later reflecting on how she was already conscious of the patriarchal nature of London's youth-inhabited street spaces:

> I was very aware of the varied manifestations of sexual violence. ... I continuously portrayed boys and men as believing they were entitled to Keisha – her body, her as a void to project their lust or rage onto.

> ... I was vividly reflecting the reality of misogyny embedded in the endz' very own patriarchal structure. (LB, 2021: 4)

In our final vignette we reflect on the projections of 'lust and rage' ever present in Keisha the Sket. Leona's relationship with her child's father, though initially exciting and passionate, eventually culminated in implosion. She describes a situation in decline, where she became for a time trapped with an abusive partner, with both of their positionings at the margins making it a particular challenge to alleviate the situation. Leona expresses concern for what might happen to him at the hands of the state, in the knowledge of the ways in which the authorities might enact violence on Black and brown bodies, while also herself having limited networks and possibilities for escape.

Yusef: What became of that relationship?

Leona: [A] very messy ending ... [it] went on a lot longer than the love. ... By this stage we'd had our daughter, I was living in a hostel ... a lot of violence went on at that stage ... I remember a point ... he grabbed me by my hair and dragged me to the shower and *stamped on my face, literally just stamped it against the tiles,* and then he turned on the shower ... obviously I was fully dressed, I had my clothes on. ... I sat in the shower and I let the shower run and I remember thinking like *what the fuck, like this is not what I want for my life* ... but he repeatedly kicked off my doors, anything that I put up, any way I tried to make this little *dump* home, I put up curtains that he ... dragged down. Anything I tried to do ... he tore it down ... like and I tried to get him out for the *longest time* ... that was the final moment when I sat in that shower, I literally just got up *soaking wet* ... I walked out there just drenched and I just said to this woman you have to get this man out of my house and she took me up the road to police officer who was standing there ... *in my heart I didn't want anything bad to happen to him, but it was impacting me so badly ... my mind was absolutely gone. So when, I stood there and I just looked at this police officer, I was like I wasn't gonna say anything ... [and] when he left, I could breathe, I could actually breathe.*

Conclusion

In this chapter we have explored the concept of 'tainted love' in the context of the lives of young adults involved in road culture. This concept reflects the ways in which love perseveres, but is often tainted by messy webs of structural violence, in the context of the situated lives of those on the margins. The issues of domestic violence, toxic masculinities and heterosexist-eroticisms are not unique to road life, and indeed may well be found in many other spaces. The marginality and connections to histories of injustice, poverty and various other forms of vulnerability make their manifestations here display acute features. The combination of ontological and existential insecurity makes for a particularly toxic mix as these young people seek to etch out a sense of self and value, while also having to be concerned with their own and their loved one's physical security, guarding against threats from the street and the state.

We can see how the search for love is integral to people, something which to experience, is to live. This leads to it being a source of sensitivity and anguish, with young men in particular, for all their machismo, afraid of the strike from the 'blade concealed in love's pinions'. We cannot hide from the grievous forms of gendered violence enacted against women, and other groups, in these spaces, something which we have only scratched the surface of. In the street, where resources are scarce, often violence is the currency used to cash in the patriarchal dividend. This though needs to be contextualised into the wider state of gendered violence in our society, as well as the fixity of racialised hypersexualisation and heterosexist-eroticism young people encounter in their lives.

However, where there is still the possibility for love, there does appear to be hope. The pathway out of the most virulently destructive elements of tainted love can be conceived in the work of deconstructing heavily racialised and classed notions of masculinity and feminity. It is necessary to 'do the work' of love, drawing on the tools handed down by the likes of bell hooks to cultivate forms of loving which we can aspire to. Work such as this must be, by necessity, compassionate. The violent work of stripping marginalised people of their sense of self, history and value was crucial in the process of cultivating the most violent experiences of intimacy on the margins, and our solutions must be generative for the psyche and the spirit. We must, from a place of love, do the work to challenge the fixities of violent masculinities and the ways in which these are intimately tied to desire, but while doing this work remembering that the cultivation of these masculinities was, and is, in itself an act of violence.

References

Amnesty International (2018) *Trapped in the Matrix: Secrecy, Stigma, and Bias in the Met's Gangs Database*. London: Amnesty International.

Anderson, E. (2000) *Code of the Street: Decency, Violence, and the Moral Life of the Inner City*. New York: W.W. Norton & Company.

Baier, A. (1991) Unsafe loves. In R.C. Solomon and K.M. Higgins (eds) *The Philosophy of (Erotic) Love*. Lawrence: University Press of Kansas, pp 433–450.

Bakkali, Y. (2018) *Life On Road: Symbolic Struggle & the Munpain*. Doctoral dissertation, University of Sussex.

Bakkali, Y. (2019) Dying to live: Youth violence and the munpain. *The Sociological Review*, 67(6): 1317–1332.

Bakkali, Y. (2021) Road capitals: Reconceptualising street capital, value production and exchange in the context of road life in the UK. *Current Sociology*, 70(3): 419–435.

Bergner, G. (1995) Who is that masked woman? Or, the role of gender in Fanon's *Black Skin, White Masks*. *PMLA*, 110(1): 75–88.

Blumer, H. (1954) What is wrong with social theory? *American Sociological Review*, 19: 3–10.

Bourgois, P. (2003) *In Search of Respect: Selling Crack in El Barrio*. Cambridge: Cambridge University Press.

Bowen, G.A. (2006) Grounded theory and sensitizing concepts. *International Journal of Qualitative Methods*, 5: 12–23.

Cherry, M. (2019) Love, anger, and racial injustice. In A. Martin (ed) *The Routledge Handbook of Love in Philosophy*. New York: Routledge, pp 157–168.

Choak, C. (2021) Hegemonic masculinity and 'badness': How young women bargain with patriarchy 'on road'. *Boyhood Studies*, 14(1): 63–74.

Connell, R.W. (1987) *Gender and Power*. Stanford: Stanford University Press.

Contreras, R. (2015) Recalling to life: Understanding stickup kids through insider qualitative research. In J. Miller and W. Palacios (eds) *Advances in Criminological Theory*. Abingdon: Routledge, pp 155–168.

Corbin, J.M. and Strauss, A. (1990) Grounded theory research: Procedures, canons, and evaluative criteria. *Qualitative Sociology*, 13(1): 3–21.

De Sousa, R. (2015) *Love: A Very Short Introduction*. New York: Oxford University Press.

Earle, R. (2011) Boys' zone stories: Perspectives from a young men's prison. *Criminology & Criminal Justice*, 11(2): 129–143.

Firestone, S. (1970) *The Dialectic of Sex: The Case for Feminist Revolution*. New York: William Morrow and Company.

Freud, S. (2006) *The Psychology of Love*. New York: Penguin Classics.

Fromm, E. (2000) *The Art of Loving: The Centennial Edition*. London: A&C Black.

Gibran, K. (1926/1991) *The Prophet*. London: Pan Publishing.

Gilroy, P. (1993) *The Black Atlantic: Modernity and Double Consciousness*. Cambridge, MA: Harvard University Press.

Glynn, M. (2013) *Black Men, Invisibility and Crime: Towards a Critical Race Theory of Desistance*. Abingdon: Routledge.

Gunter, A. (2008) Growing up bad: Black youth, 'road' culture and badness in an East London neighbourhood. *Crime, Media, Culture*, 4(3): 349–366.

Gunter, A. (2010) *Growing Up Bad? Black Youth, 'Road' Culture and Badness in an East London Neighbourhood.* London: Tufnell Press.

Gunter, A. and Watt, P. (2009) Grafting, going to college and working on road: Youth transitions and cultures in an East London neighbourhood. *Journal of Youth Studies*, 12(5): 515–529.

Hall, S. (1997) The work of representation. *Representation: Cultural Representations and Signifying Practices*, 2 : 13–74.

Hall, S. (2017) *The Fateful Triangle.* Cambridge, MA: Harvard University Press.

Hall, S. (2021) *Selected Writings on Race and Difference.* Durham, NC: Duke University Press.

Hall, S., Critcher, C., Jefferson, T., Clarke, J. and Roberts, B. (2013) *Policing the Crisis: Mugging, the State and Law and Order.* London: Macmillan International Higher Education.

Hallsworth, S. and Silverstone, D. (2009) 'That's life innit': A British perspective on guns, crime and social order. *Criminology & Criminal Justice*, 9(3): 359–377.

Heyl, B.S. (2001) Ethnographic interviewing. In P. Atkinson, A. Coffey, S. Delamont, J. Lofland and L. Lofland (eds) *Handbook of Ethnography*. London: SAGE, pp 369–383.

hooks, b. (1994) *Outlaw Culture: Resisting Representations.* Abingdon: Routledge.

hooks, b. (2001) *All About Love: New Visions.* New York: Harper Perennial.

hooks, b. (2004) *Will to Change.* Abingdon: Routledge.

Ilan, J. (2015) *Understanding Street Culture: Poverty, Crime, Youth and Cool.* London: Palgrave Macmillan.

Illouz, E. (2012) *Why Love Hurts: A Sociological Explanation.* Oxford: Polity.

LB, J. (2021) *Keisha the Sket.* New York: Merky Books.

Liebow, E. (2003) *Tally's Corner: A Study of Negro Streetcorner Men.* Boston: Little Brown & Company.

Mercer, K. (1991) Looking for trouble [review of *Robert Mapplethorpe*, by R. Marshall, R. Howard and I. Sischy]. *Transition*, 51: 184–197.

Miller, J. (2008) *Getting Played: African American Girls, Urban Inequality, and Gendered Violence.* New York: New York University Press.

Palmer, L. (2022) *The Politics of Loving Blackness.* MA Education: London. Available at: https://www.youtube.com/watch?v=l-WyWEGShC8

Patton, M. (1990) Purposeful sampling. *Qualitative Evaluation and Research Methods*, 2: 169–186.

Reid, E. (2023) 'Trap life': The psychosocial underpinnings of street crime in inner-city London. *The British Journal of Criminology*, 63(1): 168–183.

Sernhede, O. (2007) Territorial stigmatisation, hip hop and informal schooling. In W.T. Pink and G.W. Noblit (eds) *International Handbook of Urban Education.* Dordrecht: Springer International, pp 463–479.

Tagirov, P. (2018) Sexuality, love and eroticism: Methodology of distinguishing. *Advances in Social Science, Education and Humanities Research*, 283: 829–833.

Tennov, D. (1979) *Love and Limerence: The Experience of Being in Love*. New York: Stein & Day.

Tyler, I. (2013) *Revolting Subjects: Social Abjection and Resistance in Neoliberal Britain*. London and New York: Zed Books.

Willmott, L. and Bentley, E. (2015) Exploring the lived-experience of limerence: A journey toward authenticity. *The Qualitative Report*, 20(1): 20–38.

Young, T. and Trickett, L. (2017) Gang girls: Agency, sexual identity and victimisation 'on road'. In K. Gildart, A. Gough-Yates, S. Lincoln, B. Osgerby, L. Robinson, J. Street, P. Webb and M. Worley (eds) *Youth Culture and Social Change*. London: Palgrave Macmillan, pp 231–259.

4

(The) Trouble with Friends: Narrative Stories of Friendship and Violence On-Road

Tara Young

Introduction

In seeking to understand why people engage in crime and violence, social scientists have pointed out the importance of studying the social relationships between young people, especially those thought to be in, or associated with, street gangs. Early scholarship on juvenile delinquency has produced some consistent findings. One such finding consistent in these works is the homophilous nature of friendship groups. Young people are thought to gravitate towards others who are like them. They are 'birds of a feather that flock together' (Glueck and Glueck, 1950), bonding on the basis of gender, race or class, a shared sense of 'esprit de corps' derived from loyalty, respect, attachment, trust and trustworthiness (Thrasher, 1927), a commitment to a defiant counterculture (Miller, 1958) or a set of informal rules that govern interpersonal behaviour among young people including law-breaking behaviour and the perpetration of violence (Anderson, 1999). Pro-social attitudes towards offending are thought to be transmitted through peer groups (Sutherland and Cressey, 1996; Akers, 1973) and solidify group cohesion especially in the face of status challenges and external threat (Klein, 1975).

While some early scholars, such as Thrasher (1927), have emphasised comradery as the glue that gels young people together, another finding, especially in the early studies, is the view that young men who engage in crime and delinquency do not have the ability to form credible friendships.[1] For example, the view from control theorists such as Hirschi (1969) is that young people engaged in illegal behaviour are unable to make and sustain positive relationships because they lack a thorough grasp of what a friend is and do not have the social skills to be able to formulate positive relationships. Commensurate with this view is that delinquents lack self-control (Gottfredson and Hirschi, 1990), are morally vacuous and express little feelings of guilt or remorse (Cloward and Ohlin, 1960) or, according to Albert Cohen (1955), 'act with spite, malice and make the virtuous feel uncomfortable'.

A third significant theme running through the extant literature and policy documentation on crime and violence that involves young people as perpetrators and victims is the conflation between friendship, criminality and 'gangs'. It noteworthy that the term 'gang' is one that is most readily (and disproportionately) applied to friendship groups of young people from Black and other minoritised communities (Hallsworth and Young, 2004, 2008) whose violent offending is consistently defined as 'gang-related' even where there is evidence to suggest otherwise (see Williams and Clarke, 2016). A number of quantitative studies have found gang membership to be associated with violence and crime (Spergel and Curry, 1993; Saunders, 1994; Decker and Van Winkle, 1997), gang members have a higher participation rate in delinquency than non-gang members (Bradshaw and Smith, 2005; Sharp et al, 2006) and being in a gang increases an individual's offending behaviour (Esbensen and Huizinga, 1993; Klein, 1995; Battin-Pearson et al, 1998). Indeed, in the UK, gang-related violence is thought to be 'the driving force behind some of the most serious violence' including 'knife crime with injury' (57 per cent), shootings (60 per cent) and homicide (30 per cent) (MOPAC, 2018: 4).

There is a great deal of emphasis in UK criminal justice on curbing serious youth violence. Identifying the types and forms of relationships and associations that young people in gangs or 'road life' develop is an essential concern for criminal justice professionals whose goal is to disrupt offending behaviour and reduce the risks that young people 'on-road' pose to each other and the general public.

It is fair to say that the scholarship on delinquent behaviour agrees that a sizeable proportion of crime happens between and by young people in groups. These texts emphasise the importance of group dynamics and their role in the delinquency that occurs within the group. However, such views take on a pathologising gaze that desensitises public opinion towards young people and their friendships and facilitates the view that when they engage in collective offending, they do so as the 'plural subject' (Gilbert, 2000, cited in Amatrudo, 2016: 930) engaged in 'we action' (Bratman, 1984) underpinned by moral vacuity, shared intention and in full knowledge of the constituent plan.

The net result is a partial and reductive view of the friendships between young people who engage in crime and violence, some of whom may or may not be members of street-based groups labelled as 'gangs'. It is a view that has led critical scholars to vehemently argue that the narratives about friendship, gangs and youth violence is underwritten by negative stereotypes, racialisation and an over-criminalisation of certain groups (Hallsworth and Young, 2004), where the nature of such friendship is constructed as 'risky' and dangerous (Smithson et al, 2013; Young et al, 2020) and fundamentally different from young people in mainstream friendship groups.

By drawing on interviews with young men imprisoned as principal or secondary parties to murder, manslaughter or intention to commit serious harm (GBH) when young, I critically explore some of the claims about delinquent friendships that have been outlined, particularly those forged by young people 'on-road'. In doing so, I hope to offer a more nuanced perspective on who young people become friends with, the complexity of forming and sustaining 'good' relationships with peers, and the role that friendship plays in serious violence. To be sure, the aim here is not to condone the violence that young people do, but to shed some light on the existential pressures that come to bear on such friendships that lead to a violent outcome.

The findings presented in this chapter suggest that young people on the road desire what humans have sought for millennia; honest, loyal and trustworthy friends. 'On-road' friendships, however, are determined by structural positioning and influenced by street (countercultural) codes, which govern who 'flocks together' with whom, the nature of such friendships, and how loyalty and trustworthiness are demonstrated, especially in confrontational or violent situations. Based on the data presented here, it is clear that, in pursuit of friendship, some people 'on-road' do not really know their 'friends' very well until they are tested in criminal or confrontational situations, they do not always know what their friends intend to do or act in accordance to group will. Crucially, the actions these young men took in the vicinity of others had significant consequences for them, such as murder convictions and lengthy prison sentences.

The chapter begins with a brief outline of the philosophical aetiology of the concept of friendship and then progresses to a discussion of 'on-road' before presenting the narratives of young people who have been incarcerated for many years, partly because of the friendships they forged when young. I hope that by exploring and explaining the nuance of relationships 'on-road' this chapter moves the dialogue about young people's deviance and offending away from the reductionist, stigmatising and racialised rhetoric of 'gang talk' and towards a more sensitive understanding of the sociocultural conditions that preclude or encourage the formation of 'good' and or troublesome friendships.

What is friendship?

From a philosophical point of view, a life without friends is not worth living and no one would choose to live without friends even if they had all the material things they could ever need (Aristotle, 365 BC:8; Pangle, 2002; Cicero, 2018). In fact, social scientists have illustrated the importance of friendship in social-emotional development (Tack and Small, 2017) and suggested that it is crucial for the formation of self-identity (Rawlins and Roll, 1987). But what is a friend and in what ways do friendships influence our perceptions and behaviours? It has been more than 2,000 years since Aristotle suggested friendship is based on mutual goodwill between morally conscious individuals and introduced a typology of friendship (that is, friendships of pleasure, friendships of utility and friendships of virtue) but the nature of friendship and the motivation for forming close social bonds remain unclear.

Friendships of virtue

For Aristotle, friendliness 'guards against error' (Aristotle, 2020: 8). Rather than cultivating a relationship for an individual's own benefit, virtuous, or good, friendship is a relationship that benefits both parties (Pangle, 2002: 43). Friendship is not about seeking something for oneself (for example, inner goodness) but about promoting goodwill between all parties, finding the good in others and encouraging virtuosity and high moral standards (Pahl, 2000).

The truest form of friendship is the kind of friendship that exemplifies virtue. When it comes to virtuous friendships, Aristotle believes they are also the hardest to attain. The reason for this is that it is based on identifying the goodness in others – recognising their worthiness and, at the same time, recognising one's own value. Accordingly, a person who is unloved or unable to recognise their own worth – or engages in acts that are morally suspect – is not able to recognise 'goodness' and love in another person so cannot form a high calibre 'good and virtuous' friendship with anyone else. Thus, it follows that 'such friendships are rare, because such men are few' (Aristotle, 365 BC: 8:4).

Friendships of pleasure and utility

If cultivating virtuous friendships requires commitment, self-love, affection and enough emotional self-awareness to understand friendship as an end, as opposed to a means to an end, so it is likely that some people are unable to form 'friendships of the good' as Aristotle envisioned. Perhaps this is why, philosophers suggested, 'friendships of utility' and 'friendships of pleasure' (aesthetics) are more commonplace. Friendships of utility, the version of friendship that is the furthest away from perfection, is founded on necessity. These instrumental relationships are cultivated by individuals (who may or may not be 'good men') who wish to fulfil their own needs and desires. They are formed between people who are opposites, or dissimilar, but have aligned goals (for example, the acquisition of goods). For Aristotle, because these relationships are not built upon virtuous and moral foundations, they are subject to disappointment, complaint and rupture as soon as one or both parties profit from it and get what they desire (Pangle, 2002: 39). Similarly, in aesthetic friendships, people are drawn towards striking up relationships with those who they find pleasing, useful and whose companionship they enjoy; until they do not anymore, or people outlive their use. While aesthetic friendships can manifest respectful unions they too are, in philosophical terms, 'lower calibre relationships' brokered by people motivated to fulfil their own good and desires (Nichols, 2006) or 'wicked passions' (Cicero, 2018: 142:83).

For Cicero friendship is not a licence for people to indulge in 'wicked passions' or to use someone as a means to an end. Cicero's friend would not ask another to act in a morally suspect way (that is, hurt someone), to perform an evil action that would risk or undermine their honour. They would caution against being involved with someone who suggests doing something shameful. He says 'tyrants' and 'scoundrels' and people with 'poor moral characters' ask people to engage in an act they wouldn't do themselves. While such people could be considered 'friends' the relationship is one based on utility and not virtue.

People who do not behave like 'good' friends, who use or subjugate another person to their will, obstruct the possibility of true friendship. For example, the instrumentalisation of another person, for Nietzsche, erodes the mutual respect, honesty and trust necessary for friendship. While he disagrees with the idea that the foundation of friendship is *moral* goodness – and this is what people go looking for when striking up a friendship – true friendship lies in a person's concern for the welfare of others and bringing out the best in the person whom the friendship is with (Verkerk, 2019). That doesn't mean that friendship is all plain sailing. On the contrary, for Nietzsche 'a friend doesn't flatter without merit and tells you what you should hear, not what you want to hear' and '[i]f one would have a friend, then must one also be willing to wage war for him: and in order to wage war, one must be capable of being an enemy' (Nietzsche, 2017: 63).

People in 'lower calibre' friendships with (faux) friends are in relationships that are prone to break and fracture as the characters and objectives of people involved change (Cicero, 2018: 128:74), in accordance with the social context and individual needs or desires. So, in many ways, anyone seeking to cultivate a friendship that lasts, one where all parties continuously work towards the betterment of each other, is 'in for grave disappointment when some tragedy strikes and these "friends" are put to the test' (Nietzsche in Verkerk, 2019: 144:85). The advice from Nietzsche is that such 'companions' should be given wide berth as these are not capable of forming 'good' or 'real' friendships; they have nothing to give but to sap the kindness from another. The problem, as will be illustrated in what follows, is that it is in times of turbulence that the true nature of friendships becomes known.

It is possible to conclude from this brief discussion of friendship that there are many forms of friendship, and that there are ontological differences between 'common friendships' (those of utility and aesthetics) and 'rare friendships' that connect people on a deeper, spiritual and virtuous level. It is also evident from this literature that friendship can be a socially enriching experience, a necessity for personal growth, as well as a source of struggle. To achieve true friendship, one must avoid people who limit one's potential or growth or ambitions. How one finds friends in social spaces like 'on-road' is not well examined within a UK context or easy to understand.

Friendship on-road

If true, virtuous friendships are sought out for their own sake, how are these relationships realised and nurtured on the road? Are there any lessons we can learn from friendships on-road that will help us to better understand the serious violence occurring in this setting? To answer these questions, we need to consider what it means to be 'on-road' or involved in 'road life'.

What is on-road and on-road life?

The concept 'on-road' has different meanings within criminology and sociology. Nevertheless, this concept, in whatever form it takes, has been accepted by scholars looking to move away from reductionist discussions that isolate gang culture as the root cause of serious violence (Pitts, 2012). In acknowledging gangs as just one of many street collectives present in the 'on-road' world, Hallsworth and Young (2008) found that the majority of young people 'on-road' are peers or friends who hang out and do not engage in violence to any great extent, and those who do engage in low-level interpersonal fighting or other forms of anti-social behaviour.[2] Similarly, for Anthony Gunter, one of the first academics to popularise the term 'on-road', it is a place where young people 'meet up with friends', 'hang on-road', attend the youth club, rave, look up 'links' and otherwise 'catch a joke' (Gunter, 2008: 352). It is a space where friendships are cultivated, where routine activities are carried out in places that are familiar to young people. It is a social space where young people from marginalised and racially minoritised communities congregate when there are few alternative opportunities available to do otherwise. It is also a space where, sociologist Yusef Bakkali (2022) argues, young men from such minoritised communities accrue status, respect, power and 'road capital' otherwise denied to them in mainstream society. By mobilising the skills and values learnt within the 'street value systems' Bakkali's study demonstrates how 'on-road' young Black and brown men hope to transform and exchange their 'road capital' into currency useful in social settings beyond the street.

While some people are able to achieve status, respect and power 'on-road', research has shown that it is not a place where young people would choose to congregate when given the opportunity, but one where they end up by default when society fails to provide an equitable social infrastructure free from marginalisation, racism and criminalisation for them to fulfil their potential (Young and Hallsworth, 2011). Once 'on-road', youngsters inhabit a social space free from societal and familial constraints where they seek to acquire the social, emotional and material things they desire, and which are not forthcoming from the social institutions in wider society – like unconditional support, protection and 'friendship' (Young and Hallsworth, 2011).

As so conceptualised, the road is also a place where many young people find companionship, sometimes with others who engage in 'badness' (Gunter, 2008).[3] Boys and men who do 'badness' often subscribe to a 'code of the street' (Anderson, 1999) that defines the rules of 'presentation of self' (Goffman, 1990) and sets the versions of masculinity that are acceptable on the streets. Within this substratum of 'on-road', these 'rude boys'[4] or 'roadmen' are thought to conform to patriarchal heteronormative masculinity that privileges men and cultivates a culture premised upon respect, dominance, power and authority over women and subordinate males (Messerschmidt, 1993).

Levell's research on sexuality and sexual identity 'on-road' (Chapter 5, this volume) draws attention to the hierarchy of masculinity embedded 'on-road' and the pressure on boys and young men to project an identity that is impervious to victimisation, harm and exploitation. In her research, Levell (2022) catalogues the extensive domestic violence they have experienced to illustrate how such abuse helps to formulate 'on-road' masculine identities and perpetuate violence therein. Research conducted by criminologists and sociologists in the UK and further afield shows how 'on-road' young men adopt a defensiveness that protects them from the (real) possibility of victimisation, as well as a willingness (nay, expectation) to engage in 'wicked things' (for example, violence) to defend themselves and their friends when their rights are violated, none of which is conducive to formulating good friendships.

Tack and Small (2017) note that friendships forged in neighbourhoods wherein 'road life' exists are somewhat different to those cultivated in non-violent and stabilised neighbourhoods. Drawing on qualitative research with children, Tack and Small found violence and the threat of victimisation provokes mistrust and hypervigilance, which, in turn, shapes the type of friendships that are formed. Rather than forging friendships based on 'goodness', homophily or self-growth, young people exposed to unpredictable volatile environments are strategic and instrumental in their approach to relationships, explicitly forming 'friendships of utility' that provide protection from further victimisation, and where it isn't necessary to be overly emotional and invested in another person (Tack and Small, 2017). These strategies have the potential to have long-term implications for a young person's ability to recognise the internal and external goodness and worthiness required to develop virtuous friendships and possibly predispose them to form utility friendships that do not stand the test of real friendship when put under pressure.

For people deeply embedded in 'badness' the likeliness of forging friendships where it is possible to show emotions such as loss, hurt and trauma is limited. In such an environment, Young and Hallsworth (2011: 61) argue that at the extremities of 'on-road' young people adopt a fatalistic 'hood mentality' approach to life that held 'no dreams, no ambition, no drive; no nothing'. Thus, 'on-road' sensitivity and vulnerability are hidden behind the 'front space' presentation of toughness mixed with a haze of suspicion and trepidation in certain places and with people with whom they are unfamiliar. On-road, pain, loss and trauma is endured by many, but is revealed by few, and emotions are not allowed to get in the way (Chapter 10, this volume) and it is within this space that young people attempt to cultivate or continue their friendships and have expectations of the people so labelled.

However, even in treacherous environments that constitute 'on-road', some young are able to show and receive 'street love'. In their research with US-born African boys and men, Payne and Hamdi found 'street love' to manifest in multiple ways that included supporting friends emotionally and financially via bonding activities such as being on-road. For young men living in low-income, marginalised neighbourhoods challenged by structural inequalities, poverty, racism and the obvious and relentlessness of state oppression, being a genuine friend is seen as an essential expression of street love (Payne and Hamdi, 2009: 40).

The small, but growing, literature 'on-road' tells us a lot about the social context in which friendships are formed. The brief review I have produced here illustrates how 'on-road' is a space through which young people transition, with various degrees of success, on the way to self-discovery and adulthood, where some commit petty crimes and engage in a range of deviant behaviour. It is a space where professional criminals 'do the business' (Hobbs, 1999) where roadmen are trapped in a social microcosm that makes them vulnerable to failure and self-destruction (Reid, 2023). For us to understand how friendship and serious violence correlate, we must, interrogate the cultural situations where violence occurs. The narrative accounts of young men involved in serious violence provide us with insight into the issue.

Researching friendship on-road

The empirical data on which this discussion about friendship on the road is based is derived from an Economic and Social Research Council (ESRC)-funded research project (ES/P001378/1) examining serious youth violence and the legal consequences of being arrested, tried and convicted in a British court for crimes committed with others (see Young et al, 2020; Hulley and Young, 2021). The findings presented here draw on the 31 semi-structured interviews conducted with young men in custody in Category B prisons across England.[5]

Participants, data collection and analysis

Half of the participants (16) self-identified as 'Black', nine as 'White', five as 'mixed heritage' and one as 'Asian'. All were aged between 18 and 30 years old at the time of the interview. Twenty-two were convicted of murder, eight for Section 18 intent to inflict serious harm and one for manslaughter. All young men were convicted for crimes involving multiple perpetrators when in their teens or early 20s (that is, between 15 and 22 years old).

The types of violent situations these young men were caught up in moved along a continuum where the events appeared to be planned, organised events (for example, set ups and beatings that took a fatal turn, drug robberies and revenge/retaliatory acts), on the one hand, and random spontaneous events on the other (for example, the eruption of violence at house parties, clubs or in the street and alcohol-induced events). The continuum was weighted more heavily towards the spontaneous end, with serious organised violence very rare among our participants.

In the interviews, which on average lasted between one and one-and-a-half hours, we took on a narrative quality focused on the participants' life history, experiences of violence and involvement in group-related offences including the one(s) for which they had been incarcerated. A significant aspect of the interview schedule was to explore the concept of friendship and provide an opportunity for these young men to tell stories about the types of friendships they cultivated 'on-road' to understand the *meaning* of friendship in 'street life' or 'on-road', and the perceived quality of these relationships within the context of the life events they encountered (Presser and Sandberg, 2019).

It has long been known by qualitative researchers that this epistemology is less concerned with the accuracy 'or truth' of the data as retold. While retelling their experiences participants were actively involved in choosing the events and narrative devices they thought best reflected their concept of friendship. These stories may not be an accurate account of events 'on-road' in general nor wholly indicative of attitudes and beliefs about friendships. They are the tales told at a certain time and place which have been interpreted.

In the interpretation of their stories, my role was to examine the stories of friendship as told by these young men and to engage in '*verstehen*', that is, 'the interpretive understanding of social behaviour to gain an explanation of its causes, its course, and its effects' (Weber, 1964: 29). In doing so, I hope to share some insights into an unfamiliar life-world and examine the genesis and quality of 'on-road' friendships, the expectations young people have of these relationships and the pressures that are brought to bear on them. Of equal import is to comprehend how the social and cultural context of being 'on-road' shapes what sort of friendships are forged and the subsequent trajectory of them within the context of serious violence.

On-road and the expression of friendship

In ancient philosophy, friendship was conceived by men asking illuminating questions about citizenship, communal 'good' and erotic love (Nichols, 2006). Friendship in this context was an intellectual exercise curated by learned men lyricising and far removed from the sociocultural context of 'on the road' experienced by young people from marginalised and minority neighbourhoods who have, or are, creating relationships in rocky terrain where violence, suspicion and coercion loom large over social interactions. Yet, in this research, we found that some young people 'on-road' have social relationships which share some characteristics that are compatible with what could be determined as 'goodness' and 'virtuousness' in relation to their own character and that of their peer counterparts. "I've always thought if you're friends with someone, you would always do for them. … I am my brother's keeper type thing. Love your neighbour as yourself. … So, anything you want for yourself, you will always want for your mate, and vice versa" (Clifton, Black British, murder). Echoing philosophical thoughts forged across two millennia, Clifton, in his definition of friendship, recognised the symmetry of concern for himself and how this extended to those people he called friends. Here he talks about the love set aside for friends, wanting the best for them, as he would want for himself. If 'good' friendships are based on recognising the worthiness of another person and obtained by people who have a good measure of themselves, then in Clifton's reflections we can see some semblance of a friendship that, in theory, benefits both parties in positive ways. The spirit of moral concern and consideration is also evidence in Clifton's perception of friendship through his biblical references to being his "brother's keeper" and to love friends as one would *love thyself* by showing compassion and respect for another person. Being there for a friend in need was a constant predictor of friendship among the interviewees. Need in this context did not always relate to offending behaviour, but to situations where friends needed support of one kind or another:

> 'If he needs support, you support him. He's a friend of yours. When he's down cheer him up. If he's in need find out what you can do for him and try to make the situation better.' (Jason, Black African, murder)

> '[A friend is] someone you can trust. Someone you can call up, go out, grab a drink with. Someone you can chat to when times get hard. That's a friend.' (Tom, White Traveller, manslaughter)

It is evident from these narratives that young people who engage in serious violence 'on the road' believe that they are forming relationships based on virtue or reciprocal good. According to these young men, friends are akin to family and people who care about you, who see the good in you, and who will do anything for you (Jayden), even if it means spending a great deal of money:

> 'Say, if I had fucking 300 grand and my mate needed 300 grand, I would give it to him. One hundred per cent. If he needed it and he had good reason that he needed it, I would give it to him. Without even asking … without even thinking twice, I would give it to him.' (Omer, mixed-race, Section 18)

It is not important whether Omer has 300 grand to give away. Omer's willingness to part with his money symbolises the value he places on friendship. We can see, however, that the gift is conditional upon 'good reasons' for wanting the money and underpinned by what Omer's conception of what 'good' is.

When it came to conceptualising friendships, the young people exercised what Payne and Hamdi (2009) would call 'street love'. By adding street love as a concept through which we can understand friendship 'on-road' we are able to go beyond the traditional scholarship which focuses on peer influence on delinquency, anti-social behaviour and gang-related violence.

"There's mates, good mates and best mates": friends and associates

Like other studies, such as Spencer and Pahl's (2006) research on the hidden solidarities of friendship, which found a range of 'personal communities', several 'friendship repertoires' (type of friend) and 'models of friendship' (longevity of relationship) were found in our study. While Pahl and Spencer's participants talked about 'soul mates', 'best friends' and 'champagne friends', the young men categorised people 'on-road' as 'friends' or 'associates'; or as Phil (White British, Section 18) articulates, "mates", "good mates" and "bad mates". As well as outlining the different friendship repertoires he has, Phil goes on to distinguish the activities partaken with each group:

> 'Say, you're going on a night out with [the good mates] … [you'd] not [be] going out, taking drugs and all this, and walking round the streets, taking drugs and that. You'd go out to a party or something with. Best mates: I don't really have best mates, like, I just have good mates. There's good mates and there's bad mates. I just had good mates and he was a bad mate.' (Phil, White British, Section 18)

The 'bad mate' Phil was referring to was an acquaintance, someone "that my sister knew and that the people I was with knew" and was his co-defendant in the substantive offence of intention to commit serious harm (Section 18) for which he received nine years when aged 17. Like Phil, other young people noted the subtle differences between 'friends' and 'associates':

> 'Your friends are someone that you will literally have a family around and spend a lot more time with and talk to deeper. Things that you will do for them they will naturally do for you as well, without thinking. Associates is someone you come across and you can maybe have a conversation with them, you might have a laugh with them, you might get a little bit close to them but deep down you're not really friends.' (Clifton, Black British, murder)

Associates, unlike friends, are people 'on-road' that one comes across as part of the lifecycle of being 'on-road'. They are, as illustrated by Phil, friends of siblings or friends of friends who are not true friends but merely people to chat to when paths cross or to 'hang about with' when in the company of friends and family. In discussing the differences between friends and associates, one can detect something malign, malevolent and untrustworthy in the way such associative relationships are narrated. Unlike associates, friends, it seems, are constantly around and have your back. A 'true' friend:

'[W]ould tell you when you're doing right and wrong, they should tell you. An associate wouldn't care, he'd tell you to go and jump off a cliff. You would be fine but go and jump off a cliff. You might not be fine, you might be fine, but he's still pushing you to that limit to go and do it. A friend will say to you "Don't do that, that's not good for you, don't jump off, go down the ladder." They will try and give you the safest option of helping you through life.' (Kelvin, Black, murder)

In Kelvin's quotation, we see the distinction between friendships of virtue and friends of utility sharply highlighted; this time with reference to engaging in forms of behaviour that could potentially be life-threatening – like jumping off a cliff. An associate, it seems, wouldn't care about another's welfare and will push people to the limit of their capabilities – or what they would morally do. Associates were reported as not quite what they seem, presenting only a partial picture or 'cloak' of themselves, acting in a way that was unfamiliar or unexpected, and sometimes revealing their potential in confrontational contexts that included violence. Jayden, Phil and Sebastian cited being with some associates when the offence for which they were arrested, charged, tried and convicted occurred. In Ian's case, he reported being with a group of men who included "my mate, his mate's dad and some other guys that we knew" on a night out when the group set upon one of the men, beating him to death.

In certain contexts, on-road, people's 'friendships' are revealed to be something other than those based on virtue, reciprocal goodness, harmony and pleasure. Instead, they are full of trouble, strife, enmity and cruelty, especially with people who seek to create relationships of utility and aesthetics that include the engagement in 'wicked passions'. According to Aristotelian philosophy, such relationships are best to be avoided, as they erode the mutual respect and trust necessary for 'good' or 'real' relationships, but, as Rich notes within the context of the street, these types of relationships are not so easy to detect: "Back then, I thought, yes, they've got me, they'll help me, especially the ones that would buy me clothes, buy me trainers. I thought, yes, these lot are doing something for me. [Do you still feel like that about them?] No! I just knew, they were having their games" (Rich, White, Section 18). Rich, who grew up in care and was a young runaway before his conviction, would 'help' his friends by "doing whatever manoeuvres I had to do" to curry favour with the people he befriended. Doing the manoeuvres included engaging in 'badness' by dealing class A drugs (Gunter, 2008). And while he denied being a member of a gang, he acknowledged that this label was applied to him and the people he knew.

In some ways the friendship he formed with his peers was one of utility where "I would get what I wanted; I'd get a new pair of kicks or whatever" and they would get someone who was willing to sell their drugs and defend the patch. While Rich did not describe his experience as grooming or exploitation and acknowledged that the 'game playing' was beneficial to him, he admitted that he was naive to consider such people as friends; a lesson he learned after receiving a five-year sentence for a Section 18 offence in which he stabbed someone in a knife fight over a drugs robbery.

The shallow nature of some friendships of utility comes to the fore in Phil's narration of friendship, as does the lack of maturity on the part of young people to fully realise the intentions of other people, especially when they are considered as 'friends'. However, there is an acknowledgement, as Joshua (Black African, murder) notes, a lack of genuineness about some relationships 'on-road', but it is the price some young people appear willing to offset for gains (material or otherwise).

"I would jump in no questions asked!": loyalty on-road

While few young people in this study self-identified as being 'gang-involved', loyalty was viewed as a premium. Being able to trust people to be there when you need them and to 'have your back' in confrontational situations was an important condition of friendship. As Nigel (Black, murder) states, "being there for one another and supporting one another" is significant within the context of the street where young people experience hostility, uncertainty, victimisation and violence. In Nigel's case, loyalty meant watching out for friends when a fight broke out inside and outside of a nightclub in which one person was shot and another fatally stabbed.

Talk of loyalty cojoined with that of trust and respect, particularly the exhibition of loyalty in the face of disrespect, threat and the like. As expressed earlier, 'on-road' is a volatile space where some/many young men compete to survive in an illegal drug economy, where violence is commonplace, and victimisation is a reality. Within this context, being loyal includes backing your friends when asked, or when circumstance dictates. As Omer notes, loyalty is "[i]f something happens to one of us, we all deal with it. You cannot just leave. We do not ever do that". It is if a friend was fighting or in trouble, "[i]f I saw them fighting, I would jump in no questions asked" (Tom, White, manslaughter). Similarly:

> 'We would help each other in any situation. That situation he was arguing. Obviously, I've got him, and I would expect him to do the same for us, helping someone, to help me. That's just where things go wrong in life, with other people. So, it's loyalty. They see him arguing with him. That's your guy, getting involved. That's your guy.' (Rich, White, Section 18)

In many ways, some of the friendships young people formed were based on the level of risk they experienced outside of the home. Within the copious amount of scholarship on delinquent youth and 'gang' membership, ethnographers and sociologists have convincingly shown that young people band together for protection and in the face of threat from other people and groups (see Thrasher, 1927; Klein, 1975; Sanchez-Jankowski, 1991). It is the social cohesion of such groups and the loyalty shown by young people to each other that, some scholars have argued, perpetuates the misguided view that all young people 'on-road' are 'gangs', leading to the racial stigmatisation and criminalisation of all young Black and brown men as risky and dangerous, increases surveillance of minority communities and inflates the sentences imposed on young defendants presenting at court charged with multi-handed violence (see Smithson et al, 2013; Young et al, 2020; Hulley and Young, 2021).

Much of the violence, in which these young people exercised their loyalty, emerged in sporadic violent events with minimal consultation. Therefore, it is crucial to acknowledge situations in which youth accompany a 'friend' to an event or venue where they know an altercation may occur, but do not anticipate the end result. As in the case of Ian who thought "[i]t might kick-off. He might end up getting a black eye, and then it just went many steps past it and he ended up dead." Or Kaab (Black, murder), who went to support his cousin to "sort out a debt" that was owed to him and was latterly charged with joint enterprise murder involving torture.[6] Reflecting on the loyalty he showed to his co-defendant and the unfolding situation, he said, "I never thought or envisaged something like that would happen, because I've known him for a long time, he hasn't got a record of anything."

"There's no love, it was all fake. It was all lies"

While young people noted the importance of backing up friends and being loyal to them, some young people found out the hard way that people they thought of as friends were not acting in accordance to their philosophy or concept of what a friend should be. As Joshua notes, while "there's genuine love growing up, 'this is my friend, I love this person'" some people on-road have:

> '[H]idden agendas, some things are not as genuine as you think they are. I wouldn't say there's any malice in any of it, but – in reality – you're not really friends because we're still learning what friendship is at such a young age – I understand people have ulterior motives and I knew that from a very young age, so you always have to question the authenticity of what people are saying, and body language.' (Joshua, Black, murder)

As Tack and Small (2017) note, being able to spot people who have 'hidden agendas' or who is and who is not a genuine friend is difficult within the context of the street or in environments where young people are exposed to violence. The realisation that friends are not what they seem, as Nigel did, that "[t]hey're not there for you. You would have done a lot of things for them but they're not there for you when you need them. Prison is a hard place. ... Certain friendships, your loyalties to friends, it's not really worth it", can be psychologically impactful for people and affect their ontological reality for young people. As Hulley et al (2016) point out in their research on the impact of long-term imprisonment on young people, the pains of serving a long sentence result in psychological maladjustment, having a deep and profound impact on a young person's sense of self.

In reflecting on their friendships, participants like Dalton, Clifton, Mike, Omer, Nigel and Michael thought they had misplaced their loyalty and trusted those whom they believed valued their friendship, only to realise these relationships were of a 'lower calibre'. In prison, Dalton (Black, Section 18) talks about the sacrifice he thought he had made for believing in people he 'loved' but now never heard from. When asked why his friends didn't come to visit him, he replied: "Because they never loved me, there's no love, it was all fake. It was all lies. [How does that feel?] Horrible, horrible. I felt like I did all this for us."

Similar sentiments were expressed by Omer, whose friend and co-defendant, he recalled, had "snitched' on him during the trial. During the substantive offence for which he was convicted, Omer admitted that he went too far with loyalty, by hitting the victim over the head with a brick. Mike's friendship with his long-term friend ruptured when his friend also testified for the prosecution against him and "got off scot-free" despite being charged as a secondary party using the doctrine of joint enterprise, whereas he was convicted of Section 18 and sentenced to eight years in prison. Having just turned 17, Michael accompanied his friend in confronting someone he was having difficulties with. Asked why he went with his friend, Michael replied, "It was boring, and I had nothing else to do that day." He continued:

> 'I thought nothing was going on, I was just going to lend support. I didn't know anyone would get shot, I didn't know anyone was going to get beaten up, none of these things were talked about. It was a one-minute conversation asking me to follow him down the road [and] we'll go and smoke some weed after.' (Michael, Black, murder)

Consequently, Michael, because of his somewhat idealised notions of friendship and loyalty, was pulled into a confrontational situation that ended in his friend shooting someone. He was convicted for murder using the legal doctrine of joint enterprise even though he did not inflict any violence upon the victim and sentenced to a minimum of 27 years. Like Michael, Clifton said:

> 'My problem was that I was just very loyal to the wrong people. I see that now. People have always told me that. ... I've done certain things out of fear of not being part of something, not being wanted, not being ... I've done things that I wouldn't do and I've done ... for people.' (Clifton, Black, murder)

In terms of the 'street love' (Payne and Hamdi, 2009) shown between friends 'on-road' (for example, in terms of looking after relationships and the community), for some young people this evaporated on arrest and conviction. As the following quotation from Dalton starkly illustrates, the people that he committed the offence with haven't done what he thought they would with regards to 'real' friendship:

> 'No one went to look after my kid, no one even sent any money to my kid, no one even bought a pair of trainers for my son. I look at things seriously now, I've got a son and you don't even look after my son. I don't want anything to do with you.' (Dalton, Black, Section 18)

He goes on to reflect on his relationships pre-prison and concluded that there were 'fake friendships' based, it seems, on utility rather than goodness or virtue. Even though he's sitting in prison, the extent of Dalton's loyalty embedded in his sense of self. When asked what he would do to show loyalty to a friend he answers, "I would do what I had to do, put it that way", even if that meant risking his life (death or imprisonment), "if we're going through it, we're going through it together". Most of the young people in this study are imprisoned because of criminal actions undertaken with, or actions by, 'friends' or supporting their 'friends'. They, like Dalton, have "lost a lot of [street] friends since I've been in prison. I don't really have any friends anymore". Dalton noted how those who have stayed loyal to him and visited were people he grew up with who took the "straight path" and did not end up 'on the road'. It is the friends known from childhood, those he calls 'family', who visit regularly and bring his son to see him or go to visit his mother. It is not the people 'on-road'. They don't write.

Time after time, the respondents noted that when they were incarcerated the relationships they had with people who were not 'on-road' were the ones that seemed to continue after imprisonment. It was Nigel's mates in the community that came to visit and he notes that for "certain friendships, your loyalties to friends; it's not really worth it".

Conclusion

In this chapter, I drew on the extant literature and empirical data to discuss how understanding friendship is crucial when considering why young people become victims and perpetrators of violence, not least because these two factors are often discussed in tandem. Research conducted with delinquent youngsters has revealed the homophilous nature of young people who are attracted to others who are like them; especially people who share similar characteristics, life experiences and moral constitutions. Studies have suggested that deviants and criminals 'flock together' because they are incapable of recognising positive relationships or forming non-delinquent friendships (Hirschi, 1969), and instead engage with people who encourage law-breaking behaviour and promote violence (Sutherland and Cressy, 1966).

Some of these early findings are contradicted by the narratives presented in this chapter. It seems that young people know what it means to be a good friend and strive to cultivate these connections 'on-road'. By doing so, they drew on a moral philosophy similar to virtuous friendship by seeing the good in others, wanting the best for them, and expressing 'street love' by offering support in times of need. When assessing the quality of 'friendships' and who was considered to be a 'true' friend, the men distinguished between 'good mates', 'friends' and 'associates'.

For young men 'on-road' these distinctions mattered as they dictated the nature of the relationship, including what to expect from, and the commitment shown to, people so labelled. Throughout the narratives, it is evident that 'true' friends are valued. True friends are loyal, trustworthy, honest and protective, and they come to the aid of their friends when times get tough. However, it was difficult to distinguish between 'true' friends and 'faux' friends who employ tactics, tell half-truths, are evasive and are full of pretence. For some of the young men who participated in this study misjudging the authenticity of another resulted in substantial personal cost, including their freedom.

An overarching theme emerging from our study was the central importance of trust and loyalty in relationships on-road. Friendship was based on trust and loyalty, and these qualities were put to the test in situations that ancient philosophers would deem morally and virtuously suspect, resulting in 'evil acts' that undermined honour and integrity. As seen here, 'road culture' has a moral code. 'On-road' is a hierarchical, patriarchal, masculine and heteronormative space that endorses dominance and control, through crime and violence. For some young people here, being involved in a criminal, then violent, act was considered, in the moment, to be the right and virtuous thing to do to protect their honour, or the relationships they have with their friends. What is clear from the testimonies of the young people here is the complex, tenuous and fragile nature of 'on-road' relationships.

My goal in writing this chapter was to emphasise the importance of friendship in human life and to demonstrate how, in the search for friendship, young people 'on-road' engage in normative practices exercised by all, whatever social contexts or strata people occupy. In many ways, then, these relationships share similar characteristics of friendships as those between people who do not engage in serious violence. The significant difference is the sociocultural context in which the friendships are formed and maintained and what young people are 'willing' to do to express goodness or loyalty 'on-road'.

Notes

1. It is important to note that much of the early studies of delinquency tended towards a gender-blindness focusing exclusively on the experience of young men.
2. The question of what types of groups constitute 'gangs' and the criminalisation of such groups, particularly street groups primarily composed of Black and brown young men, has triggered an intense academic and political debate. This will not be rehearsed here.
3. For Gunter, the concept 'badness' refers to a social world characterised by 'spectacular' hyperaggressive/hypermasculine modes of behaviour, incorporating violent and petty crime, fraud/personal identity theft and low-level drug dealing (2008: 352).
4. The term 'rude boy' derives from a Jamaican youth (sub)culture that emerged in the 1960s as a response to unemployment, poverty, colonial oppression and injustice (see Hutton, 2010). According to Hutton, the 'rude boy' archetype is expressed in Jamaican popular music and are persons engaged in 'badness'. That is, 'wickedness and vice' (Hutton, 2010: 26).
5. The interviews were conducted by the author with Dr Susie Hulley and Dr Gary Pritchard as part of the ESRC project. It is with thanks and gratitude that I can draw on the data from this project to use in this chapter.
6. Joint enterprise is the term used to describe a complex set of legal principles in English and Welsh law that allows more than one individual to be convicted of a single criminal offence. For example, a person can be prosecuted for a crime committed by another if it can be proven that they 'intended to assist or encourage' the principal offender in the substantive offence (this is the principle of secondary liability) (Crown Prosecution Service, 2018).

References

Akers, R.L. (1973) *Deviant Behaviour: A Social Learning Approach*. Belmont: Wadworth.

Amatrudo, T. (2016) Applying analytic reasoning to clarify intention and responsibility in joint enterprise cases. *Onati Socio-Legal Series* [online], 6(4): 920–936.

Anderson, E. (1999) *Code of the Street: Decency, Violence, and the Moral Life of the Inner City*. New York: W.W. Norton and Company.

Aristotle (365 BC) *Nicomachean Ethics*. Translated by Adam Beresford (2020) London: Penguin Books.

Bakkali, Y. (2022) Road capitals: Reconceptualising street capital, value production and exchange in the context of road life in the UK. *Current Sociology*, 70(3): 419–435.

Battin-Pearson, S., Thornberry, T., Hawkins, D. and Krohn, M. (1998) Gang membership, delinquent peers and delinquent behaviour. *Juvenile Justice Bulletin*. Washington, DC: US Department of Justice.

Bradshaw, P. and Smith, D.J. (2005) Gang membership and teenage offending. *Edinburgh Study of Youth Transitions and Crime Research Digest*, 8.

Bratman, M. (1984) Two faces of intention. *Philosophical Review*, 99: 375–405.

Cicero, M.T. (2018) *How to Be a Friend: An Ancient Guide to True Friendship*. Translated by Phillip Freeman. Oxfordshire: Princeton University Press

Cloward, R. and Ohlin, L. (1960) *Delinquency and Opportunity*. New York: Free Press.

Cohen, A.K. (1955) *Delinquent Boys*. New York: Free Press.

Crown Prosecution Service (2018) *Joint Enterprise Charing Decisions: Principal, secondary and inchoate liability*. London: Crown Prosecution Service.

Decker, S. and Van Winkle, B. (1997) *Life in the Gang: Family, Friends and Violence*. Cambridge: Cambridge University Press.

Esbensen, F. and Huizinga, D. (1993) Gangs, drugs, and delinquency in a survey of urban youth. *Criminology*, 31(4): 565–589.

Freeman, P. (2018) *How to be a Friend: An Ancient Guide to True Friendship*. Oxfordshire: Princeton University Press.

Gilbert, M. (2000) *Sociality and Responsibility: New Essays in Plural Subject Theory*. Lanham: Rowman & Littlefield.

Glueck, S. and Glueck, E. (1950) *Unravelling Juvenile Delinquency*. Cambridge, MA: Harvard University Press.

Goffman, E. (1990) *Presentation of Self in Everyday Life*. London: Penguin.

Gottfredson, M.R. and Hirschi, T. (1990) *A General Theory of Crime*. Stanford: Stanford University Press.

Gunter, A. (2008) Growing up bad: Black youth, 'road' culture and badness in an East London neighbourhood. *Crime, Media, Culture*, 4(3): 349–366.

Hallsworth, S. and Young, T. (2004) Getting real about gangs. *Criminal Justice Matters*, 55: 12–13.

Hallsworth, S. and Young, T. (2008) Crime and silence: 'Death and life are in the power of the tongue' (Proverbs 18:21). *Theoretical Criminology*, 12(2): 131–152.

Hallsworth, S. and Young, T. (2010) Street collectives and group delinquency: Social disorganisation, subcultures and beyond. *The SAGE Handbook of Criminological Theory*, 21(1): 73–95.

Hirschi, T. (1969) *The Causes of Delinquency*. Berkeley and Los Angeles: University of California Press.

Hobbs, D. (1999) *Doing the Business: Entrepreneurship, Detectives and the Working Class in the Business*. New York: Oxford University Press.

Hulley, S. and Young, T. (2021) Silence, joint enterprise and the legal trap (2021). *Criminology and Criminal Justice*, 1–19.

Hulley, S., Crewe, B. and Wright, S. (2016) Re-examining the problems of long-term imprisonment. *The British Journal of Criminology*, 56(4): 769–792.

Hutton, C. (2010) 'Oh Rudie': Jamaican popular music and the narrative of urban badness in the making of postcolonial society. *Caribbean Quarertly*, 56(4): 22–64.

Klein, M. (1975) *Street Gangs and Street Workers*. Englewood Cliffs: Prentice Hall.

Klein, M.W. (1995) *The American Street Gang: Its Nature, Prevalence, and Control*. New York: Oxford University Press.

Levell, J. (2022) *Boys, Childhood Domestic Abuse and Gang Involvement: Violence at Home, Violence On-Road*. Bristol: Bristol University Press.

Messerschmidt, J.W. (1993) *Masculinities and Crime: Critique and Reconceptualisation of Theory*. Lanham: Rowman & Littlefield.

Miller, W.B. (1958) Lower class culture as a generating milieu of gang delinquency. *Journal of Social Sciences*, 14(3): 5–19.

MOPAC (Mayor's Office for Policing and Crime) (2018) *Review of the Metropolitan Police Service Gangs Matrix*. London: Mayor of London.

Nichols, M.P. (2006) Friendship and community in Plato's 'Lysis'. *The Review of Politics*, 68(1): 1–19.

Nietzsche, F. (2017) *Thus Spoke Zarathustra*. London: Penguin Books.

Pahl, R.E. (2000) *On Friendship*. Cambridge: Polity Press.

Pangle, L.S. (2002) *Aristotle and the Philosophy of Friendship*. Cambridge: Cambridge University Press.

Payne, Y.A. and Hamdi, H.A. (2009) 'Street love': How street life oriented U. S. Born African men frame giving back to one another and the local community. *Urban Review*, 41(1): 29–46.

Pitts, J. (2012) Reluctant criminologists: Criminology, ideology and the violent youth gang. *Youth and Policy*, 109(109): 27–45.

Presser, L. and Sandberg, S. (2019) Narrative criminology as critical criminology. *Critical Criminology*, 27: 131–143.

Rawlins, W.K. and Roll, M. (1987) The communicative achievement of friendship during adolescence: Predicamente of trust and violation. *Western Journal of Speech Communication*, 51(4): 45–63.

Reid, E. (2023) 'Trap life': The psychosocial underpinnings of street crime in inner-city London. *The British Journal of Criminology*, 62(1): 168–183.

Sanchez-Jankowski, M. (1991) *Islands in the Street: Gangs and American Urban Society*. Berkeley: University of California Press.

Saunders, W.B. (1994) *Gangbangs and Drive-bys: Grounded Culture and Juvenile Gang Violence*. New York Aldine De Gruyter.

Sharp, P., Aldridge, J. and Medina, J. (2006) *Delinquent Youth Groups and Offending Behaviour: Findings from the 2004 Offending, Crime and Justice Survey*. Home Office Online Report.

Smithson, H., Ralphs, R. and Williams, P. (2013) Used and abused: The problematic usage of gang terminology in the United Kingdom and its implications for ethnic minority youth. *British Journal of Criminology*, 53: 113–128.

Spencer, L. and Pahl, R.E. (2006) *Rethinking Friendship: Hidden Solidarities Today*. Princeton: Princeton University Press.

Spergel, I.A. and Curry, G.D. (1993) The national youth gang survey: A research and development process. In A. Goldstein and C.R. Huff (eds) *Gang Intervention Handbook*. Champaign-Urbana: Research Press, pp 359–400.

Tack, A.M.C. and Small, L. (2017) *Making Friends in Violent Neighborhoods: Strategies among Elementary School Children*. 224–248. https://doi.org/10.15195/v4.a10

Thrasher, F.M. (1927) *The Gang: A Study of 1313 Gangs in Chicago*. Chicago: Phoenix Press.

Verkerk, W. (2019) *Nietzsche and Friendship*. London: Bloomsbury

Weber, M. (1964) *Weber: Basic Concepts in Sociology*. New York: Citadel Press.

Williams, P. and Clarke, B. (2016) *Dangerous Associations: Joint Enterprise, Gangs and Racism*. London: Centre for Crime and Justice Studies.

Young, T. and Hallsworth, S. (2011) Young people, gangs and street-based violence. In C. Barter and D. Berridge (eds) *Children Behaving Badly? Exploring Peer Violence between Children and Young People*. West Sussex: Wiley-Blackwell, pp 59–70.

Young, T., Hulley, S. and Pritchard, G. (2020) A 'good job' in difficult conditions: Detectives' reflections, decisions and discriminations in the context of 'joint enterprise'. *Theoretical Criminology*, 24(3): 461–481.

5

The Sexual Politics of Masculinity and Vulnerability On-Road: Gender, Race and Male Victimisation

Jade Levell

Introduction

This chapter explores the lesser told stories of sexual relations on-road. Feminist and gender theorists have long since argued that sex is inherently political; summed up in the second-wave feminist slogan *the personal is political* (Millett, 1970). The premise was that how individuals and couples related in their intimate relationships was as important as the broader societal picture, connecting the micro and macro levels. Personal issues became public matters (Holmes, 2007). Feminist theorising about experiences of sex, framed as within the constraints and context of patriarchal society, have largely focused on women's experiences, however in recent years this has been changing. Aiding this change has been the critique and deconstruction of the idea of what it means to be a woman in itself. Black feminists such as Crenshaw (1991) conceptualised intersectionality to respond to the relative invisibility and lack of consideration around Black female victims of domestic abuse within refuges run by the feminist mainstream. Crenshaw urged feminists to look beyond gender solidarity and instead explicitly focus on the myriad of ways in which gender intersects with other aspects of identity, including race and class. As this has gained traction it has also brought critiques of masculinity(ies) and an understanding of the ways in which gender, race and class intersect and fundamentally change the discursive negotiations of the victim or perpetrator labels in men's lives. This is pertinent for young men on-road, who are often living at critical junctures of exclusion. Their image is constructed (both by themselves and others) in ways which resonate with protest masculinity (Connell, 2005; Levell, 2020). Toughness, invulnerability, sexual prowess and the street hustle are foregrounded in a way which leaves their experiences of vulnerability or victimisation invisible. This chapter uses an intersectional lens to examine diverse ways that men on-road discussed their consensual, exploitative, abusive or transactional sexual experiences.

Sexual prowess and gang stereotypes

Connell (2005) has argued that masculinities are defined in relation to each other as well as in relation to femininities. If this is the case, then how men view women will form a key aspect of their personal gender construction efforts (Mullins, 2006). All forms of masculinities have been constructed in contrast to a feminine other, with those that are positioned at the bottom of the masculine hierarchy somehow symbolically assimilated to femininity (Swain, 2005). One discourse around masculine capital lies in a heterosexual assumption. Panfil (2017) researched gay gangs in North America and found that '[g]ay men, especially visible gay men, are seen as a threat to male dominance and control because they are perceived as "traitors" to their sex' (Panfil, 2017: 23). Heterosexism is tied up with traditional ideas of hegemonic masculinity. Heterosexism is interlinked with the racialisation in the hierarchy of masculinities. As bell hooks said, we live in a 'white supremacist capitalist patriarchy' (hooks, 1997: 7). The system of gender and race cannot be dealt with in a vacuum. In the hierarchy of the gender order working-class and poor men are seen as at the bottom of the hierarchy, and Black working-class boys occupy an even lower space than their White counterparts. White male youth identities are 'read against a wider backdrop of structural and economic changes, black male identities are seen as hermetically sealed, self-referential and destructive, a product of a culture of poverty' (Alexander, 2000: 19). This folk devil has been legitimated by academics and policy makers blending the three concepts of what it means to be 'Black' and young and male.

In general, there is a lack of academic research on sex (both wanted and unwanted) in the lives of men on-road. Where it is mentioned, it is often centred upon dominant narratives which link hegemonic masculinity norms with the desire for sexual prowess and predatory behaviour. It is important to note concrete concerns raised around sexual violence perpetrated in gangs (Firmin, 2011; Dickson-Gomez et al, 2017; Nydegger et al, 2017). This is where the value lies in focusing not on the gang context in totality but rather the adversities that are also experienced by young people on-road (who may also be gang-adjacent or involved as well). The tension between recognising young people as both victims and perpetrators of sexual or other forms of abuse and violence simultaneously is a difficult but necessary task

(Levell, 2022). Homing in on this process of categorisation enables us to explore the sexist, racist and classist assumptions which are often at work as undercurrents. Stuart Hall et al (2013) wrote about the perceived threats of the Black male mugger stereotype, the construction of the criminal and predatory working-class Black bodies. In a White-dominant society, the preoccupation with gangs (largely constructed in the public imagination as Black-dominated) is also related to a voyeuristic curiosity around the hyperviolent and hypersexualised male youths. The concept of a 'gang', 'presents a ready racializing vessel or black "folk devil"' (Phillips, 2012: 59).

Intersectional blind spots

Awareness-raising about sexual violence and abuse as a public concern rather than a private shame has been one of the core aims of the feminist movement. Not least because the second wave of feminism occurred during the 1960s and 1970s which closely aligned and crossed over the Gay Rights movement and the Civil Rights movement in America. At this point, Black feminists started to be more vocal on the multidimensional experience of both gender and racial oppression (Haynes, 2017). Later to be coined as 'intersectionality' by Kimberlé Crenshaw (1991), this highlighted the failure of the mainstream domestic violence movement to recognise the different struggles and needs of Black survivors. Crenshaw reflected on the different meanings of domestic space, as being both avenues of refuge from White dominance in racist societies, as well as sites of male violence. In the context of male violence it has been noted that a significant 'folk devil' of sexual violence is the image of the Black male 'outsider' rapist who victimised a vulnerable White woman (Penny, 2022). This circular logic has been used in order to justify the need for a criminal justice response which enacts protection of women and maintaining racist practices that uphold White supremacy. Recent years have seen vocal critiques of White feminists' failure to acknowledge the privilege of 'political whiteness' (Phipps, 2020). As Reni Eddo-Lodge noted, the politics of Whiteness transcends skin colour, but is 'an occupying force in the mind. … It's about women espousing feminist politics as they buy into the politics of whiteness, which at its core are exclusionary, discriminatory and structurally racist' (Eddo-Lodge, 2017: 170). To be clear, the critique of White feminism is not to say that most feminists are explicitly racist, but rather that they fail to recognise the power that they wield in the wider gender order which is fundamentally intersectional. There is an inherent contradiction that the feminist movement has always focused on the structural inequality of patriarchy yet failed to see race as a political structure to be dismantled in the same way.

Accusations of exclusionary politics have been levelled at the #MeToo movement for survivors of sexual violence. It was originally created by a

Black woman, Tarana Burke, in 2006 yet it was not until it was taken up by White women years later that it gained large traction, leading to claims it was co-opted and appropriated by White women who failed to give due credit to the contributions and voices of Black feminism in its later iterations. Phipps accuses White feminism of being centred on a colonial construction of racism and privilege. She notes that 'claims to victimhood in mainstream feminism often end up strengthening the intersecting of violence of racial capitalism and heteropatriarchy' (Phipps, 2021: 81). This links to the wider racist economy, whereby 'the oppressor retains his power by encouraging this deflection of rage, and the oppressed follow the leader by oppressing those less powerful than themselves (in the case of Black men, Black women are the most likely target' (Carbado, 1999: 119). This has a long history, as Brown (2011) noted, in the masculine gender order in the history of enslavement, one of the few outlets for Black hegemonic masculinity to be expressed (with the usual markers of manhood such as property ownership outlawed), was in the dominance of Black women. In the nuances of this is the difficult truth that individuals who are faced with external marginalisation pressing down on them can also simultaneously act as the perpetrator to others who wield less power. This causes a double bind of silence for the victims who have to negotiate solidarity with their communities while also being victimised (Gómez and Gobin, 2020).

This begs the question of what position this has left Black male survivors of sexual and domestic violence? Historically positioned on the hierarchy of masculinities as beneath White men, animalised and hypersexualised by the dominant White society, yet also positioned on the patriarchal gender order to dominate Black women; gender (masculinity) takes precedence over femininity. These are far from being theoretical abstractions because they have to be negotiated in personal life and intimate circumstances by Black people almost everyday. In a poignant newspaper article, aspiring actor Obioma Ugoala (2022) discussed the ways in which gender and race intersected in his own sexual experiences, causing havoc, embarrassment and confusion on a regular basis and seriously compromising his capacity to thrive in his chosen profession. He was frequently fetishised as a Black man by White people. He spoke about the ways in which White women as intimate partners or social acquaintances shared their fantasies of what they perceived to be Black masculinity and sexuality as a unique experience.

Sexual victimisation as anti-masculine

Drawing on Connell's (2005) hierarchy of masculinity, there is also an associated pressure on men to be tough and invulnerable. This has the compounding impact of rendering male victimisation and suffering less visible. Discursively, ' "the masculine victim" is a paradox, seen both from a hegemonic masculinity angle and from an ideal victim perspective' (Burcar, 2014: 113). Men who are sexually victimised are 'subjected to a symbolic feminization process' (Bringedal Houge, 2014: 169). Male experiences of rape and sexual violence are issues which have been largely overlooked amidst the feminist characterisation of these issues as gender based, in which women are the main victims (Javaid, 2014). Rape and its association with masculinity has been driven by feminist discourse (Connell, 2005). Within this mode of thought, rape is seen as motivated by a desire to control and dominate the victim and sits within wider embodied tools of patriarchy for female domination. However, what this results in is a reinforcement of myths that situate rape as incompatible with hegemonic masculinity ideals (Ralston, 2020: 128–129). Boyle (2019) discussed the dynamics of #MeToo and the situation for male victims. She noted that male victims of rape and sexual assault may be over-represented in media portrayals and offered more sympathy than their female counterparts, but notably, 'this is not true for *all* men' (Boyle, 2019: 102; italics in original). Reflecting Connell's hierarchy of masculinities, homosexual men are more subject to victim-blaming. Boyle also noted the example of the actor and former National Football League star Terri Crews, who joined the #MeToo movement and spoke out about his experiences, but 'as a 240lbs Black Man he feared that in speaking out he would be recast as the perpetrator' (Boyle, 2019: 102). He faced a *credibility conundrum* through his gendered and racialised experience of victimhood.

Methods

In this study narrative interviews were used with the aid of music elicitation (Levell, 2019). Narrative interviews using music elicitation were selected for several methodological reasons. Open-ended narrative interviews give participants power and agency in the interview space (Mmari et al, 2017; Gausman et al, 2019). Listening to the music selected created a shared experience. It was also important to be sensitive to the way the participants' prior contact with the police might predispose them to considering interviews as intrusive and oppressive (Glynn, 2014). Participants were thus invited to 'pick three music tracks which help you tell parts of your life story'. It captured the interest of participants, with one explicitly noting that the task of choosing music encouraged him to participate in the study. Participants, eight men between the ages of 21 and 50, took part and were able to select their tracks in advance and consider what they wanted to bring. Music elicitation functioned in a variety of ways in the interviews (Levell, 2019). Several participants discussed using music as a coping mechanism in childhood when they experienced adversity and found returning to music from the past helped them to access their memories. In several interviews, the historical cathartic function of music was mentioned. In some cases, both the music tracks and their associated videos were used as a means of communication, as metaphors, or as illustrations of what they wanted to share. Some participants used the act of playing the music in the interview as a narrative tool, by changing topic through playing a new track, or using the music to give a break from a topic before moving on to the next one. This approach created an activity in which both the researcher and research could participate in the act of co-listening.

On-road as a space, place and mentality

The inclusion criteria for the study were men who had been on-road and/or gang-involved. All of the participants who came forward identified themselves as falling into both categories. However, what became interesting was the ways in which they distinguished these two categories of experience. It seemed that gang-involvement incorporated a much narrower range of experiences which were concerned more with 'a firm', alluding to organised crime groups. Shaun associated gang activity as related to coordinated violence related to the local geography of postcodes and estates.

The distinction between a peer group that is classed by young people as a gang and that which is a peer group on-road was unclear. The concept of collective action was present in Shaun's description of life on-road, as he noted that "they" (those on-road) would "protect their own". So, this indicates that 'the road' also involves a sense of collective protection, as well as a sense of who is inside the group and who is out. The coordination was discussed as a contrast by one participant, who saw authentic gang activity as part of a bygone era, in contrast with contemporary on-road youth culture. For him, the biggest distinction between his former gang-involvement and contemporary youth cultures on-road was the relative lack of senior coordination on-road. He noted that current serious youth violence was enacted due to "mindless thuggery" of young people on-road who end up "bumping into people" and enacting "stupidness". Although there may be nostalgia for his former heyday residual in there too. Shaun noted that gangs are 'part of road life', so conceptualised 'road life' as a broader background context from which gangs emerged.

The roads were also discussed in terms of locality, and the concept has an elasticity which could cover the physicality of street space, or literally the local roads. However, these roads were not neutral but rather laced with a sense of danger and hypervigilance to the perceived constant threat of violence:

'[Relaying a conversation] I said to him ... can't you see yea I'm *on the road* bruv [brother] I can't stand here for longer than three minutes, not even three minutes that's too long, like being in the same spot, like if were gunna walk along *the road* I'll walk along the side where the wall is because people jumping out of cars.' (Sam; emphasis added)

This excerpt shows two distinct references to the road, the first in the conceptual sense 'on the road' and the second in terms of the literal physical road. Often, the term 'the streets' was used almost interchangeably with 'the road', however Jordan still referred to it as somehow distinct, in being both "a man on the streets *and* the roads". Lester also talked about "street people" who then occupy the road. Jordan talked about being "on the streets" and with that was referring to the whole gang and road culture. He noted that "on the streets its awkward being in it and when you're trying to get out of it its difficult". Eric referred to his own experiences of being "*on* the streets" with the people that he grew up with. The hyperalert aspect of life on-road was not just spoken about negatively, however, it was also discussed as being both 'glamorised' and 'interesting'. A hint of the ways in which it was glamorised can be seen in Dylan's claim about the road: "Being on the road is about the girls, the money, the cars, the jewellery." This demonstrates the connection with the road as access to different commoditised lifestyle elements. 'Girls' in this context are being identified as something to be consumed, although there is an undoubtedly a sense of masculine bravado in this list. It alludes to the idea of the American dream of fame and fortune. It also hints at the money that people earn when drug dealing on-road. Indeed, drug dealing being part of road life was mentioned by all the research participants. Life on-road was also discussed as a verb, as Shaun talked about "doing road" through selling drugs. Perhaps this is where we can identify the on-road mentality. The road is also referred to as a way of being, a mentality, embodied through becoming a 'road person'. Lester noted that he knew how a "road person thinks".

On-road as a heteronormative space

The heteronormative aspect of relationships on-road was raised by Dave, who noted that being openly gay on-road was not seen as a possibility as he discussed aspects of his mental health. It is notable that these culturally feminising attributes, which are associated with weakness (through a hegemonic masculinity lens), were discussed together. He later talked about enjoying music theatre as a form of guilty pleasure. The juxtaposition of these elements is revealing.

> 'I'm alright because things are about to change, I've been at breaking point, but things are emotions you know what I mean, get back to work and stuff coz if you're out of work I've found out recently unless your gunna kill yourself or someone else they're gunna say your fit for

work. ... I think everyone should see that video. Coz like it deals with homophobia as well doesn't it, more people need to like live and let live, people aren't bothering yet, I don't see why people are so full of hate ... but you couldn't be openly gay [on-road]. ... Not that I've ever encountered anyone who's even Bi or even like say a guy is good looking would get you're a slap [laughs].' (Dave)

In this passage Dave has raised the topic of homophobia. The music video that accompanied his music choice was about a teenage boy who was singing about being suicidal while the video showed him being rejected by his family. The stereotypes of Black men and homosexuality have been explored by Han (2015). Han spoke about the way in which there was no *Brokeback Mountain* moment for Black men, who remain pathologised and othered. Han's understanding of the taboo of Black homosexuality reflects Connell's framing of the racialised gender order, noting that Black men are reluctant to identify themselves as gay as it would lead to adding a further 'disadvantaged status marker to themselves' (Han, 2015: 240).

Sexuality and sexual lives of young people on-road have been written about less than other aspects of the on-road subculture, with literature that deals with this issue often reinforcing assumptions about a virile masculinity which reproduces the stereotypes of young men being virile and unattached. Elijah Anderson (1999: 142) noted that, for young people on the streets, their perceptions on sex and pregnancy are also dictated by the code of the street. Anderson found that the main priority among men on the street was the ability to 'come as I want and go as I please', prioritising independence, freedom and male domination in relationships (Anderson, 1999: 156). In a study of 58 interviews with adolescent gang members, Quinn and colleagues (2019) found that sexual risk behaviours were a functional part of both upholding and reinforcing unspoken norms, power differentials and gendered expectations in the gang context. They found that sexual practices were used to uphold gender norms and realise group cohesion. Significantly, it was noted that high-risk sexual practices inspired 'regret and remorse over their participation but noted it was just part of "the life"' (Quinn et al, 2019: 151). Sexual risk-taking and homosocial bonding through sexual practices were a taken-for-granted aspect of life on-road.

Despite heteronormativity being pervasive, there were less discussion about steady and exclusive relationships with the opposite sex. Instead, young women were often referred to as hanging around the boys and inhabiting male-dominated space from the margins. That was pertinent especially for those who discussed perpetrating domestic violence and abuse against peers on-road.

The theme of family related to sex was also discussed by Sam, who spoke about a sexual relationship with a girl when he was on-road. What was so interesting about his account was that he focused on the functional aspects of the relationship, on the way in which his relationship brought him a wider family, which he lacked from his own blood relatives:

> 'I became the guy and then over there, there was like this country girl not from London … not bad bad bad but everyone called her a hole erm, everyone was calling her all names under the sun saying she's done this with that person, but I was there and I remember dumping the most prettiest girl on the block for her and I went off with her and how it all came about is that we just sitting there and she said to me do you want to come to my mum's house? And I said no, hell no, I don't want to go to your mum's house, who would want to go to your mum's house like who would want to? And she was like my mums cool like, she's got drugs, that's what she said, and I was like what? She has got drugs? I'm coming, so there I was, I went to her house and it was just weird, somehow I'm just going to cut the story fast, I got a mum, I got an aunty, I got a sister and a little brother and I became a father figure to the baby that was in the house and a girlfriend all at once, I found a family and they all, and we grew and we loved each other.' (Sam)

The gendered connotations in this passage are multilayered. Initially the woman that Sam sought to be in a relationship with was described as a 'hole'. This is such an evocative description of her in a purely sexual way; the hole to be used, the disembodied hole. He went on to suggest she was promiscuous and looked down on by his peers. The juxtaposition between the clear desire for a family and belonging, alongside the objectification of his partner, is jarring. It highlights the ways in which sexual life can be about both consumption and closeness, sex and family.

Child sexual abuse

Dave selected the Ludacris track 'Runaway Love' (Ludacris ft. Mary J. Blige, 2007), which conveys the story of a young girl who is being sexually abused. Dave used this track to talk about child sexual abuse. He talked about the way that the 'little sister' was centred in the music video. Dave outlined how, since being older, he has taken it upon himself to try and spot paedophiles, using examples of seeing someone on a bus who he confronted and then reported to the police. "This song, it's like perspective, the little sister and all that I'm passionate about … this like domestic violence and like paedophilia as well because that's something that I've been affected by … I had like um my mum's boyfriend was just bad. Like alcoholic, drugs and abusive and that." When he talked through that story, he noted he was "paranoid" and "looking for it" (abusers). Dave circumnavigated, and appeared anxious about, any suggestion of his own victimisation with his deflection onto the vulnerability of other victims, placing himself in the role of a knowing protector. The cathexis revealed here exists in how the emotional charge of his proximity to abuse, and awareness of its harms, continues to frame his sense of himself in the social world. He established a self-value in his protest masculinity persona, declining the privileges of hegemonical forms, or simply feeling ineligible to them, he drew the more limited dividends of this subordinated form of masculinity. He justifies the implied violence of his willingness to use threatening behaviour to redress the greater harm of predatory paedophiles. In this way he instrumentalises a rhetorical violence to manage his vulnerability and shapes his identity through the conventional logics of masculine protection. As a reaction to his experiences of victimisation, Dave spoke about how he deliberately made himself look tough and hostile. His description of 'acting crazy' or appearing to fear no limits is both a performance of protest masculinity, putting himself outside the conventions of the more controlled (and controlling) hegemonic form, but also as a consciously selected personal protection strategy. He noted he used to shave his head in order to "look dodgy" as a protection strategy. His appearance will have drawn reactions from others that would reinforce his investments in a certain kind of masculine persona, pulling him ever deeper into the kinds of protest masculinity described by Connell (1987) as the flawed refuge of men who decline the larger stages and harsher demands of hegemonic masculinity. Jefferson also notes that, for many young men, being considered the 'headcase' or 'nutter' is the most available example of the cherished hardness men like to embody because it demonstrates a young man's willingness to risk his body in performance. It shows him as 'apparently unfettered by any of the normal constraints, fears and calculations' (Jefferson, 1998: 93) and thus probably 'mad, bad and dangerous to know', someone to keep your distance from. Wilson (2003) described how some of the specifically racialised features of this masculine performance have become relatively commonplace in the UK's young offender institutions.

The blind-spot of boys' sexual exploitation

In 2022 the UK government released a strategy on male victimisation, including sexual exploitation of boys, entitled 'Supporting male victims of crimes considered violence against women and girls' (HM Government, 2022). The discursive power of the language in this report appears to focus on male victims, however it also reinforces sexual and domestic violence as issues in which, primarily, the victims are female and the perpetrators are male. Although statistically true, the discursive loop that this assertion results in can lead boy child survivors of sexual abuse to fail to recognise their own victimisation. One participant in the study, Sam, highlighted this in his narrative of hunger, poverty and theft, alongside gendered dynamics of both caring and sexual, yet exploitative, relations with older women that reversed conventional patterns of exploitation. Sam talked about stealing food for the woman whose house he lived in, engaging in sex as a transaction for food and board. The music track that Sam chose ('The Saga', Cormega, 2007) portrayed the circumstances of a young woman who is 'on-road', pregnant, hungry and sleeping in a crackhouse. In yet another example of the gaze of victimisation being projected on women and then 'owned' by a man, Sam selected this track about a woman's experience as a way to communicate his own experiences of vulnerability, being hungry, homeless and sexually exploited. The nature of his disclosure suggest that he had an internalised perception of sexual exploitation as a gendered phenomenon only applicable to women. In the following passage Sam framed his understanding with Maslow's hierarchy of needs (1943), which was part of a range of therapeutic concepts which he used to understand his past circumstances, possibly learned from programmes within criminal justice interventions. For Sam this framework enabled him to conceptualise the ways he was taken advantage of in a transactional relationship while a relatively powerless and exploited child.

> 'That is what Maslow said, you go to get your basic needs, you'll go anywhere to find it and that's why we have sexual exploitation *of women*. ... Back in the day, to stay in these people's houses I had to do sexual acts with women to be able to stay in their house, so I didn't even know what sex was, didn't even know anything about that stuff, and I was brought into it at a very young age.' (Sam; emphasis added)

This suggests Sam's reluctance to identify his own victimisation as a 'man's issue', instead he felt more understood in conveying sexual exploitation as something that generally happens to women. This indicates that, for Sam, vulnerability and victimisation were at odds with the type of masculinity that he was seeking to perform at the time. Gender stereotypes have been identified as a factor that can conceal identification of sexual exploitation and abuse, as 'gendered perceptions of masculinity mean young males are unlikely to talk about having been sexually exploited [by men] due to shame, fear, and concerns about being labelled gay due to homophobic social attitudes' (McNaughton et al, 2014: 14). Interestingly, Sam recalled that he was being exploited by an older woman by being asked to steal food which she would then cook for him in return for sexual attention. He foregrounds his vulnerability and reframes abuse to accommodate his experiences of relative powerlessness, coercion and exploitation, as well as the more conventional male violence.

Heritage of sexual violence

An unexpected disclosure from two of the participants in the study was that they had rape in their family history. Dylan found out in adulthood that he had been conceived though the rape of his mother by his father. Dylan had lived with domestic violence and abuse in childhood and had become heavily gang-involved, which resulted in a lengthy prison sentence. In adulthood, Dylan had reconciled with his father and only found out about the sexual violence involved in his conception after his father's death. Cathexis, an under-used element of Connell's theoretical framework, offers a lens to explore Dylan's disclosure and the extent of his investment in his own racial and masculine identity. This traumatic discovery was then repeated and compounded in Dylan's efforts to come to terms with his daughter's disclosure of her own rape. Dealing with this, while in prison himself, he felt compelled to reconstruct his ideas about fatherhood to support his daughter and reform his own life. The first music track that Dylan selected ('My Old Lady', Omi, 2013) was focused upon expressing his love for his mother. One of the lyrics was 'Felt the love in yur touch although we had it so rough', which Dylan explained dealt with how women, "have to go through all that pain and heartache and then get treated how they get treated". The perspective that women "have to" go through pain and heartache is revealing about the way he viewed his mother's role, bearing witness and experiencing the consequences of his and his father's violence. Dylan talked about how finding out he was conceived through rape was pivotal for him, redefining how he saw his parents and how he felt about his own identity. Dylan conceptualised his criminality and imprisonment located in retrospective guilt for the impact that this had on his mother, which becomes conflated with the guilt he felt for his own conception. It is the agency that Dylan had in the scenarios he describes in interview that is interesting because the examples of gang-related incidents are framed in such a way that he emphasises his passive position: being arrested, being shot, being imprisoned. He frames these as incidents which happened *to* him, rather than being situations he was an active agent in creating. The racialised tension of personal identity was also revealed in Dylan's narrative: "I'm mixed-race. … If I was to say I am Black that would be to deny my mum's heritage. I would rather accept my mum's heritage than my rapist dad's heritage. … Everybody looks at me being Black but I'm mixed-race." This comment shows the radical extent to which Dylan's own sense of identity was conflicted by the violence between his parents. Dylan had to navigate being in a wider 'White' society which created denigrated forms of Blackness he felt compelled to disavow even as he tried to reconcile himself to the stereotypes around gang-involved Black men in the UK. Disavowal of his fathers and his own stigmatised Blackness had somehow to accommodate his mother's Whiteness, a process additionally tangled by the cultural association of Whiteness with virtue and Blackness with 'badness' (Gunter, 2010). To be a product of both the victim and the perpetrator of a crime such as rape is an incredibly complex and affecting issue. In terms of Connell's attention to wide social relations, it is pertinent to also consider that at the time of Dylan's mother's rape, rape within marriage was not technically illegal in the UK (The Law Commission, 1992). This legal tension expresses both the social reproduction of male sexual power and its institutionalisation through marriage, where the most compelling and distressing powers of gender and race intersect. Dylan is forced to grapple with his sense of self as someone who is perceived to be Black, an identity devalued in White society, and which automatically aligns him more with his father than his White mother. The cathexis here lies in the extraordinary psychic and emotional tension generated between his exterior 'public' and ascribed identity as a 'bad' 'Black man', his interior navigation of his abusive family history and its conflicting images of virtue and value.

Sam also described antecedents of sexual violence within his family history. In his case it was his mother who was born as a result of his grandmother being raped by his grandfather. Again, it was not something that he was aware of until his adult life. When Sam found this out it offered him some important insights into his own mother's life:

> 'I found out like what my mum was going through … and this is something we don't we don't see sometimes. … My nan was a rape victim. She was raped by my mum's dad and my nan chose to keep my mum and my mum grew up as the black sheep of the family or whatever you want to call it. She didn't feel like she was a part of the family like that, and that's why she excluded us, and that's what we felt like we didn't feel like we were part of a family.' (Sam)

Sam conveyed a sense of the knowledge of his wider family dynamics once he learned about the sexual violence history within his family. It enabled him to have a different understanding of his own mother's lack of emotional availability when he was younger as being due to her working through her own rejection. The cathexis here lies in the tension between the pain of Sam's own rejection by his mother and how he had never felt part of a family himself and attempting to reconcile this with his knowledge and empathy of his own mother's abuse and rejection by her mother. In this was an inherited trauma that travelled through generations, eventually providing him with a way to understand the abuse he endured. Sam disclosed in the interview that he had been a victim of physical abuse and neglect in childhood.

In addition to the experience of rape in his family history, Dylan also discussed finding out about the rape of his daughter when he was in prison. Prior to the point of disclosure, Dylan said he had been "a bad dad, he worst of dads", however, this was his turning point. Dylan introduced the topic by talking about how, after seeing a fellow gang member being shot in the head, he vowed to "never stop avenging for the sake of him". However, this commitment to the violence and vengeance that are so valorised in the masculine imagination changed when, in prison, he found out that his daughter had been raped:

> 'I was in my jail cell and the chaplain come and asks to speak to me and ... I was thinking mum, it's my mum, it's mum and I couldn't wait to get to his office to hear what he said and then he told me that my 12-year-old daughter had been raped. So that's where the turning point come for me ... they arranged a special visit two days later ... and my daughter come up and said, "Dad please leave it the police and do something positive with your life when you come out and don't go back to jail," so that's why I turned my life around. I don't tell people; I just say family tragedy.' (Dylan)

This passage juxtaposes Dylan's experiences of domestic violence, gang violence and the sexual violence against his daughter. In this thread of his narrative around violence, the masculine roles that Dylan foregrounded changed from 'son-as-victim' to 'gang-member-as-perpetrator' to 'father/protector' rejecting violence. It also shows the desperation and desolation he felt when he thought something had happened to his mother. At that moment he was still his mother's son first and foremost, but in the moment of disclosure of his daughter's rape, his identity as a father came to the fore. This was a recurring feature among the interview group. For some of the participants finding a new sense of familial self around the prioritisation of their role as fathers, brothers and sons was transformative. In this way they looked to the wider repercussions that their behaviour had on those around them. Fathering as an identity practice can provide opportunities for men to develop different masculinities and 'expand their repertoire of emotional communication, while distancing themselves from a mothering or feminised position' (Gough, 2018: 42). Thus, fatherhood presents novel opportunities for men to enhance their 'caring masculinities' through nurturing (Gough, 2018: 58). As in Dylan's case, he moved from being an uninvolved absent father during the height of his time involved in gangs and on-road, which has then shifted through his recovery as he centralised this role in his account of himself, prompted by the double exposure to rape. The fact that Dylan doesn't tell people about the rape, but rather frames it as a 'family tragedy' reflects society's wider taboo around sexual violence.

Tough men, hidden wounds: gender trauma

It is clear that men on-road have been left out of the wider #MeToo moment. Not only due to the wider social context of the feminist movement, who have had to reconcile a racial blind-spot in the discourse, but also because Black men on-road are also within the masculine hierarchy and have been reluctant to speak out on taboo issues that are perceived as 'women's issues'. The expectations of masculinity are altered for Black men in UK society where a long history of colonial relations have generated racial structures of feeling (Williams, 1977). These structures manifest for White people and for Black people in radically different ways, being largely invisible to the former and unavoidable for the latter. Racism is not just a cultural experience but is also a 'material phenomenon' which impacts on an individual's 'consciousness of masculinity', thus racial differences directly affect gender experiences at the personal, social and subconscious level (Edley and Wetherell, 1995: 110).

In considering the impact of masculinity pressures within a wider context of patriarchy the concept of 'gender trauma' resonates. Recent work has focused on the rigid gender binary in the Western world contributing its own 'gender trauma', 'linked to patriarchal settler colonial understandings of gender' (Iantaffi, 2021: 83). Iantaffi focused on the ways in which the imposed gender norms that are both intergenerational and societally enforced cause a specific form of gender trauma, whereby the expression of diverse gender expressions have been historically limited to the preconceptions of a gender binary. Gendered responses to the trauma of sexual violence have also been explored by McGuffey (2005), who focused on the ways in which families create gender-reaffirming healing processes after sexual violence. The reassertion of traditional gender hierarchies' post-sexual violence enables families to restore patriarchal norms, which are heavily influenced by the intersections of race, gender and class. McGuffey noted that in his research he found that marginalised men often respond to sexual violence by asserting their investment in traditional gender norms through 'athleticism, emotional detachment, the promotion of hetero-sexuality, and the construction of male space' (McGuffey, 2008: 217). For Black men on-road the sexual politics of everyday life are both gendered and racialised. It is important to consider how this is relevant specifically to the on-road space. Boys and men on-road are most likely to be stigmatised as 'gang-involved' and criminalised as part of this journey. Currently the research field focuses on the aggressive sexual prowess of gang-involved men, at the expense of a focus on the vulnerabilities and victimisation that exist in the lives of men on-road, situated in the context of heteronormativity, sexual abuse, and exploitation. Black men on-road have inherited a *gender trauma* which, using an intersectional lens, is tied up with gender, race and class (and the stigma of criminality) and so it is imperative to open up a space to allow for vulnerabilities and a deepened understanding of sexual politics.

References

Alexander, C.E. (2000) *The Asian Gang: Ethnicity, Identity, Masculinity*. Oxford: Berg.

Anderson, E. (1999) *Code of the Street*. London: W.W. Norton.

Blige, L. ft. M.J. (2007) *Runaway Love*. USA: DTP, Def Jam.

Boyle, K. (2019) *#MeToo, Weinstein and Feminism*. London: Palgrave Macmillan.

Bringedal Houge, A. (2014) Sexualised war violence: Subversive victimization and ignored perpetrators. In I. Lander, S. Ravn and N. Jon (eds) *Masculinities in the Criminological Field: Control, Vulnerability and Risk-Taking*. Farnham: Ashgate, pp 165–186.

Brown, K.M. (2011) 'Strength of the lion ... arms like polished iron': Embodying black masculinity in an age of slavery and propertied manhood. In T.A. Foster (ed) *New Men: Manliness in Early America*. New York: New York University Press, pp 1–16.

Burcar, V. (2014) Masculinity and victimization: Young men's talk about being victims of violent crime. In I. Lander, S. Ravn and N. Jon (eds) *Masculinities in the Criminological Field: Control, Vulnerability and Risk-Taking*. Farnham: Ashgate Publishing, pp 113–130.

Carbado, D. (1999) *Black Men on Race, Gender, and Sexuality: A Critical Reader*. New York: New York University Press.

Connell, R.W. (1987) *Gender and Power*. Stanford: Stanford University Press.

Connell, R.W. (2005) *Masculinities*. Cambridge: Polity Press.

Crenshaw, K.W. (1991) Mapping the margins: Intersectionality, identity politics, and violence against women of colour. *Stanford Law Review*, 43(6): 1241–1299.

Dickson-Gomez, J., Quinn, K., Broaddus, M. and Pacella, M. (2017) Gang masculinity and high-risk sexual behaviours. *Culture, Health and Sexuality*, 19(2): 165–178.

Eddo-Lodge, R. (2017) *Why I'm No Longer Talking to White People about Race*. London: Bloomsbury Circus.

Edley, N. and Wetherell, M. (1995) *Men in Perspective: Practice, Power and Identity*. Hemel Hempsted: Prentice Hall/Harvester Wheatsheaf.

Firmin, C. (2011) *This Is It. This Is My Life ... Female Voice in Violence Final Report*. London: Race on the Agenda.

Gausman, J., Othman, A., Otoom, M., Shaheen, A. and Langer, A. (2019) Youth as navigators: A study protocol to incorporate narrative and visual methods into research on adolescent sexual and gender development among Syrian and Jordanian youth. *International Journal of Qualitative Methods*, 18: 1–8.

Glynn, M. (2014) *Black Men, Invisibility and Crime*. Abingdon: Routledge.

Gómez, J.M. and Gobin, R.L. (2020) Black women and girls & #MeToo: Rape, cultural betrayal, & healing. *Sex Roles*, 82(1–2): 1–12.

Gough, B. (2018) *Contemporary Masculinities: Embodiment, Emotion and Wellbeing*. Cham: Palgrave Macmillan.

Gunter, A. (2010) *Growing Up Bad: Black Youth, Road Culture and Badness in an East London Neighbourhood*. London: The Tufnell Press.

Hall, S., Roberts, B., Clarke, J., Jefferson, T. and Critcher, C. (2013) *Policing the Crisis: Mugging, the State, and Law and Order*, 2nd edn. London: Macmillan.

Han, C.S. (2015) No brokeback for black men: Pathologizing black male (homo)sexuality through down low discourse. *Social Identities*, 21(3): 228–243.

Haynes, A. (2017) 'Sex-ins, college style': Black feminism and sexual politics in the student YWCA, 1968–80. In B. Molony and J. Nelson (eds) *Women's Activism and 'Second Wave' Feminism: Transnational Histories*. London: Bloomsbury, pp 37–62.

HM Government (2022) *Supporting Male Victims of Crimes Considered Violence Against Women and Girls*. London. Available at: https://assets.publishing.service.gov.uk/government/uploads/system/uploads/attachment_data/file/1064154/Supporting_Male_Victims_2022.pdf

Holmes, M. (2007) *What is Gender? Sociological Approaches*. London: SAGE.

hooks, b. (1997) *Cultural Criticism and Transformation*. Northampton, MA: Media Education Foundation. https://doi.org/10.4135/9781412952606.n261

Iantaffi, A. (2021) *Gender Trauma: Healing Cultural, Social and Historical Gendered Trauma*. London and Philadelphia: Jessica Kingsley Publishers.

Javaid, A. (2014) Feminism, masculinity and male rape: Bringing male rape 'out of the closet'. *Journal of Gender Studies*, 25(3): 1–11.

Jefferson, T. (1998) Muscle, 'hard men' and 'iron' Mike Tyson: Reflections on desire, anxiety and the embodiment of masculinity. *Body and Society*, 4(1): 77–98.

The Law Commission (1992) *Criminal Law: Rape within Marriage*. The House of Commons. Available at: https://assets.publishing.service.gov.uk/government/uploads/system/uploads/attachment_data/file/228746/0167.pdf

Levell, J. (2019) 'Those songs were the ones that made me, nobody asked me this question before': Music elicitation with ex-gang involved men about their experiences of childhood domestic violence and abuse. *International Journal of Qualitative Methods*, 18: 1–24. https://doi.org/10.1177/1609406919852010

Levell, J. (2020) Using Connell's masculinity theory to understand the way in which ex-gang-involved men coped with childhood domestic violence. *Journal of Gender Based Violence*, 4(2): 207–221.

Levell, J. (2022) *Boys, Childhood Domestic Abuse, and Gang Involvement: Violence at Home, Violence On-Road*. Bristol: Policy Press.

Maslow, A. (1943) A theory of human motivation. *Psychological Review*, 50(4): 370–396.

McGuffey, C.S. (2005) Race, class, and gender reaffirmation after child sexual abuse. *Gender & Society*, 19(5): 621–643.

McGuffey, C.S. (2008) 'Saving masculinity': Gender reaffirmation, sexuality, race, and parental responses to male child sexual abuse. *Social Problems*, 55(2): 216–237.

McNaughton, C. and Franks, M. (2014) Research on the sexual exploitation of boys and young men. Nuffield Foundation, August 2014. Available at: www.nuffieldfoundation.org

Millett, K. (1970) *Sexual Politics*. Illinois: University of Illinois Press.

Mmari, K., Blum, R.W., Atnafou, R., Chilet, E., de Meyer, S., El-Gibaly, O., Basu, S., Bello, B., Maina, B. and Zuo, X. (2017) Exploration of gender norms and socialization among early adolescents: The use of qualitative methods for the global early adolescent study. *Journal of Adolescent Health*, 61(4): S12–S18.

Mullins, C.W. (2006) *Holding Your Square: Masculinities, Streetlife and Violence*. Cullompton: Willan Publishing.

Nydegger, L.A., DiFranceisco, W., Quinn, K. and Dickson-Gomez, J. (2017) Gender norms and age-disparate sexual relationships as predictors of intimate partner violence, sexual violence, and risky sex among adolescent gang members. *Journal of Urban Health*, 94(2): 266–275.

Panfil, V.R. (2017) *The Gang's All Queer: The Lives of Gay Gang Members*. New York: New York University Press.

Penny, L. (2022) *Sexual Revolution*. London: Bloomsbury.

Phillips, C. (2012) 'It ain't nothing like America with the Bloods and the Crips': Gang narratives inside two English prisons. *Punishment and Society*, 14(1): 51–68.

Phipps, A. (2020) *Me Not You: The Trouble with Mainstream Feminism*. Manchester: Manchester University Press.

Phipps, A. (2021) White tears, white rage: Victimhood and (as) violence in mainstream feminism. *European Journal of Cultural Studies*, 24(1): 81–93.

Quinn, K., Dickson-Gomez, J., Broaddus, M. and Pacella, M. (2019) 'Running trains' and 'sexing-in': The functions of sex within adolescent gangs. *Youth and Society*, 51(2): 151–169.

Ralston, K.M. (2020) 'If I was a "real man"': The role of gender stereotypes in the recovery process for men who experience sexual victimization. *Journal of Men's Studies*, 28(2): 127–148.

Swain, J. (2005) Masculinities in education. In M.S. Kimmel, J. Hearn and R.W. Connell (eds) *Handbook of Studies on Men & Masculinities*. London: SAGE, pp 213–229.

Ugoala, O. (2022) From being called 'an experiment' to being propositioned by a rich couple … racist myths have blighted my sex life. *The Guardian*, 26 February. Available at: https://www.theguardian.com/lifeandstyle/2022/feb/26/experiment-propositioned-by-rich-couple-racist-myths-blighted-sex-life-obioma-ugoala

Williams, R. (1977) Structures of feeling. In *Marxism and Literature*. Oxford: Oxford University Press, pp 128–135.

Wilson, D. (2003) 'Keeping quiet' or 'going nuts': Some emerging strategies used by young black people in custody at a time of childhood being reconstructed. *The Howard Journal of Criminal Justice*, 42(5): 411–425.

6

The Road, in Court: How UK Drill Music Became a Criminal Offence

Lambros Fatsis

Introduction

Urban space has long haunted the penal and criminological imagination; as a site of crime and disorder, where 'respectable fears' (Pearson, 1983) about overcrowding, mixing and safety co-exist with political ideologies and government policies that treat urban social life as a spatial, moral and socio-political problem to be monitored, regulated and controlled. In fact, the relationship between crime and the urban realm goes to the heart of criminology, as an academic discipline that is marked by an 'urban bias' (Donnermeyer, 2016: 1) due to its emphasis on studying crime as a quintessentially urban social phenomenon. Perceptions of 'society', 'community', 'deviance' and 'conflict', therefore, cease to exist in the abstract. They become designed into, associated with and represented by urban geography – as metaphors for physical locations and social spaces where hierarchies of power, social relations and social structures take shape.

Nowhere is this more evident than the areas of the city that are imagined, researched, sensationalised, suspected and policed as pockets of 'criminality' where 'incivility', violence and danger are thought to fester uncontrollably. Targeted, surveilled, securitised, walled, barb-wired and patrolled as 'no-go areas', 'urban wastelands' or 'crime-infested ghettoes', such 'dangerous' places denote more than physical *space*. They feature as 'symbolic locations' where what is symbolised is the physical and cultural presence of those who are perceived and policed as socially and politically out of *place*, through processes of state-sanctioned, racial(ised) criminalisation (see, for example, Fatsis, 2021a, 2021b). The colonial 'plantation archipelago' (Wynter, nd: 372), the Jewish quarter in medieval and Nazi Europe and the contemporary urban ghetto (Duneier, 2016), stand as symbols of such 'territorial stigmatisation' (Hancock and Mooney, 2013) as vividly as they illustrate the 'multi-racist' (Keith, 1993) ideologies, politics and law enforcement that establish and police the inner city as a 'zone of racial enclosure' (Hartman, 2021: 94).

In contemporary Britain, 'the roads', 'road life' and 'road culture' – all referring to a 'UK-specific form of street culture' (Bakkali, 2019: 13–17) – represent such a spatial and cultural reality, that is lived both as a social cul-de-sac and as an avenue for transgression (Hallsworth and Silverstone, 2009) through musical expression, dress codes and common patterns of speech (Gunter and Watt, 2009; Bakkali, 2021). While road culture should not and cannot be understood in 'exclusively racial/ethnic terms' (Gunter and Watt, 2009: 520) – especially in the context of contemporary urban multiculture – the (kin)aesthetic, linguistic and musical codes that define it are nevertheless informed by, and borrow from, Black or Afro-diasporic culture. Indeed, road culture would be – as well as sound – radically different if this was not so. Road culture would also be policed differently, if at all, if its aesthetics and 'subterraneally subversive … counterpoetics' (Wynter, nd: 218) were the cultural product of 'unpoliced populations' (Fatsis and Lamb, 2022: 17), namely, White affluent people, whose physical and cultural presence is simply not 'the prototypical targe[t] of the panoply of police practices and the juridical infrastructure built up around them' (Sexton, 2010: 48).

UK drill music or 'road rap', as it is often (and somewhat problematically) dubbed, has gradually become *the* sonic embodiment of 'the roads'. Signifying Black cultural pathology and danger in the minds of the police, prosecutors and judges, UK drill music is targeted as such and adduced with alarming regularity as 'evidence' of criminal wrongdoing in court proceedings across Britain (Quinn, 2018; Owusu-Bempah, 2020, 2022; Schwarze and Fatsis, forthcoming). Approached here as a cultural space, UK drill music is not understood merely as a rap subgenre. Rather, it is situated *within* and even understood *as* an 'urban commons' (Hartman, 2021: 4) where young, working-class, often Black, rappers 'assemble' to 'improvise … forms of life', 'experiment with musical expression', 'refuse' and resist the excluded, stigmatised, marginalised, confined and criminalised 'existence scripted for them' (Hartman, 2021: 4) by the state and its law enforcement institutions. Spatialising UK drill in such a way, however, does more than situate the music in 'a liminal space where [young people] … find a form of authentic sovereignty, freedom from the constraints they experienced at the hands of … a hostile society' (Hallsworth and Silverstone, 2009: 365). It also allows us to fully grasp why drill is targeted as a source of danger, whose proper place in public space is denied, in exchange for the defendant's seat inside Britain's courtrooms.

Drawing on the criminalisation of UK drill music by the British legal penal system, this chapter argues that what is criminalised is not drill music *per se* but what it symbolises, namely, the physical and cultural presence of Black working-class Britons as 'permanent suspects' (Ralphs et al, 2009: 485), whose forms of creative expression are perceived and policed as 'aesthetically "out of tune", culturally "out of place" and politically "out of order"' (Fatsis, 2021b: 38). What is treated as 'suspicious, dangerous and inadmissible to the national self-portrait' (Fatsis, 2021a: 144), therefore, is not the discordant sound of drill music but the disorderly presence of young Black working-class Britons, whose very 'existence' in the social world is 'apprehended as [a] crime' (Hartman, 2021: 61–62); through legal penal tactics that blame an entire music genre, its producers and audience for glorifying, glamourising and even engaging in violent crime (Fatsis, 2019b; Ilan, 2020; Lynes et al, 2020). This is not to deny, justify, downplay or condone any of the violence and misogyny in (some but by no means *all*) drill music (Fatsis, 2021b: 30–31; Fatsis, 2023). Rather, it is to stress that the British state's – or rather the Crown's – case against drill rap(pers) fails to uphold high standards of evidence, ensure procedural fairness or respect civil liberties and human rights that most people expect from and associate with the rule of law and the ideals, principles and practices that are supposed to underpin modern, liberal democratic politics more broadly.

Contrary to self-congratulatory mythologies about principles of fairness and justice in law enforcement, this chapter tells a different story, demonstrating instead how drill is selectively criminalised in ways that do violence to factual accuracy, Black cultural literacy and social justice. To do so, the following sections of this chapter will offer an overview of recurring prosecutorial tactics used against drill in court, to expose their prejudicial rationale and the discriminatory outcomes they produce, relying as such logics do on racist stereotypes about Black music genres and 'criminality' (Fatsis, 2019a, 2019b, 2021b). Starting with a brief introduction to drill music – to set the scene to its proper artistic and cultural context – a discussion of how drill lyrics and videos are admitted in court as 'evidence' of criminal wrongdoing will ensue, pointing at the flagrant disregard that the police, prosecutors and judges show for upholding high standards of (f) actual evidence and scrutinising the admissibility of what and how evidence is gathered, produced and presented – to say nothing of their failure to adequately evaluate the prejudicial impact that such material can and does have on the fairness of court proceedings. This chapter will therefore challenge the admissibility of such evidence as factually inaccurate to prove guilt, demonstrating instead how putting drill on trial normalises prejudicial assumptions about an art form, its producers and audiences. Much of the argument presented here relies on my existing and ongoing research on the long history of policing against Black or Afro-diasporic music (see, for example, Fatsis, 2019a, 2019b, 2021b) and, most importantly, on my work as an expert witness for the defence in murder trial cases that involve the use of drill lyrics and videos as incriminating 'evidence'. Bringing together a commitment to critical scholarship, ethical practice and social justice to challenge intersecting inequalities and marginalisation, this chapter aims at reintroducing drill music – not a source of danger, but a source of suspicion due to racist stereotypes about Black criminality (Gilroy, 1987; Young Review, 2014; Lammy Review, 2017; Owusu-Bempah, 2017; Williams and Clarke, 2018; Phillips et al, 2020; Fatsis, 2021a, 2021b; Paul, 2021).

What is drill music?

UK drill music is the latest rap subgenre or stylistic branch in the hip-hop/rap family tree. It originated in Chicago in the mid-2000s, but travelled across the Atlantic and took root in the UK rap music scene soon after. Unlike other rap music, UK drill is moodier and darker in sound and more graphic in its violent imagery. It is unabashedly edgy and violent in its posture, lyrics, imagery and sonic qualities. Its lyrics depict fictional larger-than-life personas who tell their story in the first person and pose as violent. As such, rap lyrics are often (mis)taken for real-life descriptions of crimes committed, rather than as first-person narratives that may be partly or purely performative, fictional, hyperbolic or fabricated even, as is the case with many other music lyrics or literary works. Crucially, drill rappers consciously exploit stereotypes of violence, gangsterism and 'ghetto life' as a sought-after commodity to be consumed online by followers whose clicks, views, likes and shares can and *do* yield material rewards (Stuart, 2020). Rather than offering a simple 'authentic' voice rappers are highly attuned to the commercial relations of their work. They deploy themes of violence and crime that they know to be very marketable. A central impetus and theme of the music is the desire to become a successful drill rapper to escape poverty and the violence in drill is part of the genre's conventions and part of its commercial appeal too. UK drill enjoys a huge popular following among young listeners of all ethnic backgrounds, as evidenced by chart-topping hits, big festival line-ups, large club events and the proliferation of YouTube and Spotify playlists. What such audiences share – regardless of their ethnicity – is a sophisticated and nuanced understanding of the genre, as an outlet for creative expression that is produced and consumed *as art* that should not be (mis)taken for literal testimony – as is unfortunately the case when drill music enters the courtroom to be (mis)judged by legal penal professionals and jurors, who are rarely conversant with the music's genre norms (Fried, 1999; Dunbar and Kubrin, 2018; Nielson and Dennis, 2019).

Evidence of things not known

Having sketched out what drill is, this section discusses the way it is introduced in criminal proceedings as 'evidence' of criminal wrongdoing – in ways that play, as well as prey, on stereotypes that inform blanket judgements about drill rappers as violent desperadoes on a gang-banging frenzy, rather than artists – amateur and professionals alike – who invent personas that narrate rather than dictate or confess to actual incidents of violence. Given the sensitivity of the matter, the gravity of charges made against drill rap(pers) and the danger to civil liberties involved when the process of making music is in turned into a criminal offence, the remainder of this section will demonstrate what is admitted as evidence in court proceedings – in order to challenge the evidential weight of such 'evidence', question the expertise of those who are instructed as such by the prosecution and highlight the problems with interpreting drill lyrics and videos in a courtroom setting and in a law enforcement context.

Drill music enters the nation's courtrooms as a source of criminal evidence in the form of lyrics, music videos and still images obtained from music videos; featuring mostly amateur, but also professional, drill rappers, some of whom are very well-known within regional and local circuits (like Skengdo x AM and Digga D). Such material is relied on as evidence of the defendants' 'bad character', involvement in 'joint enterprise', 'serious youth violence' and gang membership, or as confessions to an offence and expressions of intent to commit an offence. To introduce such 'evidence' in court, prosecutors present the material in conjunction with witness statements that are produced by relevant 'experts' (usually police officers, so-called 'gangs experts' from universities and forensic linguists), who may also be instructed to give evidence in court. The arguments that such cases are usually based on involve a matter-of-fact presentation of drill-related material, without adequately interrogating the artistic, literary or fictional nature of the 'evidence' that is brought before judges and jurors.

This may not seem problematic, especially for the Crown and its law enforcement servants. Alas, such tactics fall short of ethical conduct and evidential scrutiny and can even be challenged by the relevant Criminal Procedure Rules, Criminal Practice Directions and Crown Prosecution Service guidelines that set out the duties of experts and the procedure for admitting expert evidence. What poses as an evidence-led attempt to prosecute those who are suspected of wrongdoing based on the music they produce, therefore, starts to resemble a cautionary tale on the dangers of drawing on drill-related material without scrutinising the admissibility and relevance of such 'evidence' (Owusu-Bempah, 2020, 2022). The main objections to this alarming trend of what Kubrin and Nielson (2014), Nielson and Dennis (2019) and Lerner and Kubrin (2021) respectively call 'rap on trial', revolve around questions about:

1. the nature of drill lyrics and videos;
2. institutionalised procedural injustice in the handling of drill-based material as 'evidence' in court; and

3. a profound lack of relevant expertise of those who are instructed by the Crown as 'experts'.

These three main criticisms of putting rap on trial are taken up in turn, to set the record straight about how drill music takes the stand without sufficient evidence to prove involvement in criminal wrongdoing.

The artistic nature of drill music, denied

Starting with the nature of drill music lyrics and videos, it is worth stating the obvious: that such material are a form of fictional(ised) narrative, not autobiographical confessions (Bramwell, 2018: 484; Fatsis, 2019b: 1301; Ilan, 2020: 2, 3, 6, 13, 16; Stuart, 2020: 195). They are not intended to be taken literally, any more than first-person narratives in literature or poetry are evidence of motive, intent or identity with respect to a crime. As Stoia et al (2018: 330) argue, 'fictionalized accounts of violence form the stock-in-trade of rap and should not be interpreted literally'. Treating them as confessions means (mis)interpreting art in a legalistic context that mistakes the literary/fictional for the literal/factual. Writing about or even alluding to a real crime, therefore, cannot be interpreted as equivalent to an admission made by an actual person (rather than a character or persona) made *outside* the artistic context of a musical composition. This is a concern that has also been voiced by an open letter (*The Guardian*, 2019) endorsed by 65 signatories from human rights organisations, as well as musicians, lawyers and academics who argue that 'all artists should be afforded the same rights to freedom of speech and creative expression'. Material of this kind is produced as (self-)consciously fictive narratives that are typically characterised by extreme exaggerations in the lyrics that cannot be taken at face value. Not only is violent imagery and metaphor common to drill music, but much like various other forms of rap music (for example, gangsta rap), it tends to follow a number of genre conventions lyrically and visually too.

In other words, drill will often appear to be 'confession like' in that it describes acts of violence that rappers claim to have accomplished. Yet, it is important not to interpret these lyrics literally, but rather to understand them in full context. Such claims and performances are expected as part of the genre – a form of fictional artistic expression whose connections to literal truth are likely to be abstract and rhetorical. Indeed, these claims and performances are part of an economy of authenticity, by which artists compete for relevance and popularity through telling violent stories (Bramwell, 2018; Ilan, 2020). As such, a broader reading of the genre is required to fully understand deeply ambiguous relationships to crime and violence that cannot be trivialised or (over)simplified without sacrificing contextual literacy for prosecutorial expedience (Fatsis, 2019b; Ilan, 2020).

Dispensing justice through procedural injustice

Another worrying feature of the 'rap on trial trend' in the UK concerns the very legal logic, tactics and definitions through which drill music becomes 'evidence'. Taking 'the law' at face value obscures how legal definitions, assumptions and guidance are arrived at, what evidence they are based on and what procedures are followed by those who research and draft such legal guidance. The assumption is therefore made that such guidance must be watertight, that it is thoroughly researched and that any claims made are factually accurate and based on evidence generated by research procedures whose findings substantiate the truth and validity of what is being claimed. Even a cursory look at the relevant legal guidance on the use of drill music as evidence in court, however, reveals a considerable lack of all of these factors.

The Crown Prosecution Service (CPS) guidance on decision making in cases that involve gang-related offences provides a telling example. In a section entitled 'Gangs, drill music and social media' (CPS, 2021), such guidance readily assumes that there is a close link between drill music and gang membership, despite the dearth of any tangible evidence to suggest any such link (Fatsis, 2019b: 1303–1305). In a characteristic passage, the CPS charging guidance states that drill music videos 'often show the brandishing of weapons, include incendiary remarks about recent incidents of young people being killed or seriously injured'. While this is true, and understandable though such concerns about violent imagery might be, *reference to* a violent incident in a drill music video is not necessarily *evidence of* involvement in the incident referred to. So, unless such use of 'evidence' is challenged by independent experts with a solid understanding of the artistic conventions of rap, lyrical and visual alike, the police and prosecutors are given license to make unreliable and baseless claims about links between incidents invoked in rap lyrics and violence. Once admitted, such videos are played in court accompanied by dubious claims that (mis)lead jurors into reaching conclusions that are largely based on presupposition and *police intelligence*, rather than *hard evidence* that can conclusively prove something more concrete than inferring that lyrical references are evidence of involvement in violent incidents. To make matters worse, the assumed and taken-for-granted links between drill and violence are based on cases that relied on rap material as 'evidence' during a period (2018–2019) when the validity of such 'evidence' wasn't contested by rap experts (Fatsis, 2021c). As such, the conclusion of a trial is assumed to be the by-product of rigorous evidence-gathering procedures, or that it *must be* fair and just. Yet, convictions are secured based on logics and tactics of evidence-gathering and legal argumentation that do not observe the standards of professional conduct that we assume are followed. A successful court verdict, therefore, is simply the outcome of a court ruling which gives us no insight into how the prosecution's case was made, what evidence it was based on, whether such evidence was relevant or admissible, whether such evidence had sufficient weight to withstand scrutiny, whether such evidence is richer in prejudicial impact than evidential/probative value or whether the success and impact of such evidence depends on making an emotive case to the jury by portraying defendants in a negative light and, finally, whether the drill-related material used was even connected to the charges brought against the defendant (Owusu-Bempah, 2022).

Rather than this being a deviation from professional prosecutorial norms, such practices and the prejudicial rationale they are based on are actually informed and enabled by the law itself. To illustrate this with two indicative examples, legal definitions on gangs and legal justifications of using 'bad character' evidence are discussed in turn, to demonstrate how racist stereotypes about young Black Britons and violence stand in for actual evidence-based reasoning. Section 34(5) of the Policing and Crime Act 2009 defines gangs as a group which:

- 'consists of at least three people';
- 'uses a name, emblem or colour or has any other characteristic that enables its members to be identified by others as a group'; and
- 'is associated with a particular area'.

In the context of drill music, this means that anyone who raps on camera with at least three other people, wearing T-shirts with the drill collective's name or logo in their neighbourhood, can be identified as a gang member and prosecuted as such. Inferring gang association through appearances in drill videos, however, is hardly 'evidence' of anything other than signifying a connection – imaginative, performative or real – to a violent environment. Such a connection, however, only indicates a connection to people and places. It does not give away incriminating evidence of gang membership, association or affiliation, unless police prosecutors, judges and jurors are left to let their imagination fill in the blanks.

The same discriminatory logic is at play in relation to 'bad character' evidence. Section 98 of the Criminal Justice Act, 2003 defines bad character evidence as 'evidence of, or of a *disposition towards*, misconduct' rather than evidence which 'has to do with the alleged *facts* of the offence with which the defendant is charged' (emphasis added). Rhetoric of 'bad character' here serves to present a narrative of 'badness', rather than incontrovertible evidence of criminal wrongdoing. It is therefore reasonable to ask why would references to defendants' bad character be needed if real, tangible, concrete evidence existed? What if the material admitted as evidence simply depicts invented, fictionalised personas who rap in the first person and pose as 'bad', rather than actually being bad? Also, who decides what 'bad character' is anyway? What moral, legal, social or cultural standards determine that? Where do they come from? (How) were they agreed upon? Is the 'badness' of one's character even a legal matter that should be decided in court? Upon closer inspection, such vague moralistic allusions to one's alleged (or assumed) bad character are shown to be effective prosecutorial tools for securing convictions, rather than convincing, reliable or conclusive facts. Yet, despite mounting opposition to the use of drill-related material in court – voiced by law reform and human rights organisations (Paul, 2021), leading legal professionals (Garden Court), defence counsels, the expert witnesses they instruct, social scientists, rap experts and legal scholars (Fried, 1999; Dennis, 2007; Kubrin and Nielson, 2014; Nielson and Dennis, 2019; Fatsis, 2019b; Lutes et al, 2019; Ilan, 2020; Owusu-Bempah, 2020; Lerner and Kubrin, 2021), such guidance, and the damaging outcomes they make possible, remain in place. While the CPS has recently pledged to review its guidance by conducting 'listening exercises' with academics, barristers, civil liberties groups and youth organisations, it is nevertheless claimed that they are 'not aware of any cases where drill music had been wrongly used as evidence in the past' (Ball and Lowbridge, 2022), when the very guidance the CPS produces makes the use of such material possible in the first place; in ways that have less to do with whether it is used appropriately, but with the fact that the use of such material is inappropriate. More worryingly still, such public announcements were aired *after* the CPS heard from the author of this chapter and two other academic colleagues about how drill-related material is misused in court, in that same listening exercise that they spoke to the media about.

Rap experts needed, but anyone will do

The inclusion, interpretation and use of rap lyrics as admissible evidence in court is mired in similar difficulties, especially when rap lyrics are handled by non-experts in rap music or Black cultures. Rap is a complex form of expression, characterised by multilayered messages which leads to the possibility of misinterpretation or translation out of context. Rappers manipulate language to the point that 'complicates or even rejects literal interpretation' (Gates, 2010: xxvi, xxv). Like all poets, rappers use figurative language relying on a full range of literary devices such as simile and metaphor. Rappers also invent new words, invert the meaning of others and lace their lyrics with dense slang and coded references that defy easy interpretation, especially among listeners unfamiliar with the genre. Furthermore, rappers famously rely on exaggeration and hyperbole as they craft the larger-than-life characters that have entertained fans (and offended critics) for decades (Dennis, 2007; Stuart, 2020: 195). Listeners unfamiliar with rap culture, therefore, may have difficulty being reasonable or fair when it comes to rap lyrics or videos because it often primes enduring stereotypes about the criminality of young Black men, its primary creators. In the legal penal system, the results of this racial bias are evident in the disparate treatment that people of colour face at virtually every phase of the criminal justice process (Phillips et al, 2020; HMICFRS, 2021). When it comes to rap, research reveals similar disparities (Fatsis, 2019a, 2019b; Nielson and Dennis, 2019). When rap is routinely introduced as evidence in criminal trials, prosecutors will argue that lyrics should be interpreted literally. They are treated as confessions. As Dennis (2007) notes, however, courts tend to incorrectly assume that no specialised knowledge is required to interpret lyrics and that lyrics should be interpreted literally as reflecting accurate, truthful and self-referential narratives. This is a dangerous oversimplification which can have profound implications on the judgement of the jury or indeed the standards of ethical conduct and fairness of criminal proceedings.

Despite the caution that is displayed by rap scholars, however, the prosecution routinely seeks the expertise of people who have little knowledge or understanding of the genre – if they seek such expertise at all. Those who serve as experts for the prosecution, therefore, are usually police officers without adequate training, qualifications or knowledge of drill music, rap or Black youth culture. When it isn't police officers, it's mostly experts on gangs or forensic linguists. *All* lack the necessary expertise to evaluate rap music content. Police officers are unable and unsuitable to offer any authoritative, contextual reading of rap lyrics in an accurate, trustworthy or reliable manner. They are untrained in rigorous procedures of research and evidence-gathering and insufficiently knowledgeable to make judgements about drill music while being sensitive to context and the conventions of the genre. This is evident in the striking failure to adhere to high standards of data collection and evaluation, which compromises the value of the evidence presented, compared to rap scholars who are rigorously trained professionals, educated at doctoral level, with a comprehensive track record of rigorously peer-reviewed research publications. Similarly, experts on gangs *assume* links between drill music and gang membership, but find it difficult to *prove* them. Forensic linguists *can* translate lyrics word for word, but often out of context, as they are *not* conversant with the artistic conventions of rap. *All* aforementioned experts, therefore, draw inferences because references to gangs are common in rap. But any conclusions based on inference are bound to be weak. Gang association *cannot* be inferred through appearances in videos with known gang members, when there can be many innocent reasons for associating with gang members, including musical collaborations, or kinship and friendship ties. That is why such material have to be interpreted in the context of *rap lore* not as a matter of criminal *law*.

Criminalising road culture, one rhyme at a time

The state's failure to acknowledge, let alone recognise, such a reality leads to a situation where the use of drill lyrics and videos as 'evidence' of criminal wrongdoing resembles a story of evidence that is no evidence, legal judgments that are based on prejudice and experts that are not experts on anything that guarantees a proper understanding, contextualisation and evaluation of rap culture. This wilful ignorance of and affected innocence about how the state-sanctioned, racialised condemnation of Blackness stands in for evidence of criminality, gives us a glimpse into how road culture appears in court as an indictable offence and a moral shortcoming that stems from the corrupting influence of drill rap(pers) on the minds of the young. This could sound like an exaggeration, were it not for the fact that what the law targets as direct or indirect 'evidence' is a Black music genre that is singled out using legal reasoning that fails to question its discriminatory logic and outcomes. Were this not so, the criminalisation of drill music in the UK would not be justified by the evidence-less and culturally illiterate assumptions about an entire genre, its producers and audiences. Unlike the US, where the ignoble practice of 'rap on trial' started (Nielson and Dennis, 2019), in the UK drill lyrics and videos are interpreted with a presumption of guilt in mind – readily assuming that what is depicted in verse or on screen *must* be evidence that *should* be admitted as such in court. Yet, it is entirely possible to *not accept something as true* if it is *not known* and cannot be *proven for certain*. In fact, a newly introduced New York Senate State Bill (nick)named 'Rap on trial' does just that (Dillon, 2021). Unlike the CPS guidance, Senate Bill S7527 '[e]stablishes an assumption of the inadmissibility of evidence of a defendant's creative or artistic expression', unless prosecutors can 'affirmatively prove that the evidence is admissible by clear and convincing evidence'. Instead of assuming that drill-related material counts as reliable evidence the Crown *could* insist on the inadmissibility of such evidence. Only, it *doesn't*. Even when 'listening exercises' are conducted, the discriminatory – that is to say, *racist* – logic that shapes the relevant legislation is not called into question, or even referred to by name. As a result, an entire Black music genre is stripped of its artistic nature, so it can function as an audible sign of danger, threat and disorder to a nation's self-portrait where Black Britons do not, could not and should not belong (Fatsis, 2021a, 2021b).

Knowing as we do that 'rap is not the only art to trade in outlaw … narratives' and that it is 'not the only art form to draw from real life for its creations', it is perhaps worth pausing to think about why it becomes 'the only form of artistic expression to be mischaracterized as pure autobiography' (Nielson and Dennis, 2019: 114). As Nielson and Dennis (2019: 114) insist, 'the rules of evidence allow, in theory, for other musical genres and other art such as poetry, films and novels to be used as evidence. But that rarely happens, and not in the same manner and to the same extent as with rap music'. Much as the police, prosecutors and judges might insist on denying the racist thinking that writes itself into the legal guidance they go by in their professional practice, the racist logic and outcomes that their actions produce do not go away – without doing away with legal tools that legitimise racist thinking by codifying it in law. To deny that the criminalisation of road culture is not racialised, is to deny its aesthetic and cultural borrowings from Afro-diasporic culture(s). To claim that such evidence of institutionalised racism is new, a mishap or a deviation from the norm is to deny the long history of racial injustice in Britain as a '*default setting*, rather than a *system error*' (Fatsis and Lamb, 2022: 84; emphasis in original). To mistake legal penal reasoning and practice for justice is to do injustice to the facts of how Blackness is racially criminalised in court through drill music, by dragging people who are suspected of criminal behaviour by association with life on-road. Nowhere is this better captured than through the words of writer and interdisciplinary artist Jay Bernard (2021), whose critique of the racialisation in joint enterprise prosecutions takes the form of a monologue about a young woman whose teenage friendship ties become 'evidence' of gang association; as an 'accomplice' who is treated as 'parasitic' and 'culturally complicit' to acts of violence she never committed. Fictional though this story might be, it nevertheless speaks factual truths about how the British legal penal system relies on racist fiction(s) to blame road life for crimes the law creates.

References
Bakkali, Y. (2019) Dying to live: Youth violence and the munpain. *The Sociological Review*, 67(6): 1317–1332.
Bakkali, Y. (2021) Road capitals: Reconceptualising street capital, value production and exchange in the context of road life in the UK. *Current Sociology* [Online first]: 1–17.
Ball, J. and Lowbridge, C. (2022) CPS to review guidance on using drill music as evidence. *BBC News*. Available at: https://www.bbc.co.uk/news/uk-england-nottinghamshire-60070345
Bernard, J. (2021) *Joint*. London Literature Festival. Available at: https://www.youtube.com/watch?v=Qp8lYH0hGzg
Bramwell, R. (2018) Freedom within bars: Maximum security prisoners' negotiations of identity through rap. *Identities*, 25(4): 475–549.
Crown Prosecution Service (CPS) (2021) Gang related offences: Decision making in gang related offences. Available at: https://www.cps.gov.uk/legal-guidance/gang-related-offences-decision-making
Dennis, A.L. (2007) Poetic (in)justice? Rap music lyrics as art, life, and criminal evidence. *The Columbia Journal of Law & the Arts*, 31: 1–41.
Dillon, N. (2021) New York lawmakers introducing bill to limit rap lyrics as evidence in criminal trials. *Rolling Stone*. Available at: https://www.rollingstone.com/music/music-news/ny-state-senators-bill-legislation-rap-lyrics-evidence-criminal-trials-1258767/
Donnermeyer, J.F. (2016) *The Routledge International Handbook of Rural Criminology*. London: Routledge.

Dunbar, A. and Kubrin, C.E. (2018) Imagining violent criminals: An experimental investigation of music stereotypes and character judgments. *Journal of Experimental Criminology*, 14(4): 507–528.

Duneier, M. (2016) *Ghetto: The Invention of a Place, the History of an Idea*. New York: Farrar, Straus and Giroux.

Fatsis, L. (2019a) Grime: Criminal subculture or public counterculture? A critical investigation into the criminalization of Black musical subcultures in the UK. *Crime Media Culture*, 15(3): 447–461.

Fatsis, L. (2019b) Policing the beats: The criminalisation of UK drill and grime music by the London Metropolitan Police. *The Sociological Review*, 67(6): 1300–1316.

Fatsis, L. (2021a) Policing the union's black: The racial politics of law and order in contemporary Britain. In F. Gordon and D. Newman (eds) *Leading Works in Law and Social Justice*. London: Routledge, pp 137–150.

Fatsis, L. (2021b) Sounds dangerous: Black music subcultures as victims of state regulation and social control. In N. Peršak and A. Di Ronco (eds) *Harm and Disorder in the Urban Space: Social Control, Sense and Sensibility*. London: Routledge, pp 30–51.

Fatsis, L. (2021c) Stop blaming drill for making people kill. *The British Society of Criminology Blog*. Available at: https://thebscblog.wordpress.com/2021/10/18/stop-blaming-drill-for-making-people-kill/

Fatsis, L. (2023) Decriminalising rap beat by beat: Two questions in search of answers. In E. Peters (ed) *Music in Crime, Resistance and Identity*. London: Routledge.

Fatsis, L. and Lamb, M. (2022) *Policing the Pandemic: How Public Health Becomes Public Order*. Bristol: Policy Press.

Fried, C.B. (1999) Who's afraid of rap: Differential reactions to music lyrics. *Journal of Applied Social Psychology*, 29(4): 705–721.

Gates, H.L. Jr (2010) Foreword. In A. Bradley and A. DuBois (eds) *The Anthology of Rap*. New Haven: Yale University Press, pp xxii–xxviii.

Gilroy, P. (1987) The myth of black criminality. In P. Scraton (ed) *Law, Order and the Authoritarian State: Readings in Critical Criminology*. London: Open University Press, pp 47–56.

The Guardian (2019) Stop criminalising our musicians. *Letters*, 3 February. Available at: https://www.theguardian.com/law/2019/feb/03/stop-criminalising-our-musicians

Gunter, A. and Watt, P. (2009) Grafting, going to college and working on road: Youth transitions and cultures in an East London neighbourhood. *Journal of Youth Studies*, 12(5): 515–529.

Hallsworth S. and Silverstone, D. (2009) 'That's life innit': A British perspective on guns, crime and social order. *Criminology & Criminal Justice*, 9(3): 359–377.

Hancock, L. and Mooney, G. (2013) 'Welfare ghettos' and the 'broken society': Territorial stigmatization in the contemporary UK. *Housing, Theory and Society*, 30(1): 46–64.

Hartman, S. (2021) *Wayward Lives, Beautiful Experiments*. London: Serpent's Tail.

HMICFRS (2021) *Disproportionate Use of Police Powers: A Spotlight on Stop and Search and the Use of Force*. February. London: Her Majesty's Inspectorate of Constabulary, Fire & Rescue Services. Available at: https://www.justicein spectorates.gov.uk/hmicfrs/wpcontent/ uploads/disproportionate-use-of-police-powers-spotlight-on-stop-search-anduse- of-force.pdf

Ilan, J. (2020) Digital street culture decoded: Why criminalizing drill music is street illiterate and counterproductive. *British Journal of Criminology*, 60: 994–1013.

Keith, M. (1993) *Race, Rioting and Policing: Lore and Disorder in a Multi-racist Society*. London: UCL Press.

Kubrin, C. and Nielson, E. (2014) Rap on trial. *Race and Justice*, 4(3): 185–211.

Lammy Review (2017) *An Independent Review of the Treatment of and Outcomes for Black, Asian and Minority Ethnic Individuals in the Criminal Justice System*. Available at: https://www.gov.uk/government/uploads/system/uploads/attachment_data/file/643001/lammy-review-final-report.pdf

Lerner, J.I. and Kubrin, C.E. (2021) Rap on trial: A legal guide for attorneys. *UC Irvine School of Law Research Paper*, No 2021–35.

London School of Economics and Political Science (LSE) (nd) *Charles Booth's London: Poverty Maps and Police Notebooks*. Available at: https://booth.lse.ac.uk/learn-more/what-were-the-poverty-maps

Lutes, E., Purdon, J. and Fradella, H.F. (2019) When music takes the stand: A content analysis of how courts use and misuse rap lyrics in criminal cases. *American Journal of Criminal Law*, 46(1): 77–132.

Lynes, A., Kelly, C. and Kelly, E. (2020) Thug life: Drill music as periscope into urban violence in the consumer age. *British Journal of Criminology*, 60: 1201–1219.

Nielson, E. and Dennis, A.L. (2019) *Rap on Trial Race, Lyrics, and Guilt in America*. New York: New Press.

Owusu-Bempah, A. (2017) Race and policing in historical context: Dehumanization and the policing of Black people in the 21st century. *Theoretical Criminology*, 21(1): 23–34.

Owusu-Bempah, A. (2020) Part of art or part of life? Rap lyrics in criminal trials. *LSE Blogs*. Available at: https://blogs.lse.ac.uk/politicsandpolicy/rap-lyrics-in-criminal-trials/

Owusu-Bempah, A. (2022) The irrelevance of rap. *Criminal Law Review*, 2: 130–151.

Paul, S. (2021) *Tackling Racial Injustice: Children and the Youth Justice System: A Report by JUSTICE*. London: Justice.

Pearson, G. (1983) *Hooligan: A History of Respectable Fears*. Basingstoke: Macmillan.

Phillips, C., Earle, R., Parmar, A. and Smith, D. (2020) Dear British criminology: Where has all the race and racism gone? *Theoretical Criminology*, 24(3): 427–446.

Quinn, E. (2018) Lost in translation? Rap music and racial bias in the courtroom. *Policy@Manchester Blogs*. Available at: http://blog.policy.manchester.ac.uk/posts/2018/10/lost-in-translation-rap-music-and-racial-bias-in-the-courtroom/

Ralphs, R., Medina, J. and Aldridge, J. (2009) Who needs enemies with friends like these? The importance of place for young people living in known gang areas. *Journal of Youth Studies*, 12(5): 483–500.

Schwarze, T. and Fatsis, L. (2022) Copping the blame: The role of YouTube videos in the criminalisation of UK drill music. Special issue of *Popular Music*, 41(4): 463–480.

Sexton, J. (2010) People-of-color-blindness notes on the afterlife of slavery. *Social Text*, 28(2): 31–56.

Stoia, N., Adams, K. and Drakulich, K. (2018) Rap lyrics as evidence: What can music theory tell us? *Race and Justice*, 8(4): 330–365.

Stuart, F. (2020) *Ballad of the Bullet: Gangs, Drill Music and the Power of Online Infamy*. Princeton: Princeton University Press.

Williams, P. and Clarke, B. (2018) The black criminal other as an object of social control. *Social Sciences*, 7(234): 1–14.

Wynter, S. (nd) *Black Metamorphosis: New Natives in a New World* (unpublished manuscript).

Young Review (2014) *Improving Outcomes for Young Black and/or Muslim Men in the Criminal Justice System*. Available at: http://www.youngreview.org.uk/sites/default/files/clinks_young-review_report_dec2014.pdf

7

On-Road Inside: Music as a Site of Carceral Convergence

Chris Waller

Introduction

The character and dynamics of urban space play an important role in the lives of young men on-road and recent studies have illuminated the ways in which urban geography can foster forms of identity and affiliation (Reid, 2017; White, 2020). While urban localities or 'hoods' can engender pride, belonging and 'care' (White and Ilan, 2021), they can also be confining, limiting young people's opportunities and forcing them into narrow forms of gendered subjectivity (Reid, 2017). Across many communities, urban regeneration has played a central role in manifesting this encroaching sense of entrapment with young people increasingly priced out of housing, barred from the labour market and excluded from the physical spaces they used to freely inhabit (Reid, 2017; White, 2020). White (2020) has recently documented the effects of gentrification on Black, working-class, urban communities, describing the ways in which young people's sense of belonging is challenged by urban redevelopment which favours middle-class consumers, leading to what White describes as 'social and economic segregation' (2020: 60).

Within this increasingly bleak neoliberal landscape young people have less access to legitimate sources of employment and status and feel increasingly disconnected from their wider communities. It is within this context that Billingham and Irwin-Rogers (2021) suggest feelings of insignificance and alienation can lead young people into criminal enterprise and violence to retrieve a sense of 'mattering'. As Wacquant (2001) has noted, the withdrawal of government support from the most vulnerable and marginalised regions of neoliberal societies has tended to be matched with an increasingly punitive approach to criminal justice. The aggressive policing and criminalisation of young Black men in inner-city areas enforces these spatial demarcations leading many into contact with the criminal justice system. As Fatsis (2019) has argued, the discourse of gang warfare has played a crucial role in characterising young Black men as a threat to be contained and the intensive policing of disadvantaged areas has led to the continued overrepresentation of Black people in both youth and adult prison estates (Lammy, 2017).

In the face of political, spatial and cultural exclusion experienced by Black people, White (2020) has argued that music represents an important means of resisting marginalisation and forging significant connections to their lived environment. The relationship between music and geography within Black expressive cultures is well documented (Forman, 2002; Bramwell, 2015; Ilan, 2020) and, as Shabazz (2009) has suggested, reflects the distinctly carceral nature of Black urban spaces. While music has been shown to provide means of resisting racialised exclusion, recent work has examined the tendency towards criminalising Black expressive cultures (Fatsis, 2019; Ilan, 2019). As Fatsis (2019) suggests, drill artists have come under intense scrutiny in recent years by both the police and the media with both institutions drawing on the violent and criminal imagery within the music to align the music with gang violence. Like grime and UK rap, drill music draws heavily on local landmarks, with county-lines and postcode rivalries featuring frequently among the range of geographical references in drill tracks. However, another point of geographic reference that is referred to less in commentary but which features no less prominently within drill music is that of the prison, or 'pen'. The persistence of prison among the geographic points of reference which drill artists tend to portray suggests not only the cultural significance of the prison for those on-road, but also its social and geographic significance.

Given the significance of space and geography to on-road cultures, exploration of the role of carceral institutions as part of the lives of young men and their families is a timely addition to this growing area of research. This chapter seeks to examine the ways in which on-road culture occurs within the prison, exploring especially the ways in which the boundaries between prison and road are traversed and blurred by young people. Reid's characterisation of on-road culture as a liminal stage in young people's transition into adulthood provides a useful theoretical frame for making sense of the ways in which young people adapt both individually and collectively to the experience of imprisonment. As Shabazz's (2009) work suggests, music provides a useful lens through which to explore these continuities as they occur within subjective states of young Black men and it is along these lines that this chapter proceeds. Drawing on a quasi-ethnographic study of music in a men's local prison in the Greater London area (Waller, 2020), the chapter seeks to explore the geography of on-road cultures from the vantage point of the prison.

Entrapment

Wacquant's (2001) research on the rapid increase in the use of imprisonment in the United States illustrates the stark significance of geography alongside class and ethnicity in determining one's likelihood of being imprisoned. 'Hyperincarceration' is the outcome of political economic shifts in the latter half of the 20th century which were marked by a decisive shift from welfarist approaches to issues of poverty and crime towards increasingly punitive responses. As Wacquant has shown, the punitive turn disproportionately impacted poor Black and Hispanic communities living in disadvantaged urban areas through the withdrawal of basic social welfare from individuals and social institutions. As these ghettoes collapsed under the weight of federal indifference the middle-class inhabitants moved out to escape the deprivation, leading to an increasingly homogenous population in terms of race and class. As Wacquant (2001) argues, the rapid increase in imprisonment was not a response to increased rates of crime but rather a means of managing the staged collapse of the ghetto and the 'dishonoured' populations that it had previously sheltered. What occurred was a 'meshing' of prison and ghetto with traditional social structures of inmate solidarity within the prison fragmenting into an increasingly individualised and racialised configuration, while the urban environment begun increasingly to appear and operate in line with a carceral logic. The increased use of security infrastructure such as barbed-wire fences, code-locked gates and video surveillance within deprived urban areas constitutes part of a carceral continuity between hyperghetto and prison. While authors such as Whitman (2005) have emphasised the specificity of the cultural and political context of US punitivism, it is clear that the increased use of imprisonment across neoliberal nations has taken on a racialised character, influencing the cultural lives of marginalised communities in distinct ways. Shabazz (2009: 277) has examined the preponderance of 'prisonized subjectivities' within marginalised Black residential areas and draws on examples from the United States and South Africa to illustrate the ways in which the encroachment of the carceral state is evident in the ways that Black masculinities come to be formed. Shabazz refers to the 'prisonisation' of hip-hop culture, for instance, identifying how the idealised Black male physique as portrayed in hip-hop music videos has become more muscular towards the end of the 20th century. The bulkier and tattooed male body coheres with the 'hypermasculine logic' (Shabazz, 2009: 287) which occurs in male carceral institutions and signifies toughness and a willingness to utilise physical violence in defence of self, property and status. The diffusion of these carcerally inflected forms into hip-hop music and culture is further illustrative of the 'circularity' between urban and carceral spaces. As Shabazz (2009: 277) suggests, marginalised Black men 'are "prepared for prison" through the deployment of carceral forms into their everyday life'.

In urbanised areas of the United Kingdom, a similar encroachment of the carceral state into lives and environments of marginalised young Black men can be seen in the work of Joy White (2020). White's study of Forest Gate in the Newham borough of North London documents the attempts of urban planning policy to 'regenerate' the area by encouraging middle-class consumers to visit and settle in the area at the expense of the traditional working-class residents. As White illustrates, the effects of this gentrification are felt keenly by the young Black community in Newham who found themselves increasingly displaced from the social and economic life of their area. As they struggle with the legacy of years of government disinvestment and the poverty, homelessness and insecurity that it has engendered, young Black people are also subjected to increased engagement with the police. Deprived areas of Newham are policed with greater intensity than middle-class areas, with fears of gang activity and violence fuelling the increasingly invasive strategies such as stop-and-search. As White notes, inhabitants of Newham represent 1 per cent of the total prison population of England and Wales with high levels of overrepresentation within the probation service too. This spatial distribution is reflected more broadly within the criminal justice system with over 40 per cent of defendants in England and Wales residing in the 20 per cent most deprived neighbourhoods (Jackson, 2022). Reid's (2017) ethnography of an inner-city community in London provides further insight into the ways that social and economic exclusion come to be felt as spatial confinement. Reid's respondents are barred from mainstream housing and employment and pushed towards illicit activities from a young age. Young men are forced to adopt distinct hypermasculine subjectivities to attain and maintain their status in a competitive market of 'trappers'.

The term 'trap' refers to local drug economies but takes on greater symbolic meaning for Reid's (2017) respondents in referring not only to clients who were trapped in cycles of addiction, but also to the social, economic and psychological constraint experienced by dealers. While trapping provided alternative routes to status and financial success, it was also a profoundly risky endeavour with the threat of violence from rival trappers impacting on the lives of dealers. As Reid suggests, trappers were often scared to leave their estates alone due to the threat of violence, meaning that pathways out of their lifestyle through college or legitimate employment were often barred to them. In this respect life 'on-road' takes on the character of a prison to young people, forcing them within particular roles, identities and regions.

As the name suggests, life on-road is a geographic phenomenon as much as it is a cultural one and, as such, its dynamics, flows and boundaries require careful examination. Research has thus far examined the lifestyles of young, marginalised Black people from the perspective of urban and inner-city locals, documenting the ambivalence of these urban locales as sources of pride and identity, while also representing physical, psychological and economic constraint. However, Reid (2017) and White's (2020) accounts echo that of Wacquant (2001) in the way that urban planning and policing policy come to disproportionately criminalise young, predominantly Black men in deprived urban areas leading to a distinct spatial continuity between urban environment and prison. While urban localities tend to play a central role in analysis of on-road culture as the locus of meaning in young people's lives, it is important to examine the role of the prison as, to some extent, integrated into both the culture and geography of life on-road. In the following section we examine the impact of this convergence between prison and inner-city local through the music produced by young people subjected to racialised exclusion.

Music and the carceral

The Black Atlantic (Gilroy, 1993) provides an important framework for understanding the spatial logics that underpin Black cultural expression in the UK. As Gilroy has claimed, musical cultures of the Black Atlantic bore a countercultural significance in the 20th century due, in part, to their formation within the racialised terror of chattel slavery. Due to the complex interweaving of cultures from points across the world, whose origin stems from enslavement and its legacies of confinement and marginalisation, Black Atlantic culture is a defined by its rhizomatic movement across transnational space. Creating fusions between local and distant forms of expression, the music of the Black Atlantic enabled a disparate and diasporic population to 'create itself anew as a conglomeration of black communities' and in the face of hostility and exclusion, transition into 'a distinct mode of lived blackness' (1993: 82). White's (2011: 2) study of grime emphasises its Black Atlantic cultural characteristics, describing it as drawing on the 'cultural, political and economic history of having parents and grandparents from elsewhere', while emphasising equally the lived experiences of those in urban East London. Drawing on Caribbean soundsystem culture as well as hip-hop, drum and bass and garage, grime represents the hybridity of styles and references that characterise Black Atlantic cultures, as well as its situation within both local and transnational experience.

As White (2020) has shown, music represents a space in which the role of urban locality in the lives of young people is articulated and affirmed, enabling the Black youth at the heart of her research to 'respond to the racial terror of Black lives lived under occupation', and allowing them to resist 'the marginal roles that [had] been mapped out for them' (White, 2020: 42). The significance of rap and hip-hop in the latter half of the 20th century and into the 21st, derives in part from their capacity to provide alternative images of contemporary life, drawn from the lived experience of those pushed to the margins of society. The feeling of entrapment felt by marginalised Black subjects, which was discussed in the previous section, is well reflected in the early hip-hop which emerged from the Bronx in New York. 'The Message', by Grandmaster Flash represents a significant moment in the history of hip-hop for the inclusion of more outwardly socially and political aware lyrics into the genre. The opening verse by Mele Mel describes the sense of anxiety felt within a decaying urban space: 'I can't take the smell, can't take the noise /Got no money to move out, I guess, I got no choice' (1982).

The role of geography is significant in Black expressive culture, with scholarship on hip-hop outlining the distinctly urban culture, developed as a means of subcultural resistance to the conditions of racialised exclusion in US cities in the latter half of the 20th century described by Wacquant (2001) and others (Rose, 1994). As Forman (2002: 8) explains, hip-hop was a means for young people 'produce spaces of their own making', by redefining their local environment and imbuing them with meaning specific to localised cultural experience. By renaming roads, neighbourhoods and local landmarks, and mythologising these places by weaving them into stories, young people were able to negotiate the feelings of invisibility and dispossession by 'claiming' their urban locales and elevating their value. In the UK, the genres of grime, UK rap and drill exhibit a similar spatial focus with references to postcodes, estates and parks prominent in lyrics and music videos (Ilan, 2020; White, 2020).

It is this sensitivity to the spatial logics underpinning Black expressive culture that draws us to the role of the prison within Black Atlantic cultures as a site of increased significance in the latter half of the 20th century. While hyperincarceration does not occur uniformly across the Black Atlantic, the increased use of imprisonment and the expansion of the carceral state across North America and the United Kingdom have left a cultural impact which is perceptible in the emergent musical forms and wider cultural styles. As Shabazz (2009) and others (Waquant, 2001) have noted, the end of the 20th century engendered an increased focus on prison or 'pen' within US hip-hop. The emergence of gangsta rap in the 1980s has been thought to represent a response to and documentation of the increasingly intensive use of policing against poor Black and Hispanic people as part of the 'War on Drugs' (Alexander, 2010). It was during this era that rap music began to engage in force with the carceral state with songs such as NWA's 'Fuck Tha Police' (1988) and Ice-T's 'Cop Killer' (Bodycount, 1992) reflecting the growing animosity and distrust between poor urban communities and the police. The backlash against gangsta rap took on a predictable form, folk-devilling young Black and Hispanic men through the menacing depiction of the 'super-predator' which was understood as an untamed outcome of declining family structure. Rates of incarceration were increasing rapidly during this period as the penitentiary took on a larger role within the daily lives of people living within the collapsing urban ghettoes. Wacquant (2001: 114) cites Ellis (1993) in illustrating the depth of penetration of the carceral state during the 1980s, stating that 'three of every four inmates serving a sentence in the prisons of the entire state of New York came from only seven black and Latino neighbourhoods of New York City, which also happen to be the poorest areas of the metropolis'. Two recent iterations of the gangsta rap genre are trap and drill, which continue both the thematic traditions of gangsta rap as well as receiving a similar backlash. Trap, as the name suggests, refers to the drug economy in deindustrialised and 'crisis-ridden' (Büscher-Ulbrich, 2017) working-class communities and documents the lives of those who participate in criminal street cultures. Drill, a more recent iteration deriving from Chicago, follows similar themes and has been characterised as a violent and nihilistic 'problem genre' (Fatsis, 2019). Drill's stripped-back and haunting aesthetic found resonance with young people living in urban South London and was quickly associated with the rising rates of youth violence in the city. Drill paints a bleak and haunting image of life and death on-road with inter-regional violence, county-lines, and prison featuring heavily. The prevalence of the prison as theme in drill opens up consideration of the ways in which this institution features in the daily lives of those who produce and consume the genre.

The prison has long been a feature in Black expressive cultures and the 'prison letter', as a stylistic feature within rap music, provides an interesting point of consideration here in demonstrating the emerging continuity between prison and ghetto. Nas's 'One Love' (1994), for instance, takes the form of a letter sent to his incarcerated friend Cormega, who later built a rap career after his release. 'One Love' is thematically rooted in the description of urban decay, yet it positions the listener as a prisoner within the penitentiary hearing about the mundane news of drug dealing, violence, deceit and street politics from afar. While Nas makes reference to the pains of being rendered separate from friends and family, the song also evokes both continuity and circularity, ultimately situating the experience of imprisonment as part of a mundane sequence of events which repeat themselves endlessly within Black, inner-city communities. Furthermore, the epistolary form of the song draws our attention to the spatiality of the prison, rejecting the common tendency within music and film to render the prison as a place of exception which exists outside of the ordinary frames of reference. Instead, Nas situates the recipient of his letter as distant but present, illuminating the ways in which hyperincarceration is felt within the communities it effects.

As the track fades out Nas gives a series of 'shout outs' to other friends and associates serving time in prison, illustrating the range of impact which prison has on young urban lives.

In recent years the letter has given way to the phone, with numerous tracks including recordings of phone calls with prisoners. Joey Bada$$'s 'Piece of Mind' (2015), for instance, is book-ended with such recordings and similarly situates the listener within the prison, listening to the track down the phone. Quoting the line 'out in New York the same shit is going on' from Nas' 'One Love', 'Piece of Mind' draws on similar themes of family displacement and anxiety and presents both a deeply personal appeal to resilience while also contextualising the situation within the racial and political dynamics of the punitive turn.

> Peace to all my brothers who keep still holdin' on
> Been away so long, feel like a tickin' time bomb
> The misjudgment of my kind, whom the odds is against
> Put our backs on the fence, so we self-defence
> Followed by a series of unfortunate events
> Looking like white America got a brother again. (Joey Bada$$, 2015)

In UK rap and drill, the prison plays a prominent role and recent tracks such as 'T on the Wing' by President T (2016) and 'Wandsworth to Bullingdon' by Fredo (2021) are notable examples of a wide range of tracks which take the prison as their thematic focus. 'Intro' on Headie One's *The One* (2018) album features a collage of audio recordings of which several are recorded in prison and with the increased prevalence of smartphones within the UK prison estate, the 'prison freestyle' is emerging as a genre in its own right with hundreds of videos of aspiring and established rappers alike now accessible on YouTube. Much as the criminal justice system has adapted to incorporate Black expressive cultures within its practices of surveillance, policing and prosecution (Fatsis, 2019), so have these expressive forms adapted to the encroachment of the carceral state deeper into the communities and lives of those who constitute them. The ubiquity of the 'shoutout' to incarcerated friends and associates, as well as the frequent references to lockdown, 'seg', 'basic' and other features of prison vocabulary within drill and UK rap music suggests a deepening role of the prison within the lives of those living on-road. More subtly, the development and adaptation of these genres has served to either situate the listener within the prison, or to erode the prevalent and ideologically founded view that the prison is separate from the community. Through formal devices such as the prison letter, shoutouts and audio artefacts, the convergence between prison and daily life for young Black people living in deprived urban spaces is played out. While the phenomenon of carceral expansionism is well documented across numerous accounts (Wacquant, 2001; Alexander, 2010), what is significant here is the way in which the carceral state is 'inflected' (Shabazz, 2009: 276) by the cultures of young people who are subject to it. For the present study, the primary question relates to the role that music plays within on-road cultures in mapping out the spatial and social logics of their lived experience.

Rap and urban geography in prison

The empirical sections of this chapter draw on a quasi-ethnography of musical practice in a men's local prison in the Greater London area which will be referred to as HMP South Hill. The data was gathered over a nine-month period between 2017 and 2018 and involved 30 interviews with both prisoners and staff as well as participant and non-participant observation. While the research focused largely on the role of music within the residential areas of the prison, observations were also undertaken in the music tech classroom where a group of young Black and mixed-heritage men would dominate the classroom in a friendly and exuberant way, writing beats and recording verses while other students worked quietly on the periphery. As the research project progressed, these young men and the networks formed through their acquaintance provided important insight into the role that music, and particularly rap, played within their social lives both inside and outside of the prison. The social dynamics within the music tech classroom were largely emblematic of those across the prison, with clear social affiliation forming along the lines of age, region and race. While examples of mixing and multicultural conviviality were not uncommon (Waller, 2020), urban geography and the shared experiences and vocabularies which derived from it played an important structuring role within the social life of the prison, often creating lines of separation between prisoners. On entering the prison, inmates were asked whether they had any gang affiliations, and this information was used to reduce contact between rival groups which prison staff saw as a cause of violence. While the characterisation of 'gangs' as organised crime organisations has been subject to criticism on a number of fronts (Reid, 2017; Fatsis, 2019), the threat of violence that derived from urban regional conflicts was confirmed by some respondents:

> 'There's a guy on my wing … he doesn't go off the wing because somebody got killed in Lewisham, five years ago! And they're still fighting over it now, and they'll attack you because you come from an area where that guy came from and got killed.' (Shaun, 40s, mixed-heritage)

For this reason, the urban geography of London came to determine daily life in various ways with different regions of London tending to be placed within the same residential areas of the prison. Shaun's quote illustrates the continuity between the prison and urban communities for those living within this milieu, and as he suggested, this permeability could provide challenges for some. Crewe (2009) has referred to 'reputational networks' which act as collective adaptations to the often highly transient and unpredictable nature of social life within the prison. These networks functioned as a source of information about the integrity and status of prisoners and would often be utilised to test the veracity of a newcomer's account of themselves. For those entering new prison communities there was an imperative to represent oneself as knowable and consistent in order to avoid suspicion of hiding one's identity to conceal a disreputable index offence or rival regional affiliation.

> 'When you meet people in prison, everyone's got a story to tell, everyone's got a background innit? So when you meet someone it's like "What you in jail for, where you from, what's your name?" like. And you've gotta prove yourself, you've gotta talk [to] everyone, you get to know people, we're with people all the time.' (Elias, 20s, mixed-heritage)

While 'reputational networks' (Crewe, 2009) would operate across prisons in many cases, for the young men at HMP South Hill these networks tended to bring the 'road' ever closer to their life inside. This proximity was ameliorated by HMP South Hill's character as a local prison which was transitioning to a training prison and thus held a proportion of unsentenced prisoners from local areas as well as those at the beginning and end of their sentences. As Elias suggested, this situated the prison both temporally and spatially closer to the outside community:

> 'If someone comes on the wing (and) they're from London? Boom, cool, if you're from [my area], you either know me or you'll know someone who knows me, because it's a community innit? If you're from [my area], you're ... d'you know what I mean? We're gonna get along anyway because we're either gonna be friends or we're not gonna like each other, there's only two ways about it. If you're cool, and you [inaudible] and you're from [my area], I'm showing you love because you're from the same area as me, d'you know what I mean?' (Elias, 20s, mixed-heritage)

For George, a high-status prisoner coming towards the end of his sentence, past affiliations with notable UK rap artists, in addition to recognition for his own music, meant that his good reputation held up in most situations:

> 'Yeah [getting recognised] happens all the time. To be honest and that, I'm just paid a little bit more respect than maybe someone else

might, without having to put in any work, do you know what I mean? Because they understand that, at some point in your life you've already been there and done that and worn the T-shirt. And it's not from your mouth that they've heard it, it's from someone else's, so, they're meeting someone they've already heard about. It's not like I'm sat in a room and I'm telling you a story and you don't know … you know. I don't have to say anything or do nothing. So I'm alright.' (George, 30s, Black)

To 'prove' oneself was not only a matter of avoiding pitfalls which could lead to victimisation but also a matter of mobilising one's past achievements or 'street capital' (Ilan, 2020) as a means of achieving status within the prison community. For George, past involvement with criminal activities were verified through references in songs, which took on a greater significance as claims made by others with high status. Rap was a deeply embedded part of the cultural life of the prison for young men from on-road and, as George's account suggests, it provided a cultural space for the exchange of information that created an overlap between the prison and road. Saturday night was important for many of the young men interviewed here as it was when the two biggest national urban music radio shows came on. These shows were an important landmark in the week and respondents described how entire spurs[1] would be tuned in to the same radio shows. Instances such as this further articulated the ways in which, as Bramwell (2018) has argued, instances of 'collective listening' can provide a ways for people to participate in cultures they are physically distant from. Beyond playing drill and UK rap, which spoke in relatable ways to life on-road, these shows often had live interviews and sessions which would often include shoutouts to people in prison. As several respondents suggested, hearing artists from one's area would foster feelings of pride and relatedness:

'[Y]ou see most of these rappers from London, I either know them or I know what they're about, or I know their bredrins [friends].' (Elias, 20s, mixed-heritage)

Music thus provided a structure for prisoners to maintain feelings of involvement with on-road culture, allowing "mutual" (Tom, 20s, Black) feelings to flow through the prison walls. A common refrain among respondents of different age categories was that 'everybody's a rapper these days' and within the prison the prevalence of young men engaged in writing bars and verses was largely accentuated by the restrictive conditions of the prison as well as the booming market for UK rap and drill music at the time of the research. As the following section will discuss in more detail, the popularity of these genres presented issues in determining the authenticity of rap personae and some interviewees responded to with exasperation and scepticism to the notion that every region and estate in London was host to a representative rap artist. Despite this, there was a buoyant feeling among many of the younger prisoners who saw the democratising potential brought by new and easily accessible media technologies as a positive trend. Prison was a place for many to recapture aspirations of professional musicianship and Zach, for instance, had returned to writing bars in the sparse environment of the segregation unit. Zach described how he and the other prisoners in the 'block' would having 'clashing matches', taking it in turns to rap offensive or entertaining bars about each other. As Zach went on to state the validation of his peers had encouraged him to pursue a musical career:

> 'I was just down the block for three weeks and I just wrote everyday. I found it quite therapeutic and stuff, it was a nice meditation to reflect on stuff and, yeah, the boys down the block said "You're actually alright". So since then I've been trying to [write] as much as I can.' (Zach, 20s, mixed-heritage)

Aside from passing the time, rap also functioned as a means of self-enunciation and Zach's reference to the therapeutic characteristics of writing lyrics illustrate the ways in which music can provide space for self-reflection and identity construction (DeNora, 2000). While rap could provide a source of grounding and validation, when performed in public, the authenticity and consistency of one's lyrical content was, as Elias suggested, under constant scrutiny:

> 'You see [with] rap, it's like ... you can relate to stuff innit? So you see [if] someone's rapping about something, like, they're rapping about something you get, and then someone on the wing listens to you to see if you [are authentic/consistent].' (Elias, 20s, mixed-heritage)

As Elias's account suggests, life on-road played a prominent role in the construction of identity within the prison and the accounts within this study seemed to suggest a strong similarity between systems of status described by Reid's (2017) on-road respondents. 'Getting stripes' referred to the practices by which young people built a reputation for themselves through acts of loyalty to their friends, elders and neighbourhood. These acts would emerge as violent reprisals for perceived acts of disrespect committed against their neighbourhood and a failure to 'rep your endz' would incur accusations of weakness and cowardice (Reid, 2017: 146). As Irwin-Rogers and Pinkney (2017) have suggested, the adoption of ruthless and hypermasculine personas by young men on-road often masks feelings of anxiety and trauma deriving from complex familial contexts. Levell's (2019) work with young men on-road who had experience of domestic violence and abuse illustrates how integral music was to the lives of many respondents who, due to their experiences, were required to make sense of complex and traumatic life events. Music consumption here provided both a repository of material through which to construct masculine identities but also a resource through which difficult feelings could be encountered. As Billingham and Irwin-Rogers (2021) suggest, feelings of shame and insignificance can be linked to violence which serves as a way of attaining status or a sense of 'mattering'. The references to violence and criminality within drill music can be seen as a way of negotiating feelings of insignificance through self-aggrandising expressions that can often reach large audiences as well as enunciating one's loyalty to a specific area or social group. According to Phillips (2008: 131), territorial practices such as those associated with 'repping endz' were a way of finding 'ontological' security in unpredictable circumstances and the persistence of these urban-geographic demarcations within the prison is testament to the contingencies faced both inside and on-road. While Phillips's study of race and culture in prison found the 'importation' of culture from the community to play a large role in determining social and cultural constellations within the prisoner society at the prisons she studied, her work also emphasises the ways in which these cultural forms come to be adapted within the prison and were thus subject to negotiation.

As Shaun explained, forms of masculinity formed on-road could not be translated wholesale into the prison and required strategic adaptation when faced with high-status prison masculinities:

> 'I can understand why that generation listen to that music, because it reflects them, but it just reflects a life of violence and gang culture[2] and ultimately you get caught up in that. You're either dead or you're in jail. And then you'll come to jail and you'll see some real badman, because you can be a badman with a gun in your hand and weigh seven stone. But when you come to jail you see some real gangsters who are never getting out and jail, and you have to cool yourself because you ain't got no gun no more.' (Shaun, 40s, mixed-heritage)

The construction of masculinity on-road appeared to follow a similar framework to that of the prison, though to characterise it as entirely continuous in all circumstances would be to overlook the wider dynamics which younger prisoners faced. Tom (20s, Black), for instance, described having had 'pasta' (altercations driven by animosity) with men on another spur before being moved to a more friendly environment where he was able to relax more and integrate into the community. Thus, while on-road culture and geography influenced prison life in various ways, the distinct physical and social character of the environment presented different risks and opportunities, allowing some to strategically evade regional rivalries. Shabazz's (2009) suggestion that Black, urban masculinities are 'inflected' by carceral space appears valid since carceral space is, conversely, inflected by urban geographies. As we have seen, music provided an important cultural resource by which this inflection is both constituted and managed by those involved and the following section will examine this cultural space further by exploring the concept of authenticity.

Authenticity

The issue of authenticity is of clear importance here and examining the role of rap within the daily lives of prisoners reveals its practical role as a tool for managing the complex and challenging world of the local prison. Notably, it is the proximity of the road to the daily life for many young prisoners that presented these challenges and the accounts outlined in the previous section illustrate a sense of anxiety that derived from the intermingling of different regional affiliations. While some of those interviewed seemed relatively at ease among their associates, others, such as Tom (20s, Black), had to fight their way into a space of relative comfort. Elias's (20s, mixed-heritage) assertion that "you've gotta talk" illustrates a pressure on young people to present themselves both as transparent in their affiliations and criminal practices while also retaining a masculine 'front' (DeViggiani, 2012) in keeping with the requirements of the prisoner hierarchy of status. Within this continually shifting social space, music provided a source of information by which prisoners were able to make sense of their environment and those around them and order their social affiliations accordingly. For those entering the prison spitting bars was a way of representing oneself as a cultural insider who was fluent in both the language and attitudes required to live on-road. As Ilan's (2020) analysis of drill lyrics and audience comments suggests, the claims made by artists as to their 'criminal-acumen' are attempts to assert authenticity, rather than documentation of criminal practice. References to insider knowledge or, as Nathan (30s, Black) suggested, to the technical details of drug dealing were ways of situating oneself in relation to the nexus of authentic life experience, yet these claims also provoked concern among the respondents. First, as Ilan (2020) also notes, 'self-snitching' was a concern with drill music becoming increasingly scrutinised by the police to the point of being used as evidence in various cases. As Tom (20s, Black) suggested, overly vivid claims or those relating too obviously to real-life events risked incriminating the artist and those around them. More fundamentally though, some respondents felt that the tendency within drill and UK rap towards claims of ruthless criminal prowess reflected the ease with which authenticity could be appropriated without the requisite experience:

> '[Y]ou can just search Google or YouTube, anything … anything at all, you can put in there. And it will come up. Anything, how to get to

space, how to become a drug dealer, how to … it will come up. How to make drugs … it will come up. So people … instead of actually living it – I'm not saying they should be living it and doing it – but what I'm saying is, instead of singing about their experience they can sing about stuff they know nothing about.' (Nathan, 30s, Black)

Tobias described how rappers held a high social status within their communities and tied authenticity to the responsibilities held by rappers as representatives of particular regions or lifestyles.

'Rap used to have … you used to be able to listen to a song of an artist and learn something, it used to be about kicking rhymes, kicking knowledge. How real is this person? How … how honourable is this person? How strong of character is this person? How much integrity did this person have? Not particularly how "gangster" is this person, that was a later forthcoming from it.' (Tobias, 20s, Black)

Authenticity, as Ilan (2020) suggests, was a standard by which an artist's right to represent the lived experience of those on-road was judged and respondents would often emphasise the importance of this representation. While Elias (20s, mixed-heritage) enjoyed the music of popular Canadian rapper Drake, he was keenly critical of the highly mediated way in which this music was produced, likening the artist to a 'brand'. UK drill held a deeper significance to him because it was able to draw on a range of themes, values and life experiences which he related to in a way that other genres couldn't:

'[They rap about] [m]oney, selling drugs, doing badness … d'you know what I mean? Real shit, real life, like, everyday shit … like growing up, going to jail, like, bare man [lots of people] rap about jail. Bare man rap about dramas, bare man rap about your bredrins [friends] dying, getting stabbed, getting shot, all this bullshit. It's literally just fuckery [insidiousness, "no good"], but that's where we're from, that's what happens, that's the rules of everyday life. That's how it goes down.' (Elias, 20s, mixed-heritage)

Discussions about music and authenticity often provided ways to consider the ethics (see Bramwell, 2015) of identity within the constraining lifestyle of the 'trap' or the prison. Marcus referred to the aims of 'original trappers' as being to make enough money through selling drugs to eventually 'go legit' on their own terms without yielding to oppressive social structures. He described how growing up in poverty had influenced his music and identity by provided less 'opportunities' for him to engage with legitimate routes to success:

'It was a lot easier to go get some weed or some heroin or some crack, than [focus on school work], d'you know what I mean? Or get into a little madness or, have stealing or robbing and ... you know? So like, my lifestyle is a lot more there, innit? But the way I think is (as) a very positive person. I don't ... my mind is beyond the block.' (Marcus, 20s, Black)

For Marcus and other respondents, being 'positive' in one's mentality referred to an aspiration to achieve durable prosperity outside the trap and this term was often applied to certain adjacent genres of rap. While drill was referred to consistently as 'negative', 'positive' rap, which in mainstream parlance has tended to be equated with messages of political empowerment, referred instead to 'happy' and materialistic music which was perceived as aspirational: "they rap about girls, spending money and ... they do talk about drugs and that, but not like [drill]" (Elias, 20s mixed-heritage). While positive rap didn't capture the reality and cultural significance that the criminal and violent imagery of drill did, it was seen as a means of transcending the 'trap' (Reid, 2017) as a lucrative genre which didn't tie the artist to the same rigid requirements of authenticity. In this respect, though Elias was resolute in maintaining authenticity in his own music, both he and others were keenly aware of the difficulties of trapping while seeking to achieve legitimate success in music:

'[I]f you're still selling drugs yeah, and doing violent things X-Factor aint gonna call you like what they did to Stormzy and say "Yeah, [we] want you to be Nicole Scherzinger's friend at her house" [laughs].' (Elias, 20s, mixed-heritage)

The 'negative' themes in drill could provide a large degree of attention and notoriety for an artist, particularly, as Tom (20s, Black) suggested, when they were able to tap into dramas, controversies and regional rivalries:

'You gotta talk a lot of violence to get far. A lot of violence man. No one's gonna listen to you [if you're like] "Ah, go to school". No one's gonna listen to that [laughs].' (Tom, 20s, Black)

However, the nearer one came to prosperity the more the fear of criminal sanction and imprisonment came and the need to self-censor increased, meaning that authenticity and legitimate success were not mutually compatible within the framework of drill.

Conclusion

The data outlined in the previous sections has demonstrated that life on-road would overlap with the prison in various ways, bringing both risks and opportunities for those embedded in the social networks of these urban communities. Rap was an integral part of this cultural space, providing both the infrastructure through which ideas, sentiments and information could flow while also proving a 'cultural material' (DeNora, 2000: 46) by which the complexities of this arrangement could be negotiated. Rap functioned as a means of self-construction, allowing some to represent themselves as trustworthy and resilient by mobilising street capital. However, these practices of enunciation must be understood in terms of a broader politics of authenticity wherein one's bars were subject to constant scrutiny. The concern with authenticity first served a practical purpose within the daily life of the prison as a means of developing knowledge of one's social environment within a highly transient context. Second, the question of authenticity tied into broader questions about life on-road and about the ethics of identity within both the prison and the trap. The significance of these conversations illustrates the harsh challenges which young people face in adapting to the constraints of the trap as well as that of the prison. As Reid (2017) has suggested, the rigid masculinities which young people must adopt can further entrench the sense of entrapment which both the carceral state and the trap engender. Rap has historically provided a resource for individuals to negotiate the challenges of racialised marginalisation and Crockett Thomas et al's (2021) recent work on the role of music as a 'problem-solving' device seems particularly apt within the context discussed here. While drill has come under criticism for the predictable reasons of inciting violence and glamourising criminality, the data has shown how critically the young men in this study engaged with the genre and the legal and commercial mechanisms which underpinned it. Rather than passive consumers of the genre, drill and UK rap provided a cultural language in which ideas of self, aspiration and identity were confronted and worked out.

Notes

[1] Residential areas housing upwards of 60 people in cells. Spurs are a subdivision of prison wings with two or three spurs on a wing.
[2] While older prisoners such as Shaun did not describe their own lifestyles in terms of being on-road, the reference to gang culture and violence can be seen as a reference to the shared frame of experience held by younger generations growing up in deprived urban areas.

References

Alexander, M. (2010) *The New Jim Crow: Mass Incarceration in the Age of Colorblindness*. New York: The New Press.

Billingham, L. and Irwin-Rogers, K. (2021) The terrifying abyss of insignificance: Marginalisation, mattering and violence between young people. *Oñati Socio-Legal Series*, 11(5): 1222–1249.

Bodycount (1992) 'Cop Killer', *The Radio EP*. Prod: ICE T, Ernie C.

Bramwell, R. (2015) *UK Hip-Hop, Grime and the City: The Aesthetics and Ethics of London's Rap Scenes*. London: Routledge

Bramwell, R. (2018) Freedom within bars: Maximum security prisoners' negotiations of identity through rap. *Identities*, 25(4): 475–492.

Büscher-Ulbrich, D. (2017) Surplus trap: Crisis, gangsta rap, and trap music videos. In J. Zimmerman (ed) *African Americans: Free at Last? Equal at Last?* Austria: Königshausen u. Neumann.

Crewe, B. (2009) *The Prisoner Society*. Oxford: Oxford University Press.

Crockett Thomas, P., McNeill, F., Cathcart Fröden, L., Collinson Scott, J., Escobar, O. and Urie, A. (2021) Re-writing punishment? Songs and narrative problem-solving. *Incarceration*, 2(1). https://doi.org/10.1177/26326663211000239

DeNora, T. (2000) *Music in Everyday Life*. Cambridge: Cambridge University Press.

DeViggiani, N. (2012) Trying to be something you are not: Masculine performances within a prison setting. *Men and Masculinities*, 15(3): 271–291.

Ellis, E. (1993) *The Non-Traditional Approach to Criminal Justice and Social Justice*. New York: Community Justice Center.

Fatsis, L. (2019) Policing the beats: The criminalisation of UK drill and grime music by the London Metropolitan Police. *The Sociological Review*, 67(6): 1300–1316.

Forman, M. (2002) *The 'Hood Comes First: Race, Space, and Place in Rap and Hip-Hop*. Middletown: Wesleyan University Press.

Fredo ft. Headie One (2021) 'Wandsworth to Bullingdon', *Independence Day*. Prod: Chucks & HONEYWOODSIX.

Gilroy, P. (1993) *The Black Atlantic: Modernity and Double Consciousness*. Cambridge, MA: Harvard University Press.

Grandmaster Flash and the Furious Five (1982) 'The Message', *The Message*. Prod: E. Fletcher and S. Robinson.

Headie One, RV (2018) 'Intro', *The One*. Prod: M1OnTheBeat.

Ilan, J. (2020) Digital street culture decoded: Why criminalizing drill music is street illiterate and counterproductive. *The British Journal of Criminology*, 60(4): 994–1013.

Irwin-Rogers, K. and Pinkney, C. (2017) *Social Media as a Catalyst and Trigger of Youth Violence*. London: Catch 22.

Jackson, T., Greyson, C. and Rickard, I. (2022) Data first: Criminal courts linked data – An exploratory analysis of returning defendants and the potential of linked criminal courts data from 2011 to 2019 in England and Wales. *Ministry of Justice*. Available at: https://assets.publishing.service.gov.uk/government/uploads/system/uploads/attachment_data/file/1058219/data-first-criminal-courts-linked-data.pdf

Joey Bada$$ (2015) 'Piece of Mind', *B4.DA.$*. Prod: Joey Bada$$, Jonny Shipes.

Lammy, D. (2017) *The Lammy Review: An Independent Review into the Treatment of, and Outcomes for, Black, Asian and Minority Ethnic Individuals in the Criminal Justice System*. London: HMSO.

Levell, J. (2019) 'Those songs were the ones that made me, nobody asked me this question before': Music elicitation with ex-gang involved men about their experiences of childhood domestic violence and abuse. *International Journal of Qualitative Methods*, 18. https://doi.org/10.1177/1609406919852010

Nas (1994) 'One Love', *Illmatic*. Prod: Q-Tip.

NWA (1988) 'Fuck Tha Police', *Straight Outta Compton*. Prod: Dr Dre, DJ Yella.

Phillips, C. (2008) Negotiating identities: Ethnicity and social relations in a young person's institution. *Theoretical Criminology*, 12(3): 313–331.

President T (2016) 'T On The Wing', *T On The Wing*. Prod: Westy.

Reid, E. (2017) *'On Road' Culture in Context: Masculinities, Religion, and 'Trapping' in Inner City London*. Doctoral Dissertation, Brunel University.

Rose, T. (1994) *Black Noise: Rap Music and Black Culture in Contemporary America*. Middletown: Wesleyan University Press.

Shabazz, R. (2009) 'So high you can't get over it, so low you can't get under it': Carceral spatiality and black masculinities in the United States and South Africa. *Souls*, 11(3): 276–294.

Wacquant, L. (2001) Deadly symbiosis: When ghetto and prison meet and mesh. *Punishment & Society*, 3(1): 95–133.

Waller, C. (2020) *Tension and Release: Exploring the Role of Music in a Men's Local Prison*. Doctoral Dissertation, Royal Holloway University of London.

White, J. (2011) *From Rhythm and Blues to Grime: Black Atlantic Exchanges and the Performance of Identity*. Stanford: Stanford University Press.

White, J. (2020) *Terraformed: Young Black Lives in the Inner City*. London: Verso Books.

White, J. and Ilan, J. (2021) Ethnographer soundclash: A UK rap and grime story. *Riffs*, 5(2).

Whitman, J. (2005) *Harsh Justice: Criminal Punishment and the Widening Divide Between America and Europe*. Oxford: Oxford University Press.

8

Jeta e Rrugës: Translocal On-Road Hustle, Within and from Albania

Jade Levell and Stephanie Schwandner-Sievers

Introduction

This chapter aims to explore the similarities between Albanian 'street life' (*Jeta e Rrugës*) with life on-road in the United Kingdom. The salience of this proposed comparison is that the young people who took part in the research in Albania discussed being literally 'on the roads' as they experience international migration in adolescence, much of which involved journeys on both sides of the law in the respective countries. In drawing the comparisons between the hustle of the international 'street life' experienced by Albanian young people and the life 'on-road', we propose that some live the *translocal on-road hustle*. This chapter draws on original research findings derived from life-story interviews based on music elicitation (Levell, 2021) in Albania. This research was conducted with translocal Albanian young men between 18 and 25 years old, who had been identified as previously involved with serious and organised crime by professional gatekeepers. Interviews took place in three Albanian prisons and with young men under community probation supervision in the local community in late 2021 and early 2022. Our analysis of the life stories told by research participants through music elicitation in their own words, however, suggest that the experiences and reactions of Albanian youth who participate 'on-road' differs from their UK counterparts only in terms of very specific, contextual factors. Relevant experiences were framed as being part of 'street life' (in Albanian, *jeta e rrugës*) which resonated with the way in which life 'on-road' was discussed by men in the UK in the author's previous research (Levell, 2022a).

The stories told by the research participants reveal criminalisation pathways which emerge as contextually, rather than culturally, specific. The most notable contextual difference between expressions of urban street life in Albania and the UK on-road experience discovered, was the translocality of life on-road for many of the young Albanians. Rather than their street hustling involving 'county lines', much discussed in the UK, participants remembered different forms of migration, some regular and others irregular (including internal, external and return migration), which for many defined their youth. These suggest a continuum of marginalisation experienced along internal and external migration flows. Our wider research suggests that the discrimination experienced as *rurban* migrants within Albania (that is, those moving from rural poverty to urban promise, and once there facing rejection by the established urban elites; Simić, 1973) informs transnational migration desires. Research participants told their stories through choosing music tracks which at times thematicised such wider experiences of social exclusion and the ways it shapes desires, within and beyond Albania (see Tochka, 2017: 165–166, 172–173). To conceptualise these findings, we have threaded the concept of translocality (Appadurai, 1995) throughout the analysis, acknowledging 'on-road' as a simultaneously physical and virtual space, 'imagined, defined, and lived by different actors ... contested over time' and shaped by 'functional, imagined, or symbolic connections' which expand this locality 'beyond its mere socio-spatial dimensions' (Peth et al, 2018: 456). The concept of translocality allows us to understand the significance of the young men's neighbourhoods as they describe it, relating to spatial and social connections at home, abroad, between and in-between. Its pertinence for the character of experiences described furthermore suggests the need to widen the 'on-road' concept to be inclusive of translocal experiences, accordingly.

Finally, using a contextually sensitive, gendered lens emerged as imperative. The interviewees conveyed the on-road space (*jeta e rrugës*) as a male-dominated environment. Albania has long been considered a deeply patriarchal society, within which men take a dominant position of power both within in the family and the state. In its classic form, as documented specifically for the remote regions of northern Albania, this form of social organisation has been described as 'Balkan patriarchy' (Kaser, 2008). This is 'a social structural system where patrilineality, patrilocality, male moral authority and the formal subordination of women within the household have been the spinal core of this structure' (Michail and Christou, 2016: 967). Local neighbourhoods and communities, according to such logic, are based on kinship relations with territorial and kinship terminologies overlapping (Kaser, 2008). However, *rurbanity*, regional variations and sociocultural changes in contemporary Albania make generalisations in such terms seem potentially ahistorical and liable to stereotype. Instead, we apply Connell's (2005) masculinity theory, which emphasises the existence of multiple masculinities and hierarchisation processes, including the performance of 'hegemonic masculinity' as well as the easy emergence of 'protest masculinity' as 'street masculinity' within marginalised contexts (see Mullins, 2006). Applicable for working-class or ethnically marginalised communities, protest masculinity 'embodies the claim to power typical of regional hegemonic masculinities in Western countries, but which lacks the economic resources and institutional authority that underpins the regional and global patterns' (Connell and Messerschmidt, 2005: 847). We thus paid close attention to the masculinity pressures that the participants expressed and to the dynamics of vulnerable, protest and street masculinities (Levell, 2020). With insufficient social security provided by the state, exacerbated by the 2019 earthquake in the north and the COVID-19 pandemic of 2020 to 2022, 'Albania remains at the top of the list of Western Balkan countries in terms of absolute poverty' (Byrne et al, 2021: 17). Youth unemployment is high and has been associated with the rates of youth crime in Albania (Orgocka and Jovanovic, 2006; Byrne et al, 2021; INSTAT, 2021).

Albanian rap and gangs: myth construction and moral panic

'Albanian gangs' is a discursive trope ubiquitously found in conjunction with 'Albanian mafia', 'foreign gangs' or 'national gangs' across the press spectrum in reports on crimes involving transnational Albanians in the UK. Tabloid headlines such as 'Bad rap: Albanian cocaine gangs flaunt Lamborghinis and wads of cash in rap videos "to recruit more foot soldiers to Britain"' (Christodoulou, 2019) or 'The Albanian drug gangs who flaunt their wealth online: London-based mafia use videos to recruit more footsoldiers to the UK as Lamborghini and Rolls Royce-driving rappers glorify kingpins "linked to cartels"' (Hookham and Ryan, 2019) point to moral panics (Cohen, 2003) around immigration, organised crime and rap music with a specific ethno-national connotation. Rappers Stealth and Vinz, the artists behind the spectacular music videos referred to in these and many other tabloid articles, are declared members of the 'Hellbanianz' of Barking, East London, a transnational Albanian group variously described as either an organised crime gang using music to recruit new members, or as a rapping collective. The strategic association of rap music groups and the representation of lyrics and videos being concrete examples of crime has been an ongoing issue in the UK press and increasingly within the criminal justice system (see Chapter 6, this volume). An example of this discursive myth-making and reinforcement via the media can be found in a 2023 UK newspaper article which centres upon a local resident who was frightened by seeing a rap music video being filmed outside the apartment block. The video featured an armoured vehicle, men in balaclavas and images of a blacked-out car in Tirana (see Hellbanianz, 2022).

You just constantly hear people in their cars or pulling up or shouting things to each other, playing music or talking really loud. But it's done for a reason. … It's always worrying around here now, that's just how life is, there's so much intimidation going on. Especially as a White female living on my own in a council property. I'm a target, without doubt. (Resident Daisy O'Doherty quoted in Garner-Purkis, 2023)

This passage is revealing because it focuses on the anxieties around activities which are legal, yet 'intimidating'. This resonates with Pearson's (1983) concept of *respectable fears*. Pearson focused on the fear of crime being intertwined with the fear of youth in societal imagination, thus becoming central to young people's symbolic lives. This quote offers an example of this with racialised undertones, as the resident's identity as a 'White female living on my own' foregrounds racialised and gendered vulnerability. The message is that she is in need of protection. The instrumentalisation of White female innocence and the implied racial undertones of the outsider perpetrator is a common trope which is often deployed as a contrast to the othered threat (Ware, 2015).

Focusing on the boundaries between insiders, both in the EU, and the UK, and those who are being framed as outsiders, also refocuses our attention onto the politics of Whiteness. Too often racial politics are reduced to the contrast of Whiteness and others, however, and, as Kalmar (2022) noted in the title of his monograph focusing on Central Europeans, they are 'White but not quite'. Issues of race and racism have also been altered by the media's focus on hip-hop culture and in particular Albanian rap music as being inflammatory and reflective of Albanian 'gangs'. This is in line with UK discourse about home-grown London drill and grime music, which is increasingly being framed with a literalist lens, accused of inciting violence and lyrics holding confessionals of actual crime. Despite these tense and divisive issues occurring in the UK about Albanians, we interestingly found no equivalent moral panic about rap music in Albania. In Albanian panics about hip-hop and urban youth culture were more framed intergenerationally, with elders who grew up in the Communist period in Albania viewing rap music and aesthetics as more to do with rampant hyper-capitalism and the denigration of moral standards (Schwandner-Sievers et al, 2023).

It would be remiss, however, for us not to acknowledge the discursive loops which may be playing out in the ways in which Albanian rappers are performing 'gang' identities. The high-profile arrest of the leading members of the Hellbanianz in recent years have helped solidify their reputation as being gang-involved. Prior research by Schwandner-Sievers (2006, 2008, 2023) has explored the ways in which commonplace imageries constructed, both about and by, criminal Albanian migrants take place in feedback loops. In a similar vein there is a strong possibility that commonplace assumptions about 'Albanian gangs' or 'mafia' may be part of internal ('emic'), and external ('etic'), mutually reinforcing, myth constructions as already well documented for 'gangs' in the UK and elsewhere (Ferrell, 1999; Felson, 2006; Van Hellemont and Densley, 2019). Our social-constructivist approach, however, does not exclude the possibility that the emic reproduction of selected and established cultural scripts – here, of what it means to be Albanian, or an Albanian gangster – are part of social identity constructions which effect social lives (Gambetta, 1993; Schwandner-Sievers, 2008; Lauger, 2014). This is because such mythical constructions serve multiple purposes, including the assertion of identities of 'self' (for example, emically, to boost reputation, legitimacy, street credibility, and so on) or of 'othering' (for example, etically, to divert responsibilities for the real causes of crime, other than cultural, for example, racial discrimination and socio-economic exclusion; Hobbs, 1998: 408; Van Hellemont and Densley, 2019: 170–171). We also found that the Albanian respondents told of histories shaped by exclusion, discrimination, complicated family histories (including abandonment), and a constant battle against 'the terrifying abyss of insignificance' outside regular opportunity structures (Billingham and Irwin-Rogers, 2021).

Adultification and Albanian youth migration

Ongoing UK media panics around Albanian crime and immigration and their exploitation on the political right (Hookham, 2022; Tice, 2022) are part of a wider cross-European history, correlating with the small country's disproportionally large emigration flows since the collapse of its previous totalitarian, Communist regime in the early 1990s. Racist stereotypes invoking the trope of Albanians as culturally specifically prone to violence and criminality originally started in the early major recipient countries of Albanian migration flows, Italy and Greece (Lazarides, 1999; Mai, 2002; King and Mai, 2008). The topic of Albanian illegal youth migration has become the subject of recent attention by the UK Conservative government and media outlets. In the wider context of a looming recession, rising inflation and a cost-of-living crisis, the UK government and media's attention appeared to swing squarely in the direction of Albanian illegal immigrants and 'criminals'. Alongside these ever-tightening immigration laws is the increase in the use of inflammatory language about migrants. Current Home Secretary Suella Braverman has referred to migrants arriving on the south coast in small boats as an 'invasion. ... Many of them facilitated by criminal gangs, some of them actual members of criminal gangs' (ITV News, 2022). The language of invasion was widely condemned, and a response by the Refugee Council noted this language was 'appalling, wrong and dangerous' (Morten, 2022). The comments, alongside other specific discourse on Albanians in particular resulted in protests in London. This has relevance when focusing in on the plight of young people on-road. A report commissioned by the Mayor of London has found that in the UK there are estimated to be 215,000 undocumented children, of whom 107,000 are believed to live in London (Jolly et al, 2020: 8).

Adultification of young people who are 'othered' due to racialisation has been discussed by Davies and colleagues (Davis and Marsh, 2020). Their work primarily focused on the experiences of Black children who become involved in the criminal justice system. Although they are technically minors, being under 18, they are instead assumed to be older than their age and held more accountable for their actions (criminal or otherwise) than their White British counterparts would be. Adultification as a principle, however, is less about the facts of recording age, but more about the symbolic treatment of Black children in the wider criminal justice system. However, when it comes to the treatment of immigrant children, there have been concerning reports in 2022 that Home Office officials have been 'routinely changing the dates of birth of unaccompanied child asylum seekers to classify them as adults, according to experts who say the practice is now happening on a "horrifying scale"' (Townsend, 2022). For those who have been classified as children there has been a further scandal as it has been reported that 200 children who have been placed in hotels have gone missing, 88 per cent of whom are Albanian boys (BBC News, 2023). The discourse on this has been divisive, with MP Robert Gullis heckling in a discussion on the missing children in parliament, shouting 'well they shouldn't have come here illegally' (Burke, 2023). Comments such as this highlight the adultification of migrant boys in public discourse. Sentiments which were repeated on the BBC Radio 4 *Today* programme when their reporter Mark Easton downplayed the severity of the missing children:

> [T]hey are almost entirely people who say they are 16 or 17 [year old] Albanian males ... these young people are almost all trafficked, *sometimes willingly* to be honest, *they come knowing* they are going to be *employed* by criminal gangs in the UK. They disappear as soon as they are able and then they are found to be working in car washes or cannabis farms. (BBC Radio 4, 2023; our emphasis)

Both of these commentaries prompted outrage from migrant advocacy charities who noted that by the definition of *trafficking* it is impossible to consent, not least to imply that children *wish* to be 'employed' by gangs. The implications of this all is that these undocumented and unaccompanied migrants, many of whom are Albanian, end up on the 'translocal road'.

The semiotics of choice and agency mirror those that can be seen in debates about county lines drug dealing. The 2015 Modern Slavey Act has been increasingly applied to young people who are exploited (or 'employed') in the illegal drug trade, including as cannabis growers (Ramiz et al, 2020). Data on children involved in county lines are hard to ascertain. Police data collected since 2018 has recorded 4,000 children who are 'involved' in county lines, whereas social work assessment data suggests that there are 15,000 children in this position (Dempsey, 2021). Notable in research on county lines as part of modern slavery is the description of emotional attachment to their abusers, whereby young people cannot clearly identify their abusers or exploiters, but rather, '[y]oung people and vulnerable adults who are groomed into exploitation within county lines may identify with or feel indebted to those higher up the chain of command, preventing their acceptance of a label of victim' (Heys et al, 2022: 59–60). The line between illegal transportation via smuggling which requires payment, and debt bondage leading to modern slavery, is thin and contentious.

Methodology: music and connection

There exists little theory-guided research into the experience, language and perspectives of young Albanian men, themselves, who engaged in 'street life' and have been criminalised at home or abroad. Music elicitation as a method of unstructured interviews enables the creation of a space for listening in an ethically appropriate and sensitive manner, thereby also learning from the research participants about their social and cultural 'webs of significance' (Geertz, 1973: 5). The method was first successfully tried and tested in interviews aimed at exploring domestic and street-based violence experienced by men who self-identified as being child survivors of domestic violence and abuse previously on-road and gang-involved in the UK (Levell, 2019). In late 2021 and early 2022, Levell applied this method for the first time in Albania, as part of a wider UK-government-funded research and development project, known as RAYS.[1]

The interviews were conducted by local researchers trained by Levell in this method. In a first phase, the interviews took place at three prison sites in Albania, involving 11 men; in a second, it involved nine men on probation in the community, three of whom were also accessing support for drug addiction in a treatment programme. Reminiscent of *Desert Island Discs* style of interviewing, participants were simply asked to 'choose three music tracks which help you tell your life story'. Jointly listening to the music tracks and avoiding the asking of any direct questions generates space for the research participants to share whichever aspects of their lives they feel are pertinent, thereby mitigating researcher's bias to a maximum and protecting the interviewees' autonomy and choice (Levell, 2019). In the Albanian case, music proved to be an effective medium to explore narratives, not least because it became clear that some participants were already engaged in grassroots music creation. One participant started freestyle rapping in the interview, and another showed a hip-hop music video that had been made with his peers in his neighbourhood. However, although most of the music chosen was hip-hop, this was not a pre-requisite. Participants also chose folk ballads and classic rock tracks to tell their stories. The focus on music was not on using popular music for textual or semiotic analysis but is more about the embodied experience of music as a way to connect with people across the divides of difference. The aim of using music to connect with men, as well as to prompt the sharing of uninterrupted narratives, was in order to create spaces which were unbound by structured questioning and were authentically curious about the stories that the participants wished to tell.

Findings

Neighbourhood solidarity and marginalisation experience

> 'And then [neighbourhood name] you know, many hate us as a hood, as a unit. … But this is how people are, when you have one conflict all the good stuff that came before is forgotten … you can curse me, you can bring people, we are not a gangster hood, just, with a lot of people, you know, my circle, I just know older guys, I also hang out with people who have businesses, who are not bad at all.' (Probation interview 1)

This testimony highlights the way in which the young person shows an awareness of the external perception of his friendship group as a *gangster hood* when in fact he perceives it rather as a 'circle'. The strong identification with the local urban neighbourhood, in which the participants lived during adolescence, is apparent. The focus on neighbourhood solidarity is resonant with Rod Earle's (2011) concept of 'postcode pride'. This quotation exemplifies how, on the one hand, participants framed their collective of 'boys' as a group who hung out in their neighbourhood and enacted solidarity, which included protecting their peers and backing them up if required in fights or disputes. The various testimonies about the neighbourhood showed a range of interchangeable terms used to describe the group's organisation, including 'the street', 'hood', 'unit', or as 'hanging out together' (*vim verdall*; slang, lit. 'we went on the prowl'). On the other hand, the impression to others was important, hence being identified with a 'gangster hood', rather than a close peer circle, some of whom have 'businesses' yet are 'just human' (as in the song), is rejected in the quote. A similar sentiment around presentation of self and external image (Goffman, 1959) was expressed in another interview:

> 'I am 21 years old, the oldest boy of the family, the most problematic. I like to hang a lot. … How we say, *vim verdall* with friends. We created

problems of all kinds but, still, we are not as bad as they make us out. We like to do good, but still life is such that it didn't give us a lot of things, we didn't have the opportunity to do something better than we did in reality.' (Probation interview 4)

This passage is compelling as it talks about the collective endeavour of the neighbourhood as a street-based peer group, who are externally seen as 'bad', but who identify themselves as a group who made the best out of the little that they had. The perception of a deficit is clearly expressed, relating to a lack of opportunities or resources. This conflicting perspective between negative etic labels, on the one hand, and young people's emic perception of a street hustle, resonates with narratives of men on-road in the UK (Levell, 2020). Peer groups can provide young people with 'substantial support in dealing with problems in their life' (Hine, 2010: 174).

Young lives blighted with a range of adverse childhood experiences (Lacey and Minnis, 2019) were commonly discussed in the data. Fractured families and early experiences of loss led to lives lived on-road, with affiliations at times shifted from family to friends. As can be seen with life on-road in the UK, the street offered a spatial distinction between zones of relative safety and solace (Levell, 2022b). Despite the shift from the privacy of home to the public space on the streets, for young people living with abuse, neglect or violence, life on-road offered more than just a place to spend time, but was also an immersive reality; both a physical and a head-space. This is typified in this quote: "The street is better than the house, regardless that it's actually the opposite, we grew up there" (community participant 2).

Being viewed as 'bad' in the neighbourhood was a recurrent theme: "I was a guy who moved a lot in the neighbourhood, often, and neighbours told their children not to be accompanied with me because I was a bad influence" (prison interview 3). This suggests that these peer groups were not normalised but marginalised in their communities. Denigrating an already disadvantaged group has been argued as 'fusing the idea of the "yob" with a critique of masculinity … one result has been to further attack some of the least powerful men in society' (Collier, 1998: 87). Simultaneously, as Phillips noted, those boys who are most likely to be 'bad' and 'kicking against authority' are those 'who recognize early on that society does not provide for them a place in which they can legitimately exhibit their power' (Phillips, 1993: 28). In response, the term 'bad' has evolved to mean 'all that is strong, brave and hard. To be *bad* is to be masculine. Bad boys need to show that they are also hard' (Phillips, 1993: 28; original emphasis). Masculinity performed on-road 'can be seen as the apotheosis of the attributes which are presently being associated with masculinity's "hegemonic" form' (Collier, 1998: 74). After all, group solidarity and masculinity norms become heightened in outcast situations (Anderson, 1999).

Nacut *('the boys'): gendered solidarity*

Amar: [L]ike always the bad roads, and, like this.
Interviewer: What does bad roads mean?
Amar: With fights and things like this, on the streets, coming around, like boys you know. (Probation interview 5)

The gendered association of the roads with 'boys', *nacut*, and the ways it resonates with 'street life', *jeta e rrugës*, evident in the excerpt just cited, was a recurrent theme throughout the interviews, as in the following:

> 'The boys and the street life, not that there is something, wow, you know, I don't know what to say because there are a lot of things and sometimes I don't remember. Because now to say we are good, good boys, we can't say that. But to also say we are bad, bad boys, that we can't say either. You know? *Nacut!*' (Probation interview 1)

This passage outlines the collective aspect of being among 'the boys'. The narrator got into trouble not only for himself but acting on behalf of the collective. He described the way in which he would act with the group when "mishap falls on me" (an Albanian phrasing akin to 'when something crosses my path'). Street solidarity is tied up with the protection of the group's pride. Central to this is being willing to engage in violence, both with and on-behalf of the peer group. Masculinity can be constructed in being (or not being) a 'tough guy', as in the previous quote, but how this can be rooted in vulnerability is evident from the following interview excerpt:

> 'There have been cases where, two people fight, and to do good, I entered in the middle [got involved], and I got cursed, then for myself we fought more for teenage fights, because I'm like, how can I explain, for example you are here with me now, if someone comes here and talks to you and curses you, I can't let that happen or to do something like this. Because after all this I also know what it means. Because I grew up without a dad and I don't want that, I don't want it to be done badly when I'm present. So that's why I entered for others [defended others].' (Probation interview 1)

The relationship between violence as a reaction to feeling intense vulnerability has been explored in prior research (Levell, 2020, 2021, 2022a). The way that this participant described the impact of being fatherless denotes a specific form of sociocultural vulnerability: experiences of denigration for it (he knows "what it means" to get cursed). Masculine pride, a paradigm of the code of the street, here is restored by standing in for others and not permitting offence. Violence as a response to the existential vulnerability of childhood migration is alluded to in the following passage:

> 'The first year there [abroad], the wind took my mind [*ma mori era mend* [*sic*] – 'I became foolish'], I hung around with bad friends, I was chilling with a group of people that never thought, hey let's go eat some desserts, they always thought, hey let's go hit someone.' (Probation interview 3)

In this statement, there is a foregrounding of being violent as a core part of the group mentality among young men on-road. Instead of the participant's friends "eating desserts" (referring to leisurely indulgence in contrast to risky action), they would look for opportunities to fight. Young's research into young people on-road 'locates violence along a spectrum where it is the people most deeply immersed in "road culture" who are capable of lethal violence' (2016: 10).

Women and girls (other than as mothers and sisters) were rarely discussed as part of the street scene, although occasionally in an objectified manner:

> 'I know I am *haram* [shamed], cause when I left my house, at that age, to go hang out with the boys that I hung out with, I was *haram*, with guys that mess with women, like guys that don't care, is she older or not, you know guys that will say the word regardless. You know I know the type of guys, the type of guys in the street that as soon as they get on the street, you know, immediately saying "wow" or gesticulating, harassing her.' (Community participant 3)

Clearly, women do mot occupy an equal footing in on-road space. Instead, they are objectified and harassed. The use of the term Ottoman-Turkish, originally Arab, term *haram* ('forbidden' or 'shame') suggests that the participant knew that he was transgressing a moral code. It is not clear whether such self-denunciation indicated regret and facing a disjuncture with spiritual moral codes, or perhaps a shifting of codes in the presence of a female interviewer. Be this as it may, asserting status among peers through the competitive pursuit of women has been well documented as a masculinity strategy anywhere (Kaufman, 1993). Kaufman asserted that 'men construct their masculinity amid a triad of violence: men against women, men against men, and men against themselves' (cited in Adams and Coltrane, 2005: 237).

Code of the street

When participants discussed the dynamics of the neighbourhood groups, they mentioned 'rules' (*rregullat*) as underpinning important social norms within the groups. Some related this to a *kanun i rrugës*, the 'code of the street' (see Anderson, 1999), which bears some resemblance to but also considerably differs from, the historical *kanun* of the mountains. Originally deriving from Greek *kanōn* for 'rule', *kanun* was the Ottoman-Turkish administrative term for any local customary law through which the Ottoman empire extended indirect rule across its provinces until its dissolution in the early 20th century (Reinkowski, 2005). The term, and subsidiary concepts such as *besa*, were adopted into Albanian and international usage regardless of its Ottoman heritage and the availability of alternative Albanian terms for local customary rules and practices (for example, *doket*, *zakonet*, *traditat*). The polysemic concept of *besa*, etymologically deriving from Latin *fides* ('faith', 'trust', 'faithfulness', 'loyalty', 'trustworthiness', 'honour of the house'), in both the media, by law enforcement, or in the criminological literature, is usually conjured up as integral part of the *kanun* honour code, sometimes explained as reminiscent of the Sicilian *omerta*, the Italian mafia's historical code of silence (for example, Xhudo, 1997; Raufer, 2003). A prescriptive, normative ideal-type of existing historical *kanun* codification attempts (for example, Gjeçov, 1933), *besa* requires loyalty and protection beyond death within families as well as with in-laws, friends, former enemies upon ritual reconciliation and towards guests (Schwandner-Sievers, 1999). Both terms have been documented to serve culturalist stereotyping of Albanians by outsiders (for example, UK media, in asylum proceedings, or by police) as well as emic, self-essentialising identity constructions (Schwandner-Sievers, 2006, 2008, 2023).

The code of the street as discussed by the research participants is evident in the following narrative, which describes an altercation in a neighbourhood. Initially focused on the protection of a little girl, the situation escalates to require regulating by the local street boys:

> 'Some days ago, a motorcycle almost ran over that little girl. The biker wasn't that fast, [a] pizza guy. The biker avoided her and pushed her aside with the leg. And the girl – thank God – was saved. The biker stopped … [the father] took the girl and put her inside, and he came out, and he started hitting the biker. The biker wasn't moving himself you know, a young guy … he was saying "I'm sorry, I see what I did, I'm really sorry" – still [the father] hit him and cursed him. And he went inside and got a knife. I swear to god, I'm not lying these words. [The young boy] tells me, oh shit he is coming out with a knife. … Cause I was the only one there in the hood. … In that moment the boys came, all my boys … and … I told the guy, at the doorstep of his house, like go and come out of your house, dare to come out of your house with that knife, but look how many boys we are here. We will break your ribs. You can do the action to come here to this

boy, but you can't do that action. As long as I am here I said in the neighbourhood, maybe you can do that in your family, but here, in this neighbourhood there are rules. Cause I am angry, cause the other guy didn't mean to do it, this is also something, you as a parent, don't make your child nervous so your child leaves from the door of the house, to get out of the house, like on the street, where, to be honest, cars also go fast, but you as a parent, why do you let your child go out alone, the child doesn't understand what street it is. And he put down the knife. Cause I touched him.' (Probation interview 3)

This rich narrative constructs the group's masculinity in their role as the rule-enforcers of the neighbourhood. The comment that, "maybe you can do that in your family, but here, in this neighbourhood there are rules", first, refutes any traditional *kanun* understanding according to which an outsider nearly harming and pushing the daughter in front of the father's house could be interpreted as an offence to personal honour, which 'the strong man ... has every right to avenge ... by the spilling of blood' (Gjeçov, 1933: 129–130). Such understanding disregards questions of culpability. To 'the boys', however, this was a relevant part of the street code. Second, it indicates the juxtaposition between private and public space. The public space of the neighbourhood is owned by "my boys", who, as a group, disrupt traditional masculine hierarchies and overrule the older father.

Some of the discussions around the 'code of the street' explicitly evoked *kanun* or *besa* in rhetorical recourse to a cultural script which permits, first, an identification with both local and national traditions, thereby generating a sense of collective pride and solidarity; and, second, explaining street-life expectations and conjuring up trustworthiness and reliability among both kin and peers through a rhetoric of old: "You would go out with a knife, with a bat, or a lot of friends, with cousins, of course, with *besa* ['trustworthiness'] also my friends did not let me down, I always had them behind me" (probation interview 6).

Questions of reliability and trustworthiness, however, are universal norms in street codes, here simply expressed through the readily available rhetorical repertoire rather than indicative of specific sociocultural traditions *per se*. Meanwhile, taking recourse to local traditions, specifically blood feuding, explicitly, can serve to justify violence, threats and demands in street conflicts and rivalries, such as in this explanation of community participant 2: "I have my uncle's son, he is suffering a prison sentence for stabbing and that affected a lot the other side, *gjaku*, my cousin." *Gjaku*, 'the blood', is part of traditionalist *kanun* rhetoric evoking expectations of kinship solidarity and liability. In summary, traditions and familism might become evoked in recourse to the readily available cultural scripts and thus can, but do not necessarily have to, play a role in negotiating street solidarity.

Kam marrë rrugët *('I took to the streets')*

Migration stories are stories of different life stage stories, reflecting a multitude of individual experiences, social situations, and directionality: "I don't know any childhood because I have grown in the streets of foreign countries, from one country to another" (prison interview 2), one incarcerated participant shared. Another, whose parents had emigrated to make money abroad, remembered being left behind: "I had a very difficult childhood. I had to work where I could, since I was 6–7 years old. My parents were not present in my life because when I was six years old, they migrated [to Italy]. I felt lonely" (prison interview 1).

Another incarcerated participant illuminated the potential effects of involuntary return migration. Following two years spent as a child of asylum-seeking parents in Germany, when he attended school and had to "grow up fast", he disengaged from school upon return to Albania and his situation deteriorated. Several participants had migrated during adolescence, either in regular or irregular ways, yet none ascertained a process of grooming or exploitation underlying these experiences. Rather, the participants framed it either as a family decision involving collective out-migration, or as an individual escape from family conflict. The following passage exemplifies the transnational hustle 'on-road', both, figuratively and literally:

> 'Everything started when I was 16 years old, not like the boys that studied, we were a little cheeky [*capken* – 'mischievous'] at school, and we didn't feel comfortable anywhere. And at that age, I took the road to Italy [*kam marrë rrugët*], alone. I fought my parents, saying that I will go to Italy. I took the roads, walking. … Meaning, I paid someone, and did the way with him, Serbia, Croatia, Slovenia, Italy. And every border, we crossed on foot. We took a taxi from Slovenia to Italy, and at the border, we went out and crossed by foot. But what I went through for two weeks at that time, only God can know. I went there then, and there I had bad friends. I started selling weed, prison there, prison here. Three to four times, meaning. … A total of six to seven years all together. Not that I needed anything you know, but it's like written that you will go there.' (Community participant A1)

Such stories of 'taking the road', that is, irregular migration leading to criminal engagement at a young age, were ubiquitous. Yet the role of the parents was not always clear-cut. Sometimes a 'family friend' played a role, suggesting their involvement; for others, family conflict prompted escape. Several narratives framed migration as both a strategy and a sacrifice for the family, with different actors possible in performing the required role (for example, parent or child).

Conclusion

The music elicitation data offers a unique insight into the viewpoints of criminalised young men in and from Albania. Despite the wider UK media and governmental interest into Albanian gangs, the young people involved focused on aspects of street life which seemed more akin to life on-road. The life stories revealed the role of the neighbourhood, both locally and in the transnational context, in providing solidarity among the boys on-road beyond kinship ties. The commonality of international youth migration within our small sample indicated that for many young men, 'street life' is a transnational experience. Travelling across borders both with and without their families at a young age was a defining part of several participants' childhoods. The fracturing of families in this way has been part of a normalised Albanian experience since the downfall of Communism, which resulted in the migration of 'at least one, usually male, member of nearly every Albanian family into the wider world' (Schwandner-Sievers, 2008: 111). Saying this, international travel is not uncommon among many European families that are part of the Schengen Agreement. However what is distinct in the Albanian context is the way that the street-life on-road hustle is part of the travel story, not least as obtaining a legal UK visa for citizens of non-Schengen countries is contingent on providing proof of steady employment or education. Young men, in solidarity with 'the boys', engage in street codes, male-dominated peer groups, and engage in low level criminality to get by. As outlined in the introduction, upon arrival into the UK (as just one possible host country), as irregular migrants who are without the privilege of formal visa approved migration routes, Albanian young men are then constructed as gang-involved (in a process of both emic and etic myth-making) and often adultified within a system which frames them as the outsiders. They are measured by the legal system against the idealised constructions of victimhood (White women) and then framed as actual or potential criminals. At the point of engaging in the translocal roads their legal status as minors (under 18 years old, according to the UN Convention on the Rights of the Child) is overlooked as they are framed as offenders upon arrival.

In contrast, the life stories that we collected revealed a much more nuanced picture, which resonated with the concept of life on-road. Albanian 'street life' was laced with male friendships and gendered neighbourhood solidarity, a street hustle (including some level of criminality), and a code of the street. This code could be arguably could be described as reflecting a modernised and transformed *kanun*. Yet, while the availability of distinct cultural scripts appeared in some of the explanatory rhetoric and was identified as part of the repertoire for making sense of self, there was little similarity between the *kanun* of old and the 'rules', *rregullat*, which the research participants described as forming their code of the street. Rather, their recollections revealed strong similarity with on-road masculinity struggles described in street life elsewhere, including in the UK (for example, Anderson, 1999; Levell, 2022a).

Family was relevant, but the complex, diverse and problematic social relations discovered, including abandonment, pressure and neglect, forfeit any singular, culturalist typologisations. Rather, they point to a broader understanding of the pull of life on-road for marginalised young people who experience a complex milieu of adverse childhood experiences which lead them to affiliations with a street-based peer group. Being on-road emerged as a translocal, masculine hustle which involved male peer groups, street violence, criminality and aspirations for financial and family independence as well as desires to matter, sometimes as a provider and protector of family members, for others in terms of the street code and heightened masculinity norms. The latter related particularly to stories about adolescence on-road interspersed with adjoining experience of marginalisation and discrimination, of which the narrators were painfully aware. Notably, within the multidirectional and translocal marginalisation continuum described, experiences of discrimination, conflict and poverty experienced in Albania stood out as being intertwined with on-road life.

Note

[1] RAYS stands for 'Reconnecting Albanian Youth and Society'. The authors wish to thank Palladium International Ltd for commissioning this music elicitation research led by Levell, Bristol University, in conjunction with a wider array of UK government-funded participatory action research led by Schwandner-Sievers, Bournemouth University.

References

Adams, M. and Coltrane, S. (2005) Boys and men in families: The domestic production of gender, power and privilege. In *Handbook of Studies on Men & Masculinities*. California: SAGE, pp 230–248.

Anderson, E. (1999) *Code of the Street*. London: W.W. Norton.

Appadurai, A. (1995) The production of locality. In R. Fardon (ed) *Counterworks: Managing the Diversity of Knowledge*. London: Routledge, pp 204–255.

BBC News (2023, January) About 200 asylum-seeking children have gone missing, says minister. Available at: https://www.bbc.co.uk/news/uk-politics-64389249

BBC Radio 4 (2023, January) *TODAY Programme*. Available at: https://www.bbc.co.uk/programmes/m001hfp2

Billingham, L. and Irwin-Rogers, K. (2021) The terrifying abyss of insignificance: Marginalisation, mattering and violence between young people. *Oñati Socio-Legal Series*, 1–28.

Burke, D. (2023, January) MP demands Tory Jonanthan Gullis makes public apology for 'fanning hatred'. *The Mirror*. Available at: https://www.mirror.co.uk/news/politics/mp-demands-tory-jonanthan-gullis-29065436

Byrne, K., Kulluri, E. and Ilir, G. (2021) *Situation Analysis of Children and Adolescents in Albania*. Tirana: UNICEF. Available at: https://www.unicef.org/albania/media/4071/file/Situation%20Analysis%20of%20Children%20and%20Adolescents%20in%20Albania.pdf

Christodoulou, H. (2019) BAD RAP Albanian cocaine gangs flaunt Lamborghinis and wads of cash in rap videos 'to recruit more foot soldiers to Britain'. *The Sun*, 14 July. Available at: https://www.thesun.co.uk/news/9503813/albanian-cocaine-gangs-rap-videos-cocaine

Cohen, S. (2003) *Folk Devils and Moral Panics: The Creation of the Mods and Rockers*. London: Routledge.

Collier, R. (1998) *Masculinities, Crime and Criminology*. London: SAGE.

Connell, R.W. (2005) *Masculinities*, 2nd edn. Cambridge: Polity Press.

Connell, R.W. and Messerschmidt, J.W. (2005) Hegemonic masculinity: Rethinking the concept. *Gender & Society*, 19(6): 829–859.

Davis, J. and Marsh, N. (2020) Boys to men: The cost of 'adultification' in safeguarding responses to Black boys. *Critical and Radical Social Work*, 8(2): 255–259.

Dempsey, M. (2021) Still not safe: The public health approach to youth violence. *Children's Commissoner*, February. Available at: https://www.childrenscommissioner.gov.uk/wp-content/uploads/2021/02/cco-still-not-safe.pdf

Earle, R. (2011) Boys' zone stories: Perspectives from a young men's prison. *Criminology & Criminal Justice*, 11(2): 129–143.

Felson, M. (2006) The street gang strategy. In M. Felson (ed) *Crime and Nature*. London: SAGE, pp 305–324.

Ferrell, J. (1999) Cultural criminology. *Annual Review of Sociology*, 25: 395–418.

Gambetta, D. (1993) *The Sicilian Mafia*. Cambridge, MA: Harvard University Press.

Garner-Purkis, Z. (2023, January) Life on the London estate 'taken over by Albanian gangsters with constant armed police raids and huge knives left in the bushes'. *MyLondon News*. Available at: https://www.mylondon.news/news/east-london-news/life-london-estate-taken-over-26080466?utm_source=twitter.com&utm_medium=social&utm_campaign=sharebar&s=03

Geertz, C. (1973) *The Interpretation of Cultures*. New York: Basic Books.

Gjeçov, S. (1933) *Kanuni i Lekë Dukagjinit – The Code of Lekë Dukagjini*. Tirana: Gjonlekaj.

Goffman, E. (1959) *The Presentation of Self in Everyday Life*. New York: Doubleday.

Hellbanianz (2022) *Vinz x Stealth – Poppin Smoke*. AVD Digital.

Heys, A., Barlow, C., Murphy, C. and McKee, A. (2022) A review of modern slavery in Britain: Understanding the unique experience of British victims and why it matters. *Journal of Victimology and Victim Justice*, 5(1): 54–70.

Hine, J. (2010) Young people's 'voices' as evidence. In W. Taylor, R. Earle and R. Hester (eds) *Youth Justice Handbook*, 1st edn. Cullompton: Willan Publishing, pp 168–178.

Hobbs, D. (1998) Going down the glocal: The local context of organised crime. *Transnational Organized Crime*, 37: 407–422. https://doi.org/10.4324/9781315084565

Hookham, M. (2022, August). Four in 10 Channel migrants are from ALBANIA – not a country devastated by war of famine – secret military file reveals. *Mail on Sunday*. Available at: https://www.dailymail.co.uk/news/article-11088107/Four-10-migrants-arriving-Britain-boats-war-free-Albania.html

Hookham, M. and Ryan, J. (2019) The Albanian drug gangs who flaunt their wealth online: London-based mafia use videos to recruit more footsoldiers to the UK as Lamborghini and Rolls Royce-driving rappers glorify kingpins 'linked to cartels'. *The Mail on Sunday*, 13 July. Available at: https://www.dailymail.co.uk/news/article-7244811/Albanian-gangsters-UK-flaunting-wealth-online-PR-drive.html

INSTAT (2021) *Children, Adolescents and Youth-Focused Well-being Indicators 2016–2019*. Tirana: Albanian Institute for Statistics and UNICEF. Available at: https://www.instat.gov.al/en/publications/books/2021/children-adolescents-and-youth-focused-wellbeing-indicators-2016-2019/

ITV News (2022, November). Suella Braverman faces criticism for Channel migrant 'invasion' claim. Available at: https://www.itv.com/news/2022-10-31/braverman-deflects-blame-for-manston-migrant-saga-as-she-denies-blocking-hotels

Jolly, A., Thomas, S. and Stanyer, J. (2020) *London's Children and Young People Who Are Not British Citizens: A Profile*. London: Mayor of London. https://doi.org/10.13140/RG.2.2.13839.12964

Kalmar, I. (2022) *White But Not Quite: Central Europe's Illiberal Revolt*. Bristol: Policy Press.

Kaser, K. (2008) *Patriarchy after Patriarchy: Gender Relations in Turkey and in the Balkans, 1500–2000*. Vienna: Lit Verlag.

Kaufman, M. (1993) *Cracking the Armour Power, Pain and the Lives of Men*. Toronto: Viking.

King, R. and Mai, N. (2008) *Out of Albania: From Crisis Migration to Social Inclusion in Italy*. Oxford: Berghahn.

Lacey, R.E. and Minnis, H. (2019) Practitioner review: Twenty years of research with adverse childhood experience scores – advantages, disadvantages and applications to practice. *Journal of Child Psychology and Psychiatry and Allied Disciplines*, 61(2): 116–130. https://doi.org/10.1111/jcpp.13135

Lauger, T. (2014) Violent stories: Personal narratives, street socialisation and the negotiation of street culture among street-oriented youth. *Criminal Justice Review*, 39: 182–200.

Lazarides, G. (1999) The helots of the new millennium: Ethnic-Greek Albanians and 'other' Albanians in Greece. In F. Anthias and G. Lazarides (eds) *Into the Margins: Migration and Exclusion in Southern Europe*. Farnham: Ashgate, pp 105–121.

Levell, J. (2019) 'Those songs were the ones that made me, nobody asked me this question before': Music elicitation with ex-gang involved men about their experiences of childhood domestic violence and abuse. *International Journal of Qualitative Methods*, 18: 1–24.

Levell, J. (2020) Using Connell's masculinity theory to understand the way in which ex-gang-involved men coped with childhood domestic violence. *Journal of Gender Based Violence*, 4(2): 207–221.

Levell, J. (2021) On masculinities: Navigating the tension between individual and structural considerations. *Journal of Gender-Based Violence*, 6(1): 227–234.

Levell, J. (2022a) *Boys, Childhood Domestic Abuse and Gang Involvement: Violence at Home, Violence On-road*. Bristol: Policy Press.

Levell, J. (2022b) Internal homelessness and hiraeth: Boys' spatial journeys between childhood domestic abuse and on-road. In H. Bows and B. Fileborn (eds) *Geographies of Gender-based Violence: A Multi-disciplinary Perspective*. Bristol: Policy Press, pp 50–62.

Mai, N. (2002) Myths and moral panics: Italian identity and the media representation of Albanian immigration. In R. Grillo and J. Pratt (eds) *The Politics of Recognising Difference: Multiculturalism Italian Style*. Farnham: Ashgate, pp 77–94.

Michail, D. and Christou, A. (2016) Diasporic youth identities of uncertainty and hope: Second-generation Albanian experiences of transnational mobility in an era of economic crisis in Greece. *Journal of Youth Studies*, 19(7): 957–972.

Morten, B. (2022, November). Minister warns on language after Suella Braverman 'invasion' comment. *BBC News*. Available at: https://www.bbc.co.uk/news/uk-politics-63466532

Mullins, C.W. (2006) *Holding Your Square: Masculinities, Streetlife and Violence*. Cullompton: Willan Publishing.

Orgocka, A. and Jovanovic, J. (2006) Identity exploration and commitment of Albanian youth as a function of social opportunity structure. *European Psychologist*, 11(4): 268–276.

Pearson, G. (1983) *Hooligan: A History of Respectable Fears*. Basingstoke: Palgrave.

Peth, S.A., Sterly, H. and Sakdapolrak, P. (2018) Between the village and the global city: The production and decay of translocal spaces of Thai migrant workers in Singapore. *Mobilities*, 13(4): 455–472.

Phillips, A. (1993) *The Trouble with Boys: Parenting the Men of the Future*. London: HarperCollins.

Ramiz, A., Rock, P. and Strang, H. (2020) Detecting modern slavery on cannabis farms: The challenges of evidence. *Cambridge Journal of Evidence-Based Policing*, 4(3–4): 202–217.

Raufer, X. (2003) A neglected dimension of conflict: The Albanian mafia. In J. Koehler and C. Zürcher (eds) *Potentials of Disorder*. Manchester: Manchester University Press, pp 62–74.

Reinkowski, M. (2005). Gewohnheitsrecht im multinationalen Staat: Die Osmanen und der albanische Kanun. In M. Kemper and M. Reinkowski (eds) *Rechtspluralismus in der Islamischen Welt: Gewohnheitsrecht zwischen Staat und Gesellschaft*. Berlin: de Gruyter, pp 121–142.

Schwandner-Sievers, S. (1999) Humiliation and reconciliation in northern Albania: The logics of feuding in symbolic and diachronic perspectives. In G. Elwert, S. Feuchtwang and D. Neubert, Dieter (eds) *Dynamics of Violence: Processes of Escalation and De-escalation of Violent Group Conflicts*. Berlin: Duncker & Humblot, pp 133–152.

Schwandner-Sievers, S. (2006) 'Culture' in court: Albanian migrants and the anthropologist as expert witness. In P. Sarah (ed) *Applications of Anthropology: Professional Anthropology in the Twenty-first Century*. Oxford: Berghahn.

Schwandner-Sievers, S. (2008) Albanians, Albanianism and the strategic subversion of stereotypes. *Anthropological Notebooks*, 14(2): 47–64.

Schwandner-Sievers, S. (2023) Albanian culture and major crime: Challenging culturalist assumptions among investigating UK police. In J. Been, T. Bierschenk, A. Kolloch and B. Meyer (eds) *Policing Race, Ethnicity and Culture*. Manchester: Manchester University Press, pp 267–288.

Schwandner-Sievers, S., Berry, M., Sheppard, N. and Thartori, K. (2023) *Local Perspectives on Young Albanian Serious Organised Crime (SOC) Risks*. Available at: https://www.bournemouth.ac.uk/research/projects/sounds

Simić, A. (1973) The peasant urbanites: A study of rural-urban mobility in Serbia. In *Studies in Anthropology 1*. New York and London: Seminar Press.

Tice, R. (2022) *Sunday Sermon: Why are 4 in 10 Channel Migrants from Albania?*. Richard Tice on Talk TV, 7 August. Available at: https://www.youtube.com/watch?

Tochka, N. (2017) Cosmopolitan inscriptions? Mimicry, rap, and rurbanity in post-socialist Albania. In M. Miszczynski and A. Helbig (eds) *Hip Hop at Europe's Edge: Music, Agency, and Social Change*. Bloomington: Indiana University Press, pp 165–181.

Townsend, M. (2022, November) Child asylum seekers detained as adults after UK Home Office 'alters birth dates'. *The Guardian*. Available at: https://www.theguardian.com/uk-news/2022/nov/27/child-asylum-seekers-detained-as-adults-after-uk-home-office-alters-birth-dates

Van Hellemont, E. and Densley, J.A. (2019) Gang glocalization: How the global mediascape creates and shapes local gang realities. *Crime, Media, Culture*, 15(1): 169–189.

Ware, V. (2015) *Beyond the Pale: White Women, Racism and History*. London: Verso Books.

Xhudo, G. (1997) Men of purpose: The growth of Albanian criminal activity. *Transnational Organized Crime*, 2(1): 1–20.

Young, T. (2016) *Risky Youth or Gang Members? A Contextual Critique of the (Re)discovery of Gangs in Britain*. London: London Metropolitan University.

9

'He's shown me the road': Role Model and Roadman

Peter Harris

Introduction

This chapter outlines a conceptual framework for understanding the relationship between male adult youth work professionals characterised, or *positioned*, as 'role models' and young men positioned as 'roadmen'. It begins with a critique of social policy that promotes male role models for young men in the UK, as it relates to both formal and informal education settings. It then sets out a theoretical perspective on masculine subjectivities using positioning and psychosocial theory and highlights some implications for our understanding of relationships between male youth professionals and young men. Using a closely observed case study of a young Black man and his older White male youth worker, this chapter argues that male youth workers seeking to proffer alternative 'roads' for younger men need to develop a deep, reflexive awareness of their own and young men's identity constructions. The chapter concludes that social policy making and professional training regimes may need to be more acutely attuned to the complexity of these professional relationships.

Role models and roadmen: policy and positioning

Role models

Considerable political capital has been spent, both in the United States and the United Kingdom, on 'solving' the problem of youth crime and violence via the promotion of appropriate 'role models' and 'mentors' for 'alienated', and especially Black, young men. Politicians from both of the main British political parties have promoted this common-sense notion despite that it seems to consist of a set of assumptions that have come to be accepted 'on the basis of limited evidence and challenge' (Robb, 2014: 238). Drawing on classic social learning theory (Bandura, 1977) and/or sociological, dramaturgical formulations of identity performance (Goffman, 1959), young people are understood as potentially being redirected along new, non-deviant pathways or 'roads' when these are set out or 'shown' by an older role model/ mentor. This is assumed to occur through a process of imitation and eventual inhabitation of preconceived social roles, which are usually presented as more respectable, law-abiding and successful. Arguably, though, it remains unclear what the precise meaning and function of these male role models might be, and how the process of modelling and behavioural change occurs on the ground in face-to-face youth work practice.

This lack of clarity can be observed in debates around the role of male teachers within formal education settings. Responding to calls for more male teachers in primary education in the United States, Sevier and Ashcraft (2009) argue that research urgently needs to inquire into the meaning and usefulness of the male-teacher-as-male-role-model discourse. They interrogate the confusion surrounding the concept and the consequences of that confusion. They warn that the illusion of clarity afforded by the taken-for-granted nature of the discourse prevents examination of what it means to be a male role model and risks a return to traditional, normative and essentialist beliefs about gender.

Sevier and Ashcraft identify several problematic assumptions behind this discourse. First, a supposition that more male teachers are needed to compensate for the lack of positive male role models in many boys' lives, especially in the light of rising numbers of single-parent households. Such calls come close to suggesting that the presence of men is a necessary corrective to the damaging effects of over-exposure to single mothers or other women. Second, they argue that the promotion of more male teachers in primary schools also assumes that male teachers, by virtue of their very maleness, will serve as desirable models of masculinity. This simplistic conceptualisation of the male role model suggests that (all/any) men will bring 'masculine' pedagogical styles to the 'feminised' school environment, without articulating *what kinds* of masculinities are being modelled. In some instances, the hope expressed is that male teachers will broaden children's conceptions of appropriate masculinities by providing examples of 'nurturing' men. However, Roulston and Mills (2000) have showed how male teachers often engage in hypermasculine behaviour to compensate for the perceived feminine nature of their occupation and that other teachers, administrators and parents frequently call on them to perform more typically 'masculine' tasks. Other studies (for example, Allan, 1997) have also raised concerns about male teachers' efforts to secure masculine legitimacy by performing and reproducing hegemonic (dominant) forms of masculinity in their classrooms.

This rhetorical call for more positive male role models for young men has also featured heavily within youth work and informal education circles, both historically and more recently. For example, Batsleer (2015) argues that in the 20th century the Boys' Club Movement and Boys' Brigades had the effect of ensuring the continued socialisation of young people in binary gender norms and the reproduction of patriarchy. She points to contemporary examples of what she sees as politicians reinscribing normative discourses around nuclear families and absent fathers, such as when David Lammy, who set up an all-party group on fatherhood, was reported as saying:

> In areas like mine, we know that 59% of Black Caribbean children are looked after by a lone parent. There is none of the basic starting presumption of two adults who want to start a family, raise children together, love them, nourish them and lead them to full independence. The parents are not married and the children have come, frankly, out of casual sex; the father isn't present and isn't expected to be. There aren't networks of extended families to make up for it. We are seeing huge consequences of the lack of male role models in young men's lives. How do you find your masculinity in the absence of role models? Through hip-hop, through gang culture, through peer groups. (Lammy, cited in Batsleer, 2015: 17)

More recently, the role model concept has been mobilised in relation to youth work and mentoring projects for young men seen as at risk of involvement in gangs and knife crime, especially in socially disadvantaged urban neighbourhoods. Inspired perhaps by the much-viewed film footage of Ian Wright's emotional reunion with his boyhood mentor, the No More Red campaign at Arsenal FC seeks to reinvigorate calls for 'safe spaces' and 'mentors' for young men. Other prominent male figures from the world of sport, for example the professional footballer Marcus Rashford (who himself was brought up in single-parent household) have also been proselytised as positive role models for young men. In other gang intervention projects, older men who have had some personal experience of crime and violence but have since 'reformed' and are seen as 'down with the kids' (Harris, 2020) are promoted as uniquely and advantageously positioned to engage with young men who may be embarking on 'roads' towards crime and violence. Positions within this debate about role models can appear polarised with, on the one side, strong support for Lammy's dystopian vision coming from voices both inside and outside communities affected by violence. Equally, academic analyses, argued from feminist and psychodynamic perspectives, have sought to problematise the push for more 'respectable' role models and mentors for young men and pointed out both the assets and shortcomings of the 'ex-gangster' professional identity (for example, Batsleer, 2015; Harris, 2020).

Roadmen

A range of commentators (including in this volume) have charted how some marginalised young men, especially in urban environments, position themselves, and are positioned by others in a contemporary youth identity, colloquially referred to as the 'roadman'. The 'roadman' identity can be understood as a subcultural identity associated with transgressive behaviours such as 'on-road' or 'underground' activity in the drug trade (Gunter, 2008). The life of the roadman has been portrayed in popular TV dramas such as *Top Boy* and *Blue Story* and can arguably be heard reflected in some forms of popular music such as grime and drill (Boakye, 2017). The term roadman can also be understood to refer, at least in part, to a masculine identity rooted in reserves of masculine and street social capital (de Visser et al, 2009; Sandberg, 2014). The development of street social capital theory can be traced back to Bourdieu (1984) as the originator of the phrase 'cultural capital'. Cultural capital theory helps explain how resources of cultural power and confidence are differentially acquired by different social groups. The concept is elastic enough to be applied to subcultures; that is, marginal groups defined in relation to the dominant, hegemonic or 'parent' culture. Capital, in its street social guise, can be conceived as a form of currency which is both prized and competed over within subcultures, including those within deprived urban communities, and notably by young men. Once acquired, this 'street' form of social capital allows young people to claim credibility and status within their own social milieu.

Elijah Anderson's description of the 'savoir faire' of the street world in his ethnographic study of street corner subculture in Philadelphia (1999) captures the relational characteristics of street social capital. It consists of 'knowing how to deal coolly with people, how to move, look, act, dress' and is:

> [A] form of capital, not a form middle-class people would respect, but capital that can nonetheless be cashed in. … This kind of capital is not always useful or valued in wider society, but it is capital nonetheless. It is recognised and valued on the streets and to lack it is to be vulnerable there. (Anderson, 1999: 105)

Psychosocial and positioning theory

The foregrounding of male *vulnerability* as a feature within young men's identity formation points to how some young men's projection of masculine power and strength might be a tactic aimed at defending themselves from feelings of vulnerability. Work within the growing field of psychosocial studies (for example, Frosh et al, 1998; Gadd, 2006; Hollway and Jefferson, 2013; Harris, 2020) draws on contemporary psychoanalytic thought to theorise subjectivity as incorporating *unconscious* forces that drive personal psychic investments in discursive identities. These accounts stress how, for every individual, their psychological *investment* in an identity will be driven by a range of emotions as well as societal and subcultural expectations of appropriate gender roles. For young men in relatively deprived urban neighbourhoods the identities that are available to them are limited and often highly gendered and racialised due to the pervasive influence of subcultural and dominant discourses. Their embodiment of discursive identities such as the roadman can be read in part as aimed at resolving psychic vulnerabilities that may arise out of biographical experience, as well as the humiliation caused by disempowerment and discrimination. Displaying physical or emotional vulnerability has consequences for peer credibility and could trigger sanctions that compromise physical safety. For certain young 'roadmen', hypermasculine practices, such as competitiveness and attraction to risk, may therefore serve the purpose of recovering self-esteem while defending against fears regarding weakness and social dependency.

Positioning theory (Harré, 2006; Harré et al, 2009) is an approach in social psychology that examines interactions between individuals and details the mechanisms through which roles are assigned. It suggests that how we are positioned is intricately connected with how we perceive ourselves and how others perceive us. Both the role model and roadman subjectivities arise out of self-initiated positionings within discursive structures which continually position subjects. In interaction, individuals may react to or even refuse to accept the positioning of himself by the other. What one person says can position another, either intentionally or unintentionally, and it can be difficult to ascertain how each conversant conceives of themselves and the other participants. Disentangling this complexity can only be revealed by in-depth analysis of conversation. Without a shared understanding of how utterances are understood by each speaker, any conversation (the primary tool of engagement of youth workers) cannot be fully understood and replicated. Identities such as the roadman and role model are ascribed identities; that is, they emerge as a product of the ways in which people are positioned as particular 'kinds' of people by others. These identities are intertwined with participation in particular sets of cultural, and especially subcultural, practices. Subjects are called or 'hailed' into these kinds of subject positions, but they are also subjectively appropriated (or psychologically invested in) by individuals. As Stuart Hall explains:

> The notion than an effective suturing of the subject to a subject-position requires, not only that the subject is 'hailed', but that the subject invests in the position, means that suturing has to be thought of as an articulation, rather than a one-sided process, and that in turn places identification, if not identities, firmly on the theoretical agenda. (Hall, 1996: 6)

Relationships between adult male youth workers and young men will involve each man drawing on their knowledge of these ascribed social identities and the degree to which they wish to agentically invest in (or resist) whatever identity is offered to them. Each will imaginatively position oneself and the other in a role, and this will influence how they act in any situation or interaction. Adults such as male youth workers who are perceived to possess more or less masculine or street social capital may be positioned (or position themselves) in or out of mainstream and subcultural milieus. This raises questions of how the actions of young men and older men seeking to engage with them are perceived by those on the 'inside' and 'outside' of subcultures, including the degree to which each identifies (psychologically) with the other.

Deploying psychosocial and positioning theory highlights the shortcomings of an under-theorised notion of role models by foregrounding processes such as investment, identification and positioning within interactive relationships and practice. Older male youth workers may be particularly well placed to engage with young men outside of formal educational settings in spaces that have become segregated and dominated by young men. Workers seeking to inhabit these spaces will do so from a range of subject positions, some more or less proximate to subcultural or mainstream forms. How a male youth worker positions himself will be central to his capacity to build relationships with young men and respond meaningfully to the challenges they face. The worker's own embodied identity performance can become a tool for young men to reimagine themselves, but this raises the question of how male workers position their own gendered and racialised performance and how this then positions them relationally to those with whom they seek to engage or 'reach'. The 'reach' of a male youth worker (the extent to which he makes his presence felt) may depend on the degree to which he is perceived as being part of the same subculture inhabited by young men. Questions arise as to what extent (and when) it might be productive for a male youth worker to challenge practices, subject positions and performances that have kept young men physically and emotionally 'safe'. How can male youth workers both acknowledge the utility and necessity of perceived strengths such as physical prowess and local knowledge that form part of existing 'roadman' identities within local subcultures, while leaving space for young men to also acknowledge and concede various forms of vulnerability? As we discussed earlier, there are political and ethical tensions that can emerge where aspects of masculinities that could be viewed as complicit in the continued sustenance of patriarchal power form part of professional identity. There is a danger of idealising heteronormative, charismatic male youth workers who may also be defending against their own feelings of vulnerability. This idealisation can obscure how such workers continue to implicitly reinforce the forms of self-concept that lie behind some young men's sexist attitudes and more destructive behaviour patterns.

The following case study seeks to illuminate the subtle issues of positioning and psychosocial dynamics that feature within a relationship between an older male youth worker (Steve) and a younger man involved on crime and violence (Germaine). It highlights how each man initially positions the other, but how shifts in power and positioning open the possibility of alternative readings of each other's subjectivity. The analysis that follows then seeks to illuminate how reading the relationship between Steve and Germaine through the fixed cultural frame of 'role models and roadmen' does not adequately account for the complexity of how their relationship develops or the true nature of its transformative potential.

Germaine

Germaine was a 19-year-old young Black man living in a large town in the West Midlands. He was introduced to me by Steve, his youth worker, to whom he attributed his desistance from involvement in violence. Steve was an older White, working-class man in his 30s who had grown up in the same area as Germaine and had spent some years in the army before training as a youth worker. He worked at a local gang intervention project.

Germaine began by telling me that he and his younger brother had not known their biological father when they were young and that they been brought up almost entirely by their mother. Although he was keen to stress his mother had "always been there", he later disclosed that when he was aged four his mother was sentenced to eight months in prison for a "serious" offence. During this time, he was cared for by his grandmother and his mother's new partner. When I asked him again about his birth-father he told me vehemently that if he saw him today he would not speak to him. He had only met him "a couple of times" and "didn't have any respect" for him.

Germaine remembered being bullied by other boys in his final year of primary school and experiencing disorientation borne out of "not knowing who his friends were at the beginning of the day". By the time he reached secondary school (aged 12) he had begun to establish a reputation for being one of the 'bad ones' in his area. "I was bad as in, if I had a weapon on me, I am using that weapon. If anyone tries it on me I am going to do something." The area he lived in was bereft of opportunity:

> 'It is like a black hole. There are no dreams in [area]. It sucks you in, like, there is nothing you can see. There is nothing to motivate you round here. It is just drugs, violence – that is all you see round here. But when I mean it is a black hole, there is no ambition in the Hood, basically. Like in the roads where I live, everyone knows each other and everyone knows everyone's business. So, when I first used to walk

to school I used to see crackheads, people selling to crackheads – that is first thing in the morning.'

Germaine felt there were no older men in the area to whom he could look up to; no "role models". He considered the White male teachers at the school to be all "aggressive bastards" and "idiots". He remembered that the headteacher at the school had once told him that he would "never amount to anything" and that he would only ever be "just another Black person on the streets". Germaine "wanted to prove people wrong": "If the teachers used to tell me to do something I used to tell them to, 'Shut up,' 'Fuck off,' all of that. But that is the way I was. So, I wasn't really listening to anything." His older cousins were involved in drug dealing locally and he remembered being "intrigued" by the "fast money" they were earning. He was asked to drop off some cash to a local dealer and began to think "I want to be like that".

Germaine began to get involved in fights at school with groups of Asian boys and he joined a local gang. In one incident he witnessed a 12-year-old boy being stabbed four times by a "12-inch blade", leading to life-threatening injuries. He became increasingly fearful and reckless and began to carry around a wooden bat to protect himself. Germaine felt his mum was struggling and "couldn't handle" him. In her desperation to steer Germaine away from the gang, she asked her brother who had just been released from prison for drug dealing to show Germaine where the "road" he was on might lead. He took Germaine to a crack den.

> 'He was just opening my eyes because my mum couldn't handle me. No one else couldn't handle me. I wasn't listening to anyone in my family. But she knew that if he spoke to me he could show me how the life would be if I wanted to carry on down that road. So, he picked me up from my house, took me to [place]. First, he took me shopping just to say, "Yes, this is what you can do with about 10 grand." He was showing me, "If you want to do this, this is what you're going to have to do." But he knew I never had it in me to do that. I didn't find it very comfortable because I was sitting on the bed and there were needles around me. I was thinking, "This is fucked up." I don't really want to do this.'

Soon after this, Germaine met Steve, a local youth worker at the youth club he attended with his friends. He remembered being very reticent to talk to Steve when he first met him, partly because of Steve being "White":

> 'Back then, me and all my friends were thinking, "Who is this White guy? What's he doing here? We don't know him, he doesn't know us."

We used to say he is "Booky" [weird]. So, we never used to show him any respect. When he used to come we used to ignore him or laugh [at] him. We would say, "You can't eat Black people's food!" but then he would say, "Well, you like our White girls anyway!" That is the way everything started for me – the banter. It was like, "Yes, we like this guy."'

Germaine continued to get to know Steve in the local youth club where his friends were making grime music videos, "dissing other people" and "wanting to be violent". Then when Germaine got into trouble at school, Steve was called in to offer some support. Germaine was suspicious at first and felt Steve was "stalking" and "spying" on him. Steve took him out for a meal and visited his house. Germaine gradually began to feel he could talk honestly to Steve.

> 'I never used to talk to him about anything to be honest. When I was younger I never felt comfortable around anyone, to talk to anyone about my stuff. I never used to tell my mum anything. When I used to speak to Steve it wasn't anything, like, "off my chest" to be honest, but that was at the start. Then when our relationship started to progress, that was the person I could turn to and tell him my problems and stuff. So, I used to tell him, he used to give me advice.'

Steve would "pop into school randomly" and sit in on any disciplinary meetings Germaine had to attend. Germaine felt that Steve always had his "corner" and even began to see Steve as "family". Germaine remembered that at this time he felt he faced a distinct choice of "roads" and that his mum just did not have the capacity to exert enough influence on him:

> 'I didn't know what road I was going down. I needed … Steve was my guidance to keep me on the straight and narrow because my mum tried it … you need someone to keep drilling it in you to not go down this road that your friends are down. So, Steve was pushing me down the right road.'

Germaine began to "realise" that he was also going to have cut contact with his chosen peer group to block out "all the negativity". He still felt the absence of a father figure in his life:

> 'If I had a dad as a role model in my life maybe I could turn to someone to talk to about my problems. But as my mum, you don't really think you could talk to a woman about your problems on, say, my problems on the roads. Because if I had a dad to turn to, he could be more stricter and tell me where to go to do this and to do that.'

Germaine noticed that Steve was "putting in time" and was "checking up" on him, keeping him "on his toes". His mum would often remind him that Steve had still "got his eyes" on him. He saw that Steve was supporting his mum too, and that she "had time" for him, which he seemed to find gratifying and comforting:

> 'Sometimes I used to be upstairs playing my PlayStation. I used to hear a knock on the door and he wouldn't come straight upstairs to me. I would hear his voice, I would go downstairs and he and my mum were having tea with biscuits and just talking. I was like, "Yes!" [*significant change in tone to indicate feelings of triumph*].'

Steve became an "angel" – a "quiet voice" in Germaine's ear who could tell when he was lying and would show him the fruits of taking a different road though life.

> 'When you are in your feelings and you think, "Oh I don't want to do that," Steve is there, like, keep pushing you and telling you it is not good and everything. He is showing you certain things, as in, he used to take me out and say, "This is what you can have." He used to take me to posh restaurants, like, "This is what you can have if you're not on the streets." But when you are on the streets you can have anything you like, but it is not legit. Steve would tell me what to do to get legit.'

By 15 Germaine had begun to extricate himself from his violent peer group. He was spotted by a local football club who then offered him a professional contract. Since then, he said, he had managed to stay mostly clear of trouble and was determined to not go back to his old way of life: "Because I am not going down that road. I am no longer going down that road. I am going down that road that I am on."

Analysis

As a story of a young man extricating himself from a violent pathway while coming under the influence an older male youth worker, this case study could be cited as evidence for the efficacy of the role model and mentoring schemes currently in favour in youth policy discourse. Viewed through the lens of psychosocial and positioning theory, though, the story reveals a more complex picture. Germaine and his peers felt blocked by the lack of opportunity for young people locally – the "black hole" of social disadvantage. At school Germaine felt positioned by his older White male teachers as just another "Black kid on the streets" and he, in return, positioned the teachers as "idiots". Germaine's psychological investment in a 'bad' man identity can be seen as a self-initiated response to this positioning that at least enabled him to see himself (and be seen by others) as powerful rather than a powerless victim.

Germaine's drift into violence could be read simplistically as a product of his association with deviant peers and negative role models in his neighbourhood. But there is more to his story. His childhood must also have included a period of dealing with loss and abandonment when his mother was suddenly absent due to her incarceration. The bullying at primary school left him unsure as to whether he could rely on his male friends. At this young age this must have undermined his confidence and self-esteem, leaving him feeling very vulnerable. This early vulnerability may explain the beginning of his efforts to deny it through the construction of a 'bad' roadman identity. His decision to carry a weapon for self-protection is one made for reasons of physical self-defence but also psychological defence against uncertainty and vulnerability, possibly accentuated by witnessing the brutal assault his friend experienced.

His determination to never see his biological father was also perhaps a defence against exposure to further rejection and pain. His growing defensiveness materialised in a reluctance to talk about his feelings to anyone (to get things "off his chest") or to listen to any advice. He saw the lack of a disciplinary presence in his life as something that could only be provided by a male parent and this detrimentally affected his appraisal of his mother who he perceived could not "handle" him. His account shows how his investment in the 'male role model for young men' discourse meant he began to conflate his mother's struggle to "handle" him with a highly gendered notion that only men and fathers can be "strict". This notion persisted and drove his longing for a man whom he felt could support his mum and/or provide the guidance he felt he needed. Germaine believed he could not talk to her about his "problems". It was only when his mother recruited her brother (an active drug dealer) to administer some shock treatment that Germaine felt he experienced the disciplinary male presence he felt he lacked. It was actually this encounter with an older criminally involved man, as opposed to a respectable positive role model, that initially triggered him beginning to reconsider his life trajectory.

When he met Steve their different racial and generational identities were, at first, a barrier to psychic identification, despite a shared allegiance to the local area and similar class background. The exchange between Germaine and his friends, and especially Steve's riposte "You like our White girls", is intriguing. What kind of masculinity was Steve modelling in this response and what was the nature and function of this comment? What 'road' was Steve showing these young men in terms of their ongoing identity choices? Was Steve competing for masculine and street social capital with these young Black men, immovably locating himself and Germaine within a normative heterosexual and racialised matrix? Did his 'banter' endorse sexist notions of male ownership of women and objectify White females as trophies to be competed for within racialised male enclaves? The possessive pronoun 'our' could certainly signify Steve's complicity with patriarchal power and racial privilege.

However, this appraisal of Steve's approach can be augmented by analysing it via psychosocial and positioning theory. Germaine and his friends may have been investing in hypermasculine roadmen identities (one of the few viable subject positions available to them in the local context) to avoid any acknowledgement of more open, sensitive attitudes to women that would leave them open to ridicule. Their investment in this identity would also have strongly influenced how they appraised, gendered and racialised Steve in that local context.

Steve initially told me that his use of the term "our White girls" was meant to be tongue in cheek; an attempt to caricature and parody racial and gender stereotypes through humour. Both Steve and the young men could then poke fun at the stereotypes, themselves, and their own contradictory attitudes. Steve's confidence to venture into the subcultural male-dominated landscape did seem to win Germaine and his friends over enough to the extent that they began to revise their preconception of Steve. His comment, although questionable in its intent, did seem to have the effect of short-cutting the process of building rapport with young men.

Building on the leverage acquired through this breakthrough, Steve became a consistent presence in Germaine's life who could withstand Germaine's initial disparaging and racialised positioning of him as a "booky" White man. Steve then positioned himself (and was positioned by Germaine) as an older man who was willing and able to spend time with him and his mum and with whom there was space for authentic, challenging communication. Steve then simply stayed around long enough for Germaine and his mum to begin like and trust him. Steve's presence in his mum's life and support for her seemed to lift Germaine's spirits. Germaine felt his mum finally had what she needed. He then began to invest his relationship with Steve with a 'he has shown me the road' motif. Steve's 'reach' extended beyond the geographical and he became a transformative presence; a 'voice' in Germaine's ear, showing him a different 'road'.

Two years after the events described in this study, Steve and I discussed Germaine's transcript again and the questions it raised for his practice and professional identity. On reflection he felt that the comment about "our White girls" and his bodily and linguistic practices may well have been triggered by a strong sense he had at the time that he could not afford to be seen as vulnerable by this group of young men. In these early stages of his relationship, he felt he needed to avoid being 'emotionally undone' (Anderson, 1999). We agreed though that the 'banter' could equally have been interpreted by the young men as condoning sexist and racist attitudes. Steve began to further reflect on his own background and subjectivity and how this had featured within his relationship with Germaine. We discussed how a simple notion of role modelling could never capture how that relationship was permeated with disowned vulnerabilities on both sides, involved shifting investments in multiple discursive motifs, and developed within fluid chalk-lines of gender, ethnicity, class and sexuality.

Conclusion

This example of a male youth worker working within the sphere of gendered performance in a local subculture shows the necessity for a continued commitment to critical research which uncovers the forces that shape young people and youth workers' positioning within relationships. This case illuminates how the 'youth-worker-as-male-role-model' subject position may not offer the self-evident answer to young men's violence in the way in which public and policy discourses often imply. It highlights the complex factors at play within youth work relationships that academic analysis needs to keep pace with and find ways to accurately portray. Male youth workers' distinctive professional positioning means they are well placed to offer themselves to young men involved in violence as role models. This subject position contrasts neatly with the positioning of other professionals such as teachers as more disciplinary and mandatory. To maximise the transformative potential of their practice though, male youth workers need a highly developed sense of their own and young men's gendered and racialised identity constructions within subcultural spaces. Viewing identity construction through psychosocial lens allows us to see that cultural ideals of race and masculinity penetrate and construct individuals in ways in which those individuals are often unaware. Building a sensibility to unconscious psychological processes can allow consideration of how male youth workers' professional relationships with young men might become (unconsciously) rivalrous and competitive. Recognising the unconscious drivers behind male personas is also key to understanding how male youth workers might disrupt gender norms and promote desistance (cessation from crime). This disruption requires a delicate balancing of empowerment and simultaneous disempowerment. How and why young men construct their identity may depend on early experiences of loss and abandonment and male youth workers may need to develop the necessary understanding of how these experiences drive young men's identity construction to formulate meaningful practice responses. Sometimes this identity construction process might involve relationships with negative role models in young people's lives that, paradoxically, can still have transformative potential.

The deployment of reserves of masculine and street social capital by older male workers may secure access to (and engagement with) youth subcultures such as the life-world of the 'roadman'. But those male workers also need to be equipped with the skills and self-awareness to enable the lowering of psychological defences on all sides and introduce alternative, less toxic forms of masculine identity in the longer term. This is a level of understanding to which the current youth policy and training regimes may need to become more attuned. Positioning and psychosocial theory can help, enabling fuller recognition of how identity construction is more complex than 'character' formation through role models.

If calls for more male role models for young men are balanced with an awareness of insights generated from analyses such as presented here it becomes possible to avoid the reinforcement of forms of self-concept that lie behind some young men's sexist attitudes and more destructive behaviour patterns. Male youth workers like Steve can then seek to provide a route for young men to travel towards less defensive identities. This involves a mixture of practical advice, emotional support and building of a relationship where male youth workers act less as role models for young men to imitate, and more as figures with whom they are able to negotiate challenges and co-construct new identities and futures. The business of working with young men, rather than the imposition of one identity in the shape of a role model, becomes about enabling young men to be reflexive about a range of possible identities and to come to terms with their own psychological development. Male youth workers situated within local youth subcultural contexts need to be able to move fluidly around that subculture to encourage changes in young men's thinking. This requires reflexivity, not only as part of youth work practice, but also in research and policy making, and some subversion of settled orthodoxies regarding the social reproduction of youth identity.

References

Allan, J. (1997) *The Persistent Fewness of Men Elementary Teachers: Hypotheses from Their Experiences*. East Lansing: National Center for Research on Teacher Learning.

Anderson, E. (1999) *Code of the Street: Decency, Violence and the Moral Life of the Inner City*. New York: Norton.

Bandura, A. (1977) *Social Learning Theory*. Englewood Cliffs: Prentice Hall.

Batsleer, J. (2015) Against role models. Tracing the histories of manliness in youth work. The cultural capital of respectable masculinity. *Youth and Policy*, 113: 15–30.

Boakye, J. (2017) *Hold Tight: Black Masculinity, Millennials and the Meaning of Grime*. London: Influx Press.

Bourdieu, P. (1984) *Distinction: A Social Critique of the Judgement of Taste*. London: Routledge.

De Visser, R. Smith, J.A. and McDonnell, E.J. (2009) 'That's not masculine': Masculine capital and health-related behaviour. *Journal of Health Psychology*, 14(7): 1047–1058.

Frosh, S., Pattman, R. and Phoenix, A. (1998) Lads, machos and others: Developing 'boy-centred' research. *Journal of Youth Studies*, 1: 125–142.

Gadd, D. (2006) The role of recognition in the desistance process: A case analysis of a former far right activist. *Theoretical Criminology*, 10(2): 179–202.

Goffman, E. (1959) *The Presentation of Self in Everyday Life*. New York: Doubleday.

Gunter, A. (2008) Growing up bad: Black youth, road culture and badness in an East London neighbourhood. *Crime, Media, Culture*, 4(3): 349–366.

Hall, S. (1996) Cultural identity and diaspora. In P. Mongia (ed) *Contemporary Postcolonial Theory: A Reader*. London: Arnold.

Harré, R. (2006) Positioning theory and moral structure of close encounters. *Oxford Handbooks Online*, 296–322. doi:10.1093/oxfordhb/9780195396430.013.0010

Harré, R.F.M., Cairnie, T.P., Rothbart, D. and Sabat, S.R. (2009) Recent advances in positioning theory. *Theory & Psychology*, 19(1): 5–31.

Harris, P. (2020) 'I needed to go backwards before going forwards': A psychosocial case study exploring the interweaving of desistance from violent offending and professional youth worker identity formation. *Journal of Psychosocial Studies*, 13(2): 193–208.

Hollway, W. and Jefferson, T. (2013) *Doing Qualitative Research Differently: A Psychosocial Approach*. 2nd edn. London: SAGE.

Robb, M. (2014) Disseminating research: Shaping the conversation. In A. Clarke, R. Flewitt, M. Hammersely and M. Robb (eds) *Understanding Research with Children and Young People*. London: SAGE.

Roulston, K. and Mills, M. (2000) Male teachers in feminised teaching areas: Marching to the men's movement drums. *Oxford Review of Education*, 26(1): 221–237.

Sandberg, S. (2014) Street capital: Ethnicity and violence on the streets of Oslo. *Theoretical Criminology*, 12(2): 153–171.

Sevier, B. and Ashcraft, C. (2009) Be careful what you ask for: Exploring the confusion around the usefulness of the male teacher as male role model discourse. *Men and Masculinities*, 11(5): 533–557.

10

Diary of an On-Road Criminologist: An Auto-Ethnographic Reflection

Martin Glynn

Provocation

Who engages research participants who come from communities deemed 'high risk', 'hard to reach', 'hard to identify', 'hard to access' or just plain frightening? Who is qualified to access those same communities and is required to demonstrate credibility in order to receive that access and gain valuable insights alongside the data? What does a researcher do when he or she is faced with an emerging situation that is 'spontaneous' and 'instant', which requires an 'improvised' approach to the gathering of data? What happens when such encounters are captured with sensitivity, when ethical considerations for the safety of those involved are taken into consideration, even when the site where the events took place is chaotic? Who decides that these encounters are not valid forms of understanding the social world? And who discounts the gatherer of such information, as merely acting like a journalist? These are all questions I myself face, have faced and continue to face. Welcome to the autoethnographic reflections of an 'on-road' criminologist.

First, I want to make my position clear. Based on the sheer awkwardness and barriers imposed upon my own work over the years, this chapter sets out to develop a position which is less dictated by institutional protocols, and more within a paradigm where research is part of a process of reflecting hidden and silent research narratives.

On-road researcher

'On-road' is a term broadly used to depict the code of the streets. For me, an 'on-road' criminologist is 'a credible researcher who has been granted permission, alongside access to the lives and stories of individuals not accessible in the traditional routes of engagement when conducting academic research' (Glynn, 2021). The key to gaining access to people in my constituency comes through my own lived experience, which like theirs has also been fraught with danger and fear, although in my case not because of a criminal lifestyle. My implicit knowledge of, and connection to, the 'road life' from which they come is also a prerequisite. In addition, powers of persuasion, street level reasoning, and navigating the code of the streets must become embedded in the 'on-road' researchers' 'modus operandi'. Failure to do this and you will lose respect and disjoint the research process overall. There are times when both prisoners and community people I engage with get angry, and at times, exhibit the kind of distress that, to many, would be frightening. Much research is predicated on well planned, resourced, committee approved, university backed, theoretically driven, work. 'On-road' research, on the other hand, is where an encounter, incident or moment happens spontaneously, and in the observation and dialogue with the situation, significant insights, understandings and conclusions can be drawn and inferred. It is also important to note that many 'on-road' encounters and situations cannot be mediated within traditional methodological tools, such as: observing spontaneous street violence; bumping into ex-offenders returning to the community; or closed community gatherings where those invited are allowed in on a 'need to know' basis. These encounters can be brief or last for hours. The practice reality of 'on-road' research is less about an academic report, testing a hypothesis or presenting at a conference. It is about making sense out of chaos, reflecting on the events as they happen, and disseminating the findings in culturally appropriate ways. In most cases, it is the community itself that has need of the information that emerges from the 'on-road' encounter, whereas universities may see them as merely anecdotal.

On-road criminologists versus carwash sociologists

DuBois (1978) refers to researchers who do not venture into communities as 'carwash sociologists'. Katz (1988) similarly criticises those social scientists that can 'graciously transport themselves' to worlds they have never been to before by making claims from a 'safe vantage point' of the 'ivory tower'. Rich (2009), when recounting his experiences on the stories of young Black men who had experienced trauma because of street-based violence states, 'without any access to their voices, we could easily formulate solutions that are out of sync with the reality of their lives and that would be ineffective and downright destructive' (Rich, 2009: xv). These accounts clearly make a point that demands to be discussed. Namely, the world at times is messy, dangerous and chaotic. Failure to understand and take account of the events that occur can severely affect those who are on the receiving end of oppressive forces in their lives. Denzin (2010), in his attempt to draw attention to the need to transcend the confines of the 'ivory tower', directs his efforts to a 'call to arms' for all those scholars who believe in the connection between critical inquiry and social justice. Matthews (2009), too, puts forward a proposition that there needs to be the development of a more coherent realist approach that is able to get beyond the existing forms of what he refers to as 'so what' criminology. Green (2010) likewise calls for new frameworks to be developed when researching sensitive issues or marginalised perspectives from populations who have been 'pathologised' more than 'respected' and 'understood' within the research domain. The previous responses form a backdrop from which to address those researchers like myself working with 'high risk' and 'difficult' populations, who are not only excluded from research bids, but are never taken seriously by other academics who feel that 'objectivity', 'longitudinal' studies and responding to abstract concepts takes precedence over using research for an equally as noble cause such as social justice.

Who am I?

What happens if the insider perspective you assert, wherein you position yourself, is seen as too subjective and labelled as radical by the orthodoxy? I see myself in this context as a critical researcher – inasmuch as I position myself in relation to research that is connected to social, political and cultural transformation and change – I still see my work as connected to, and focused on, areas that build and sustain 'social capital' and that are designed to make the residents where I live more autonomous and flourishing human beings. In doing so, I have to contend with a toxic mix of poverty, crime, urban decay and, more importantly, legions of people who do not see themselves as part of anything that will liberate them to a happier and trouble-free life. I frequently talk to my White colleagues about their privileged ontological position, which at times is met with silence, restless body language and the kind of abstention from comment that can make me feel like a blind man in a room full of people trying to hide from me. Being grilled about my cultural awareness, Black politics and connection to the streets still is, and always has been, all part of my initiation into researching complex, messy and challenging subjects.

Whose story is it?

All the participants in my work have a story to tell. Stories of pain, hurt, loss and trauma push you on all levels to ensure you do not let your personal feelings get in the way. With traditional forms of research, the ethics of 'going native' are clearly important in relation to not breaching the boundaries between the researcher and the subjects of the inquiry. As an 'on-road' researcher getting embroiled in the telling of someone's story, you can get seriously (physically) hurt, as well as destroying your credibility in the community. The community, when it suffers pain, oppression or trauma, demands that you not only listen, but that you take a side. In essence, the 'on-road' code places you as a researcher in a position where you're truly made accountable for your ethical position. This situation transcends signing a release form. When you're dealing with the dark world of drug dealers, gangsters, ex-offenders, victims of crime and numerous other cohorts who languish at the tail end of society, the vernacular is named at times, not by me, nor the academy, but the community itself. The community makes the demarcation, not about whether you are a researcher, but more about the kind of researcher you need to be if you want access to their stories. So, in the UK, I'm referred to as an 'on-road' researcher. Those dominant conservative research paradigms at times can be oppressive, disempowering, controlling, and can marginalise an 'on-road' researcher, like myself, whose 'Blackness' is also frequently contested by the oppressive Whiteness.

Blackness

'Blackness', which is shorthand for 'Black consciousness', centres on the understanding of the history of Black oppression and subordination, combined with acquiring the physic tools and ability to transcend its impacts. Freire (1998) argues that researchers are neither impartial nor objective. Becker further argues that the researcher who favours officialdom will be spared the accusation of bias (1967: 243). Both Becker and Freire locate their argument less within the research process, methodology or analysis, and more in the politics of the research.

So, what is my role as an 'on-road' criminologist? I see my role therefore as a researcher that recognises the need to contest and challenge the way the racialisation of crime and criminal justice systems impacts on minoritised communities and the wider community. How then do I negotiate and balance my own interests and research agendas with those of my research participants, which may be inconsistent with or diverge from my own? In relation to the notion of my Blackness as a researcher, working with Black men forces me to confront my own subjectivity and ask that question. Frequently, Black men I research with demand that I have a level of political and cultural Blackness as a way of gaining access to their hearts and minds. It is also apparent that White researchers do not have to account for their 'Whiteness' or demonstrate their understanding of 'Blackness', yet as an 'on-road' criminologist I do. Therefore, if the researcher focuses purely on the research outcomes, without understanding that there are 'by-products' that emerge from that interaction, such as improved confidence, self-esteem and improved self-concept, then something important is being lost. It could be argued that a researcher that possesses knowledge notions of Blackness with Black men has more to offer subjects of inquiry who have traditionally felt powerless and subordinate to White researchers. I argue that offenders generating and creating their own agency involves confronting what society presents as both obstacles and aspirations. In doing so, it is hoped that they will further interrogate the cultural context and examine and explore notions how to transcend society's limited expectations on their ability to desist. However, a White researcher with a hypothesis to test the centres of criminal activity may not pick up or see the relevance of social, historical and cultural factors that not only informed their criminal activity, but could enable it to terminate or desist. So I ask myself, how do Black researchers (like myself) who are involved in a fight for validation – not for the integrity of their abilities as researchers – exercise the right to have a worldview that differs from their White counterparts; one that is no less valid, just different? Much the same as feminist researchers, 'on-road' researchers want freedom to operate within a context that validates notions of Blackness, free from constantly having to defend themselves against because of fears of the backlash coming from White academics. Therefore, I see an integral part of my role as an 'on-road' criminologist researcher to make visible the experiences of denied or marginalised subjects, and to talk back, challenge, contest and problematise dominant representations and assumptions made about them. The following autoethnographic reflection is an example of what would be loosely termed 'on-road' research in action.

Case example: on-road with 'T'

The following reflexive account was not planned. I was parked up waiting for my son to appear from his school during the 2011 August riots, as the streets were pretty dangerous at the time on account of some serious disturbances that had taken place. As I waited for my son, 'T', a known gang member, was walking around the community like a ticking time bomb. On seeing me, he smiled and greeted me warmly before jumping into my car. He informed me about what was happening in his life and wanted to share his testimony with me in case he never made it through the 'street war' that was taking place at that time. The following is an account of what happened.

'T', a tall, powerfully built young Black man, baseball cap peak tipped forward, masking his face, looks from side to side like a prowling hyena, marking his territory. We lock eyes and realise I know him. I pull over and invite him into my car. His greeting is warm and friendly. We touch fists.

'T's fists are scarred. In close proximity, I notice 'T's face is troubled with an expression that suggests all is not well. 'T' is angry, traumatised, grieving and in a dark place right now.

Our conversation centres on catching up with each other; inquiries about work, children and life in general are the kind of formalities that most people who see 'T' from a distance don't notice. All they see is a 'bad man', 'thug', or some other label that makes those who judge feel better. I see 'T' as a bright guy whose pain is carried around like a sack full of heavy stones. I inquire about 'T's wellbeing. I can see from his face that he wants to talk but is struggling with how to broach the things on his mind.

A change of facial expression, a clenching of fists, combined with tightening of neck muscles gives me a sense that 'T' is emotionally connected to recent tragic events all in the name of 'street warfare'. 'T' reveals that he's lost four 'tight bredrins' in a space of 18 months. Describing one murder, 'T' meticulously recounts the sounds, sights and smells of that fateful day. The painstaking detail of his description hits me hard when I realise that these memories will be etched on his soul forever.

I further learn that 'T's sleep pattern is erratic, interrupted and deteriorating rapidly. The assumption can be that 'night people' always sleep well during the day. 'T's sleep pattern has been interrupted as part of a psychological trauma that will ultimately lead to health risks later on in his life. 'Street runnin's' no compensation for a good night's sleep. I continue to listen to 'T's pain and learn how the cumulative impact of these events has created a domino effect, with nightmares that are locked in his subconscious memory much the same as a prisoner of war. 'T' is clearly grieving over the first murder, but the stockpiling of the others in his thoughts and memories is torturing his soul.

I see 'T' as someone who is experiencing inner-city post-traumatic stress disorder. However 'T's condition is not brought about by war, but is an internal struggle comprising a sense of isolation, a lack of social inclusion and belonging. This makes it almost impossible for guys like 'T' to self-actualise. 'T's social labelling as 'deviant', 'anti-social' and 'nihilistic' also creates impossible odds for him to go from a so-called 'liability' to an 'asset'. The pessimist in me holds back slightly, but deep down I know that I have to be realistic about his 'T's chances of survival in a world that repeatedly criminalises young Black men.

As I journey through 'T's current experiences a constant thread running throughout is the issue of 'rage'. This type of rage is dark, disturbing, menacing and very dangerous. Not just in terms of the threat it may pose to someone who may became an innocent victim of 'T's projected anger, but more importantly to 'T' himself, who despite his power, strength and courage, also demonstrated a scared, vulnerable and fatalistic approach to his life. His inner conflict of pain, loss, helplessness and a desire for revenge is a perfect illustration of W.E.B. Du Bois's analysis of young Black men in America, where he refers to this condition as 'double consciousness'.

'Double consciousness' centres on the inability to reconcile those parts of us that are competing with each other for space and validity. In 'T's case the 'double consciousness' is 'justice' or 'revenge'. An inner conflict that many marginalised young Black men in the UK face on a regular basis.

With no means to decode, reconcile and negotiate this dual dilemma, 'T' feels that to act out what he feels will make him feel better and in turn solve his problem of his 'rage'. He and I both knew that this was not the case, but as he said several times, "What am I supposed to do?" I try to explain that violence is not the way, but in my comfortable position I suppose it is easy to say. Focusing on ways to prevent 'T' from venting his anger was very testing at times but I knew had a responsibility that I couldn't abdicate.

'T' reveals the desire to make someone pay for crimes committed to his bredrins. An all too familiar scenario, which tends to bring out shocked responses from a society that seldom attempts to understand guys like 'T'. I see 'T' less as a bad man, thug or gangsta but more as a young guy symbolic of a generation who've been forgotten, let down and left to raise themselves as men. Society, on the other hand, sees another scapegoat, someone to punish and exclude from getting the rewards that society tends to reserve for those who seldom question or challenge the status quo.

Blighted by marginalisation, social experiments and punitive responses to their social reality, we have a generation of young Black men like 'T' who have grown to normalise violence as a way of articulating their masculinity. In the discourse centring on young Black men, we hear agencies and professionals citing various theories, schemes, programmes and so on, all designed to impact on the lives of guys like 'T' as a way of getting him to conform, behave himself and be controlled. Seldom does the dialogue focus on the impact of father deficit or the inability to repair masculinity in crisis. Nor does the recognition of processes such as rites of passage or manhood development become a targeted and focused activity that guys like 'T' can begin a process of personal transformation.

'T' becomes restless; his body language, deep sighs, exhalations, long pauses, and staring into the video of his memories for long periods of time, make me wonder about 'T's relationship with older men. 'T's sense of outrage, shock and disbelief was running through every ounce of his body and has infected his internal functioning that is poisoning his very essence. To a guy like 'T' losing control was an assault on his manhood. A choice that was non-negotiable. 'T' reaffirms his position that someone is going pay for his losses. I ask 'T' about coping strategies. A shrug of shoulders, another deep sigh, and a pursing of lips tell me exactly where he's at in respect to managing his trauma.

'T' cites singing and cage fighting as temporary releases for his inner turmoil. Pushing him further, I ask 'T' how he feels about community representatives who attempt to put his case forward in meetings, make grant applications on his behalf, and to those agencies who claim to be making a difference for youth like him. 'T's level of anger rises swiftly, and he refers to those people speaking on his behalf as taking "money under false pretences". Despite his outburst 'T' expresses a sense of feeling powerless and tired of taking on a fight that's not his. He restates his position. Namely, "I'm tired of being seen as an experiment." Suddenly this powerfully built young man looks sad, lonely and despondent. Yet another problem becomes attached to an already large list of things pushing 'T' further towards psychological self-harm.

I am both humbled and saddened when 'T' reveals I am one of the few people he can trust. He goes on to say that most of the time he can't even trust himself and there is a point where he will not hesitate to act aggressively or violently if he loses the capacity to ground himself in rational thinking. I realise when talking to 'T' how many of us speak rhetorically about helping guys like him, but do so from a distance and in the security of an office.

Being accountable to 'T' is scary but vital if trust is to be built with a generation whose sense of loss and helplessness is not being listened to, until it comes into contact with the criminal justice system, where the response is punitive not restorative. 'T' gives me a valuable insight and perspective into the dangerous world of how the streets are now. It sounds strangely familiar to me, which is all the more disheartening as I have to concede things haven't changed in spite of the new technology revolution. What hasn't changed is that guys like 'T' still need love, understanding and support. The paradox of this situation is that it is guys like 'T' who should be seen as someone who can play a key role to play in enabling the wider community's understanding of the complexities of 'T's environment.

At no stage in our conversation did 'T' cite any agency or group that had asked for his opinion, thoughts or ideas about solving his problems. It could be argued that 'T' should access what exists. The counter-argument is to question how appropriate, relevant or effective those current services are. Or is the kind of targeted outreach designed to reach guys like 'T' outside the scope and remit of most organisations? Accessing 'T' is not just about doing a job, it is understanding masculinity, fathering, listening, hearing, and connecting to the kind of pain that is so real that it's frightening. 'T's conversation switches to 'street loyalty'. He talks passionately about how extreme punishments can be meted out if the 'code of street respect' is broken. From 'T's point of view, there is a job to be done and those who didn't sign up for it are part of the problem also.

He reveals how a lack of trust between bredrins can send an individual into a state of paranoia, by not knowing 'who's got your back' at a time when it's needed. Yet another problem for 'T' to internalise. The current inter-cultural/inter-faith conflicts on the streets bring an angry response and another key issue to the forefront. The issue of cultural factors in masculinity and its impact upon the various warring factions provides a powerful insight into how young Black men articulate their manhood.

'T' knows that some of his adversaries come from difficult family backgrounds, strong religious bonds, war-torn zones, and so on. All competing for space and articulating control and ownership of that space in their own way. He says there is no blueprint or template for a cohesive approach to masculine articulation on the streets, but stresses that love, security and a sense of belonging are in short supply. The more I listen to 'T' the more I see an erosion of processes designed to build and develop vulnerable young men into grown men with a strong sense of purpose. The need to 'take a scalp' or an 'eye for an eye' coming from 'T' highlights that he has no desire to 'turn the other cheek', something that faith communities need to be aware of when intervening with young men like 'T'.

Having a pathological hatred of an individual for harm done is one thing, to move that onto a whole community gives society a reason to place the forces of social control on red alert with the power not only to stop the outcomes, but to send a clear message to guys like 'T' that any attempt to disrupt the balance in society will be met with force. I push 'T' further and discover something I already know, namely, all of his crew feel the same as he does. I'm welling up inside and feeling sad. I connect to 'T' as I see my younger self but I know that I am not him and have to accept that times are now different.

An army of young men like 'T' are poised and ready to take on whatever is thrown at them, not worrying about the personal cost to them or their intended victims. The clarity of his statement suggests this is beyond hatred and into the realm of 'the dark zone' where there are no rules other than survival. Insulated by a massive amount of hurt and surrounded by a similar dark energy creates an awesome 'street power' that can be oblivious to reason unless the outcomes bring a result that will satisfy all 'street soldiers' involved in a war that cannot be won by any one side. "T' talks about revenge being a dish best served cold. It's chilling!

By now I'm taking in every syllable, breath, gesture, emotional outburst, eye contact, shift in mood, as part of his powerful testimony. Failure to do so will result in creating more distress for a young man who hasn't been listened to or heard in a very long time. Moments like this put many things into context and make me realise how ineffective many of us have been, and still are, at enabling young men like 'T' to live meaningful and productive lives. Cars pass by, making my heart skip a beat; a young Asian man walking towards the car makes me wonder whether or not 'T' will hand out a punishment beating.

He smiles and refrains out of respect for me. I reassure 'T' that if he needs to talk I'm available. In these encounters you never force someone to take up the offer, but by making it available you give a lifeline as a gesture of support. A persistent weakness of policy making in terms of the young Black men like 'T' is its failure to examine the aspirations and goal striving patterns of Black youth and to measure these in relation to the social/political ambitions and the real opportunities available to young people as a whole. If policy addresses only the criminal intent, desire and behaviour of young men like 'T' without taking responsibility for the socio-historical conditions that created it, then policies will be not be relevant or appropriate in understanding and addressing the right issues. African American criminologist Amos Wilson states that 'a young Black man with no self concept, will be motivated by self alienation, exhibit an ignorance of his ethnic heritage, engage in unbound hedonism, manifesting in deep insecurities, regarding his masculinities and masculine courage' (Wilson, 1991: 35).

If young Black men like 'T' cannot develop a positive self-concept it is questionable whether they can maintain a focus that will enable them to desist from destructive behaviours that will harm both themselves and others. Engaging young Black men in processes that will liberate them from the pain of social neglect and denied access can play a significant role in taking 'T' from a social position of being seen as a *social liability* into the realms of being acknowledged as *an asset* to his peers, his family, and in turn the community.

'T' looks at his watch and knows it is time to go and get 'back on-road'. I look in his face and see fear, sadness and a real uncertainty of his future. As we hug and bid farewell to each other I'm struck by how passionate he is about the need to defend his community, honour and the principle of gaining justice for past wrongdoings to his bredrins. His final reflection brings out a beaming smile. It's both an optimistic and bright moment. 'T' is about to become a father for the first time. He knows the dangers and threats to him not being able to fulfil that role, but somehow he knows that he must make the best out of a bad situation for sake of his child.

As he disappears into the darkness, I breathe deeply, and fight back tears. Maybe I'm crying for myself or could it be that like 'T' I'm upset at what history and society has turned him into. My encounter with 'T' forces me to confront my own inner fears. Can I judge 'T'? Do I throw him away because of fear of accessing him? Does he become part of my own analysis of the situation? No! It's much simpler than that. For a few brief moments I became a father figure, uncle, brother, a man who needed to listen to another man. At that moment I was neither a researcher, professional, practitioner nor a representative of an agency designed to help guys like 'T'. I was merely a temporary support for someone who needed to be listened to.

I took no great pleasure in hearing and feeling 'T's pain, but it does connect to my own. It also reveals an insight into a world that many vulnerable young people will continue to face if the current state of affairs is not checked, addressed and acted upon. We can all sit in judgment and be rhetorical about what needs to be done. However, several fundamental questions need to be asked: How many more 'T's do we need to see going to jail, committing suicide, behaving violently, struggling with fatherhood, not managing their masculinity, and so on before we act to change things? How long will it be before we individually and collectively recognise real action has been transcended by a culture of talk shops, complacency and apathy?

I'm sad seeing 'T' escape into the shadows as I don't know when I'll see him again or if I'll see him again. Talking to 'T' highlights the need to capture these types of 'in the moment' encounters as the basis for educating, informing and preventing others from going down the same road.

Discussions: breaking the fourth wall

My reflections here are poetic. By sharing and disseminating my thoughts in this way I am not only co-producing my research journey (autoethnography), but I am also co-sharing in a way that moves beyond merely satisfying the traditional academic edicts regarding the form in which research findings are disseminated. In the theatre we would refer to this approach as 'breaking the fourth wall', where the actor talks directly to the audience.

Gate keeper (Glynn, 2021)

> First person accounts from offenders are often distorted 'N' misunderstood As simply a 'records of events' or what others deem what's bad 'N' what's good Many theories are created 'N' generated 'N' at times are flawed 'N' conflated By those who should be challenged, contested, discredited 'N' not exonerated Those responsible for this confusion, present an illusion, merged with delusion Where the production of new knowledge has promoted a 'zone of exclusion' For many women 'N' scholars of colour 'N' offenders themselves
> These differing views are frequently confined to history 'N' sit on university shelves
>
> While the gatekeepers celebrate with rhetoric 'N' biased inferences Crime 'N' criminal behaviour becomes the subject of many workshops 'N' conferences That paints a distorted picture of crime while at the same time laying claim By owning the stories of those who become the targets 'N' victims of blame
> Where flawed agenda's 'N' biased assumptions examines only a part, seldom the whole While others focus attention on the individual 'N' ignore structural power and control While the criminology circus roles into town looking at the numerous role

of the offender Administrative justice pushes out numbers 'N' stats, ignoring race, class 'N' gender

Unable to tell their stories the undetected silences of the marginalised still remain While harm done to victims does not heal their hurt 'N' repair broken links in the chain These stories are ontological, epistemological, criminological 'N' metaphorical Sometimes allegorical and can even be rhetorical

Narrative is made up of fragments of stories that inspire and constrain Every movement, every action, what Merton calls the 'strain'
These stories of crime explains criminal behaviour and other harmful action Of the stories that we tell, the whole thing or just a mere fraction

These stories can motivate, highlight, or legitimise the harm
Can be told thru' raw anger or depression or thru' calm
These stories evaluate, report, inform 'N' recount
'N' tell us about the motivations, intentions, 'N' the amount
Of experiences that reveals how the past shapes the future
Explores the dreams, visions, 'N' desires of nature versus nurture
Could be counter factual propositions or even anecdotal
Stories look at factors of desistance or behaviour that's anti-social

These stories reveal insights into criminogenic factors
The influence of peers 'N' who are the real actors
These stories set out to show who we are 'N' what we do
How we occupy the world 'N' what becomes lies 'N' what becomes true Some stories are unconcerned with empirical veracity
Are influential, consequential 'N' has the human capacity
To reveal hidden truths 'N' present many propositions
Exposing beliefs, values, 'N' insights with many juxtapositions

Whether they be true or false stories that motivate our actions
Offender's and victims testimonies will always provoke reactions
While stories told by elites are presented in the form of propaganda
Where the ignorant are manipulated as the snake like narrative meanders Through falsehood 'N' on-line distortions 'N' generated social lies
The media dissolves and buries the truth 'N' blinds us in our eyes
The masses then consume 'N' support this harmful action
That creates conflict 'N' division thru' societal reaction

Where riots, police shootings 'N' mass incarceration converge 'N' clash While the state machinery devours freedom 'N' conspiracies they hash The rules are then corrupted in this manipulative 'N' dangerous game While some academics and policy faker's, stake 'N' make a claim
That whatever is said is factual, correct, 'N' rooted in the truth When those in control define validity, reliability 'N' false proof This evidence is then presented thru' numbers 'N' thru' stats Ignoring the stories of the marginalised 'N' negating how the powerful acts

Whereas the narrative of the oppressed reveals participation and consent The order of how things happen 'N' how freedom comes from dissent Silent voices scream about how deceit is used to control and prevent Where they expose the real motivation behind history's and society's intent Where passive tolerance sees harm done and not just that of the crime Told through a series of critical events which are sustained 'N' maintained over time Where understandings of legal 'N' not just illegal acts
Are obscured from our gaze with exaggerated empirical facts

While, we're not told the stories behind the myths with openness 'N' sensitivity Some stifle real progression, going from inclusion into exclusivity
Stories reveal what is narrated and who narrates 'N' what
What are the key factors in the story 'N' also what it is not?
Characters 'N' metaphors 'N' the making of meaning
Constructing new scenarios with emotion 'N' of feeling
Who or what drives the story? Understanding the self?
Knowing and showing how harm is done from action into stealth

Uncovering the moments and fragments of the legitimacy of this harm 'N' learning how the rulers 'N' powerful react 'N' sound the alarm
By signifying, relying 'N' pushing 'N' applying the rules of moral panic While the media inspires 'N' conspires with behaviour that is manic 'N' as this conspiracy unfolds many call for honesty 'N' integrity
While those in charge turn a blind eye and operate extremely sneakily To prevent deflection from the truth designed to pacify the masses
The establishment laughs and smiles as they clink their white collar glasses

Our stories are genres, redemptive 'N' all seeing
They justify or repel 'N' in some cases are very freeing
Our stories are constructed 'N' deconstructed over time thru' transitions Bring us together while restating our numerous 'N' diverse positions Synchronic stories reveal the plot at one small point in time
While diachronic stories shows the development, evolution 'N' revolution of crime These stories are not static 'N' are open to full interpretation
Have multiple voices, change 'N' unfold, from death to liberation

Stories are always co-produced, manufactured 'N' tailored to suit the occasion Influenced by setting, environment 'N' are full of arguments 'N' persuasion Meaningful adaptations with selective reconstruction
Non-linear, sequential 'N' powerful, layered with deduction
We act upon our stories through language 'N' thru' power
Whether they're reciprocal or volatile in the telling we must scour
For hidden meanings 'N' truths to find the emergence of new codes
Counter narrative's contest 'N' challenge 'N' take us down new roads

Disputes emerge over telling while dispelling common held beliefs
Challenging labelling, confronting terror, or toppling white collar chiefs To liberate this narrative data must be found
Voices must be heard 'N' reflected in the sound
Of the telling 'N' the knowing 'N' the hearing of the story
In the pain 'N' in the suffering 'N' in the victory 'N' in the glory
In the characters 'N' the scenes 'N' the plots 'N' twists 'N' turns
In the endings 'N' the beginnings 'N' the lessons we must learn

In the truths that we must seek 'N' the mission 'N' the quest
In the methods 'N' of our analysis 'N' in the hypotheses we test
As we connect 'N' collide 'N' collaborate in the lives with whom we share We must never let their stories die, fade, drown, or disappear.
What do stories about racism tell us about being Black 'N' Black oppression? How do we understand racist insults, slights 'N' the philosophy of micro aggression? How do these stories challenge negative experiences of race 'N' racialisation? 'N' how we challenge 'N' contest 'N' transcend notions of integration 'N' assimilation?

How do we move beyond the pain, the hurt, the loss, towards a stronger sense of worth? 'N' how does the telling of stories of *black pain* bring racism right back down to earth? How do we then respond, make sense of 'N' find comfort in our collective humanity? When racism erodes our ideas of self, who we are 'N' our combined racialised identity Black people in telling their stories opens a window into ignored or alternative realities Where dominant groups impose privilege, leading to many 'N' numerous black fatalities These stories facilitate understandings 'N' meanings by 'bridging this *'racialised gap'*. Reveal different everyday realities, giving wisdom and guidance to avoid this psychic trap

These stories reveal betrayal, white privilege, violence, where racism colludes and conspires 'N' grounded theory emerges, enabling codes of racism 'N' white privilege to die or retire The stories that are told are funny, painful, satirical, meaningful, important 'N' ironic While the majoritarian narrative speaks loudly, which is pathetic, painful, 'N' chronic So when do the oppressed 'N' marginalised find the time 'N' space to breathe 'N' feel free? 'N' when do the power of these stories, change, transform, 'N' allow black people to jus' be? Maybe, the strategy that's required to operate on 'N' remove this racialised tumour Is engagement with, embracing 'N' presenting our stories through the use of humour?

Conclusion

This chapter called for the acknowledgement that some aspects of the research encounters are not uniform, do not take place in safe environments, and at times struggle with notions of objectivity. Why should 'on-road' researchers working 'outside the box' accept notions of subordination based on irrelevant and inappropriate methods? Black researchers, qualified as we are, are still rendered powerless in an academic system that privileges one group over the other, where policy responses, legislative changes and other responses do not provide us with a sense of equal justice in terms of access to validating both our research and the methods we employ. How then do 'on-road' researchers like me maintain the balance between challenging the status quo, while at the same time not get sucked into the very machinery that grinds our energy down, forcing us away from research that is meaningful and important? The inability of Black researchers who suffer racial disparities in criminal justice research to successfully operate independently of street-level bureaucrats, policy makers and strategic agencies is also problematic and requires a new approach that provides a shared platform that has power to determine its own destiny. Central to this proposition is in the way the narrative of Black researchers is produced and produces change. The dominant narrative, which restricts and renders counter-narratives invisible, suggests a reframing of what constitutes a counter-narrative. If 'on-road' researchers are to seek transformation as a way of transcending their subordination, then they must seek transformative spaces where the interrogation of the obstacles and barriers to their freedom is given voice, complete with the development of an action plan designed to push their counter-narrative into a strategy for meaningful and productive change. This strategy must not replicate a structure that has kept them down, but instead create a more equitable and empowering way to function and live in a society that still privileges different groups over each other. In the course of this study, the helplessness of many Black men became obvious. The current state of affairs leaves little room for intellectual growth, when these very definitions create a powerless and subordinate group who languish in the research abyss, hoping something will turn up. Future research must challenge dominant social and cultural assumptions regarding Black researchers' ability to name their own reality. In doing so any future research must develop counter-discourses through storytelling, narratives, chronicles, biographies, and so on, that draw on our real lived experiences in relation to the barriers we face.

References
Becker, H. (1967) Whose side are we on? *Social Problems*, 14(3): 239–247.
Denzin, N. (2010) *The Qualitative Manifesto: A Call to Arms*. Walnut Creek: Left Coast Press.
Du Bois, W.E.B. (1978) *On Sociology and the Black Community*. London: University of Chicago Press.
Freire, P. (1998) *Pedagogy of Freedom: Ethics, Democracy and Civic Courage*. Lanham: Rowman and Littlefield.
Glynn, M. (2021) *Reimaging Black Art and Criminology: A New Criminological Imagination*. Bristol: Bristol University Press.
Green, L. (2010) The sound of 'silence': A framework for researching sensitive issues or marginalised perspectives in health. *Journal of Research in Nursing*, 16(4): 347–360.
Katz, J. (1988) *Seductions of Crime: Moral and Sensual Attraction of Doing Evil*. New York: Perseus Books.
Matthews, R. (2009) Beyond 'so what?' criminology. *Theoretical Criminology*, 13(3): 341–362.
Rich, J. (2009) *Wrong Place, Wrong Time: Trauma and Violence in the Lives of Young Black Men*. Baltimore: The Johns Hopkins University Press.
Wilson, A. (1991) *Black on Black Violence*. New York: Afrikan World Info System.

11

Conclusions, Compromises and Continuing Conversations

Jade Levell, Tara Young and Rod Earle

As we discussed in the Preface, an edited collection is by nature a collaboration, a milieu of different perspectives and experiences which together create a provocative mosaic of scholarly work. In a similar vein, an editorial group is an alliance of people with a shared interest but from differing perspectives. This is what makes it so wonderful to work as a team. To reflect our cultural and gender diversity as a team we have decided to organise this concluding chapter into three parts, where we each reflect on the aspects of the collection which speak most to us and our own work, and most importantly, what the next steps are for this field of study. What questions need to be further posed.

Jade's reflections: feminist lens on the soundtracks to subjectivity, relationality, love and community

As some contributors in the collection have noted, adult anxiety about the generation beneath them is perennial (Powell, 2011). Although the concept of 'youth' is relatively recently conceived. From the mid-17th century young people started to be seen as separate from both adults and children, with the concept of 'adolescence' coined by G. Stanley Hall (1904). In this text he discussed 'several "problems of youth", including: unbridled sexuality; rejection of parents/teachers; lack of concentration; extremes of emotion including aggression; and unpredictability' (Powell, 2011: 11). The causes for this were attributed to both social context and biological changes in the shift to adulthood. The reason for this increased focus on the *teenage years* came from an enhanced concern around deviance, delinquency and social reform (Garland et al, 2015). The focus on youth has been said to be laden with symbolic value. The concept of youth has 'served as a metaphorical device to embody both the aspirations and anxieties of a particular historical time ... a harbinger of change, an emergent consumer, a signifier of hope, or a portent of social decline' (Garland et al, 2015: 2). Therefore, it is important to focus on the wider meanings and social context of the current youth moral panic and what it indicates about contemporary social and political change. This collection has sought to go beyond the individuals that are often viewed as a collective who are on the periphery or in the throws of 'gang-involvement'. However, at times this label is laden with baggage that interrupts the curiosity we have around the term 'on-road'. This term allows for the continuum of vibrancy and despair, of hopes and dreams. In this way, and drawing on the definitions of life on-road as outlined by Hallsworth and Young (2004) and Gunter (2010) in the introduction, life on-road could be said to be a relational culture. Clifford Geertz defined culture as a combination of a worldview and an ethos, 'a people's ethos is the tone, character and quality of their life, its moral and aesthetic style and mood; it is the underlying attitude towards themselves and their world that life reflects' (1973: 127). The academic appraisal of the on-road space certainly includes these aspects.

To me, this collection is reflective of the second-wave feminist slogan, 'the personal is political'. As Kate Millet wrote, the reference to 'politics' in sexual politics is to describe 'power-structured relationships' (Millett, 1970: 23). She was focused on patriarchal relationships and the interweaving of intimate connections and the ways in which these can reflect wider power imbalances. This was revolutionary at the time as it classified the feminist principles of disrupting the private/public split by blowing open the 'closed doors' which allowed inequality and abuse to reside. By focusing politically on intimate and personal relationships women were able to foster solidarity over their domestic circumstances which had so much weight in their lives. Interestingly, this shift of exposure has not happened in writing about the lives of men and boys. Instead, within criminological literature, they are still overly represented in terms of writing about their criminality and criminal sociality. However, friendships, love, music, the richness of life, is sorely neglected. To focus back onto the personal as political is a feminist lens on subjectivity, viewing people in their wholeness, in their relational selves. In the 1990s postmodern period, feminist theory was said to experience a 'turn to culture', focusing less on 'things' and more on the social processes of 'symbolization and representation ... and attempts to develop a better understanding of subjectivity, the psyche and the self ... and towards a more cultural sensibility' (McRobbie, 1994: 173). It is an act of *resistance* against the dominant narratives of criminality. This refocusing is part of looking at taking a holistic view of young people's lives on-road rather than the boundary-making claim of 'gangs'. There is of course a place for enquiry about crime and desistance but choosing to look beyond this can be an act of defiance against morbid fascination with deviance. In doing this we choose love, hope and humanity.

As shown throughout this collection, life on-road is an interconnected and relational space. It is focused on the lives that are lived through community, whether that be in friendships, families or with youth workers. This represents a resistance to the modern focus on the 'atomic self' (Sacks, 2002: 150). This collection emphasises the antithesis of that, and instead draws on a *relational ontology* which resists the individualised appraisal of people's lives and instead focuses on their relationality (Richardson and Woolfolk, 2013: 27). The relational aspects of life on-road are often neglected as the focus through the criminal justice lens homes in on the use of connections between young people as evidence of collusion or joint enterprise in 'gangs'. We value this collection in the way that it holds a space for vulnerability, for softness, for friendships and relationships. Not to romanticise the life, as it can also include vulnerability, pain and trauma, as the chapters have shown. But opening up the space to discuss friendship is so important, as friendship relies on consent not coercion, and this is a gap in scholarship of life – we all experience the trials and tribulations of interconnectivity, yet often reduce young people's relationships to folly. bell hooks focused on the subjectivity of love and described love as a practice which offers hope of resistance against White supremacy and in decolonising the mind. She noted that, '[l]ove was the force that empowered folks to resist domination and create new ways of living and being in the world' (hooks, 2012: 195). She went on to note that, 'anytime we do the work of love we are doing the work of ending domination' (hooks, 2012: 195). hooks framed love as a combination of five aspects: 'care, commitment, knowledge, responsibility, and trust' (hooks, 2012: 195). She likens these to baking ingredients, all of which are needed in order to make the final product; love. hooks writes about capacity and practice of love, including self-love, in the face of a racist society. Noting that there can be the development of a split self, whereby individuals internalise racism in their own self-image and so viewing oneself in wholeness is challenging. The solution, for hooks, is the practice of love for both selves and in community. Love in the sense that she conceptualised it is grounded in feminist thinking and practice (hooks, 2018). The relevance of this to the collection is that it returns to love, relationships and community as a direct focus of enquiry.

In doing this, however, we are not blind to the structural inequalities that limit and restrict the opportunities for young people on-road. We know that through using intersectionality (Crenshaw, 1991) as a frame we can make visible the ways in which gender, race, class (among others) are all implicated in the sustenance of marginalisation for young people. In recent years there has been wider acknowledgement of the impact of racist policing through the controversy of the UK gangs matrix (Williams, 2015;

Amnesty International, 2018). We are also seeing a contemporary moral panic in the UK around Albanian 'gangs' and associated illegal migration. Although the target of othering changes over time, the trend of creating racial boundaries on 'outsiders' remains constant. Taking a feminist lens to this material positionality is important. Bob Pease (2019) calls us to face up to the fact that despite feminism and gender equality being somewhat mainstreamed, patriarchy is alive and well. What he deals with so well is the tension that feminists can face when they are presented with the superficial acknowledgement of gender mattering, and gender-sensitive responses to violence and abuse, but at times feeling that it is there to tick a box. As we discussed in the Introduction, there has also been much less research that has focused criminologically on the lives of boys as victims, and of girls as agentic. The tide is beginning to turn on this, but we need to have fuller conversations about the ways in which young people live and relate beyond gender stereotypes.

Life on-road can be a site of artistic creation and consumption, which was highlighted through the focus on music throughout the collection. Being attuned to the soundtrack of young people's lives gives us a small insight into the soundscapes of life on-road. Music and friendship are parts of the universal human condition, and that is what is so powerful if viewed holistically. Music when taken as part of the 'ethnographic imagination' can provide a rich and evocative way to hear the stories of young people's lives. Rap tracks in particular '[enable] listeners to gain insights into meanings of human existence from the standpoint of insiders, and to uncover the world of everyday life' (Barron, 2013: 532). Music is inherently relational, in both the production and consumption. Even when music is enjoyed alone it provides an asynchronous connection between the artist and the individual. It is this connection between artists and listeners, or peers within a subculture, which has become so tense in the on-road context. As noted in the collection, music and lyrics are now being used as evidence of criminality. In doing this the state is fundamentally changing the purpose and function of the music and its relationship to the fans and artists. In focusing on the richness of music in the lives of young people on-road, as well as during migration, and in prison, we are opening up a space to hear how young people themselves perceive their relationship with music. As Stokes noted in a timeless way, 'what we know about ourselves and others and the spaces we create for ourselves is also built out of sounds' (Stokes, 1997: 673).

The questions of researcher subjectivity, authenticity and positionality were also threaded throughout the collection. With research that focuses so heavily on such a marginalised young people it is important for the question of power to be constantly considered. As was mentioned in several chapters, the idiom of the 'ivory tower' is laced with symbolism of White supremacy, of colonialism, and of scholarly gatekeeping. As Glynn's chapter

(Chapter 10) so provocatively asked: Who is the right person to conduct research with young people on-road? What are the conditions which create an authentically non-exploitative on-road scholarship? Similar questions were posed in a different context by Harris (Chapter 9), who focused on gender and youth workers, asking whether gender matters in building relationships with young people. The chapters in this collection, as well as our preface on gatekeeping, have posed more questions than they have answered in many ways. However, to be opening up space for these discussions without anyone needing to have the last word is part of feminist praxis. We cannot make change without hearing each other. My hope for the next steps in the small field of on-road studies is that interdisciplinarity is viewed not just as a happenstance for many scholars in this field, but as an active strength.

Feminist theory has a lot to contribute to the focus on the political relationality of young people, as well as on the gendered ways that marginalised young people cope with their lives. Feminist praxis in on-road scholarship also promotes ways of thinking and writing which are aimed at flattening the hierarchies of researcher/researched and instead find ways to authentically collaborate with participants, for instance in the mutual appreciation of music. Anthropology and the associated field of ethnomusicology offer us ways to understand the role of music in dominant and sub-cultures in non-limiting ways. Drawing in a sociological understanding of relationality opens up a space to consider the inter-related ways that young people's lives entwine, as well as the structural inequalities and social harms that create and reinforce multiple oppressions, often on the axis of race and gender. Finally, criminology has a stake in this work. Instead of focusing down at deviance and crime, there is an emerging turn to look instead at how young people flourish (Billingham and Irwin-Rogers, 2022). Taking a humanising and strengths-based approach to understanding young people's struggles with adversity feels like choosing hope. We are looking at children first, and this lens opens a space for compassion, empathy, love and community.

Tara's reflections

> We live in a world where there is more and more information, and less and less meaning.
>
> Baudrillard (1981: 6)

In the early 2000s, when I started researching the life experiences of young offenders and young people 'at risk' of offending, there was increasing concern within statutory agencies about the rising level of gang, gun and knife crime and the link to street-based gang groups. Policy and academic research at the time associated persistent offending (Stelfox, 1998), increased levels of knife possession among young people (Lemos, 2004), sexual violence against girls and young women (Firmin, 2010, 2011), rioting and public disorder (Cameron, 2011) and using dangerous dogs as weapons (Harding, 2012) with gangs. Journalists distilled the gang crisis for public consumption in reports headed by straplines such as 'It's lawless out there' (Helm, 2000), because of youth knife crimes of 'epidemic proportions' (Alleyne, 2008), somewhat consolidating the gang as 'Britain's deadly new menace' (Townsend, 2006) constituting a significant threat to the general public. Positing a view similar to sociologist Charles Murray (1990) who attributed anti-social behaviour and (violent) criminality to the 'underclass', David Blunkett, the then Home Secretary in 2003, said that the primary threat came from 'unfettered feral yobbish kids' who cause a whole heap of misery (Blunkett, 2003, cited in Johnston, 2003) some of whom are associated with gangs. Gangs, it seems, were everywhere, operating in prisons (Wood and Adler, 2001; Wood, 2006), within/outside the school estate (Alleyne and Wood, 2014; Home Office, 2015) and associated with the emerging terrorist threat (Rose, 2012). In short, in the mid-2000s gangs were 'the new face' of youth violence despite some being 'reluctant gangsters' (Pitts, 2008).

Amidst this storm of research, and arguably a period of deviancy amplification (Young, 1971; Cohen, 2003), there have been some dissenting voices seeking to offer a critical and alternative view of youth violence. Acknowledging the real crime and violence involving young people as victims and perpetrators and the devastation this caused to the lives of people it touched – direct and indirect – these scholars sought to situate youth-related offending within structural violence, marginalisation and racism. Casting their epistemological net wider than the gang trope that problematised populations, such as the Black and minoritised, this research challenged the criminal justice paradigm. Hallsworth and Young (2004, 2008, 2010) argued that there was no empirical evidence supporting the claim that gangs were on the rise in the UK and challenged the evidence underpinning such claims. In addition, they claimed that gangs and violence were only causally related due to the lack of data, which served to incite moral panic and justify ever-more punitive responses to youth crime. Similarly, Shute et al's (2012) critical analysis of the policy response to the gang crisis concluded that the criminal justice rhetoric was based on a simplistic elision of youth violence based on evidence that was in danger of reifying the very thing it was trying to control. Their assessment of the Ending Gang and Youth Violence initiative – which followed the Tackling Gang Action Programme (Home Office, 2008) designed to eliminate serious gang violence – was that it was evidentially suspect, discriminatory and lacked 'intellectual/moral coherence' (Shute and Medina, 2014: 26). In short, the focus on 'gangs' was nothing but 'blunderbuss' and an exercise in 'hunting Gruffalo'.[1] Moreover, the Ending Gang and Youth Violence strategy and other government initiatives were adopting the 'gang' label to fuel moral panic about youth offending, instigating fear and panic about marginalised groups and justifying ever-more surveillance and punitive control over certain communities, continuing the historical stigmatisation and pathologisation of particular social groups, most notably working-class and Black and minority ethnic young men (Shute and Medina, 2014). Hallsworth and Young's research recognised 'gangs' as one of a number of delinquent collectives and not necessarily equated with street-based crime and violence. Gunter's ethnographic research popularised the concept 'on-road', using this to explore the social cultural life-world of young people. Hallsworth and Silverstone (2009) utilised the term 'on-road' rather than the language of 'gangs' to illuminate the experience of young men involved in weapons-related offending. Critical scholarship drew attention to the lack of neutrality when attributing youth violence to 'gangs', uncritically applying this moniker to describe groups of Black and brown people and the offences committed by them as 'gang-related' in spite of evidence to the contrary (Williams and Clarke, 2016), effectively stereotyping and pathologising people of colour (Alexander, 2008). Noting the increasing surveillance of communities of colour within the paradigm of risk (Smithson et al, 2013), more recent scholarship has pointed to the incorrect assumption of Black men and Black culture as 'criminogenic' (Gabbidon, 2010) and the elevation of gang-related offending in youth justice policy in the UK and across Europe (Fraser et al, 2018). Indeed, Fraser and his co-authors caution against the slow creep of 'gang talk' into the justice paradigm and the shaky foundations upon which discussions on youth violence is framed. They point to the continuing influence of 'gang talk' that pervades the discussion of social control, drawing our attention, as have other scholars, to the introduction of gang databases such as the stigmatising 'Gangs Matrix' (Amnesty International, 2018; Williams, 2018) as monitoring tools, gang injunctions and the increase use of legal doctrines such as joint enterprise to incarcerate young people associated with gangs (Crewe et al, 2014; Williams and Clarke, 2016; Hulley et al, 2019; Young et al, 2020; Hulley and Young, 2022).

At a time when the Home Office (Home Office UK, 2018) is raising public awareness of 'county lines' gangs who use coercion and violence (including sexual violence) to intimidate children and vulnerable adults to deal, move and store drugs, there are academics and practitioners who are calling into question the legal tactics and evidential basis upon which these claims are made. In addition, there is a new and burgeoning body of work dedicated to challenging the use of social media, especially certain forms of urban music such as rap and drill, by legal practitioners, operating within a paradigm of risk and justice for the victims(s) as evidence in criminal cases involving young people; disproportionately Black and mixed-raced young men (Fatsis, 2019; Ilan, 2020; Lynes et al, 2020; Bakkali, 2022; Young and Hulley, forthcoming). Joining the critical scholarship is Janhine Davis's (2022) research on the adultification of Black children. According to Davis there is a persistent and ongoing act of dehumanisation, which explicitly impacts Black children, and influences whether they are accorded the status of 'child', viewed as 'innocent', and how they are safeguarded and protected. For Davis (2022: 5), adultification occurs outside of the home and it is always founded within discrimination and bias and is evident in criminal justice discourse.

For me, this collection adds to the critical chorus and it is unashamedly a British voice. As I have already noted, without disregarding the serious crime and violence committed by young people 'on-road', the empirical, theoretical and historical analysis of 'on-road' presented here attempts to disrupt the criminalising and pathologising of young people. This work invites the reader to assess in a more nuanced way the attitudes and behaviours of young people by, among other things, introducing narratives of compassion and steering our primary focus on offending towards the systemic mistreatment of young people. As Billingham and Irwin-Rogers (2021) note, if we are to tackle the crime and violence young people perpetrate and experience, we need to switch our attention to the failure of social institutions to provide what is required for them to realise a prosperous and fulfilling life. We need to understand what matters to young people. I believe this volume goes some way to doing that.

Rod's reflections: roads taken, lessons learned, no detour ahead

The opportunity for me to work on this book extended a collaboration that emerged through supervision of Jade's PhD. It represents much of what I have found most valuable in working at The Open University, a commitment to collaborative forms of work enlarging opportunity for the many rather than the few, as has historically been the case for universities. Although my contribution has been smaller than either of Jade's or Tara's, I think the combinations have been mutually enriching and lasting in effect. Reconnecting with Tara was too good an opportunity to miss because a long time ago we shared office space as we both made tentative steps into academic life, feeling like outsiders for various different reasons. Conversations and diverging experiences then about race and gender did not exactly fall on deaf White ears, but I have been slow to appreciate how thoroughly mired I am in the structures of White privilege, structures that propel some people upward and onward, while holding others back and down. It was inconceivable that Jade and I, as two White academics, could enlarge her project without the input of an academic who shared at least a few more of the characteristics of the young people whose lives we wanted to know more about. Tara's track record speaks for itself and her long-standing determination to combine race and gender analysis provided an ideal fit with Jade's.

We wanted this collection to register in the world of practice, in the places where people work with children and young people. All three of us have aspects of this world in our past. Several of the contributors have taken me back to where I began as a well-intentioned but perhaps poorly equipped youth work practitioner in the South London borough of Lambeth in the 1980s. As I struggled to make sense of what the work was becoming, perhaps what I was becoming, I turned to evening classes in the sociology of crime and deviance, and then to a day-release Master's degree in criminology at Middlesex University to make better sense of what was happening. There I met Paul Andell who was also working with young people in South London but through the voluntary sector. We shared notes on our encounter with a young American PhD student who was researching gangs in London. He had come to Brixton to find its legendary but characteristically elusive '28s', the gang that everyone seemed to know about, but to which no one seemed to belong. My Black colleagues in Lambeth were sceptical to the point of amusement: another White academic with an interest in deviant young Black men. When this student discovered Paul and I were also Master's students at Middlesex he asked us whether we intended to become academics. We both snorted with laughter. We could not imagine any other way of making our work and interests more irrelevant. We thought that becoming an academic meant becoming socially redundant, retreating into abstraction. It has been sobering to meet with some of the contributors to this book who share this scepticism and it has been challenging to persuade them, in good faith, that 'it is worth it', that this kind of work is not irrelevant and is far from abstract. Sometimes I can scarcely convince myself.

Martin Glynn's closing contribution to the collection spells out his answer to this dilemma by contrasting his own deeply engaged and reflexive approach as an 'on-road' criminologist with the approach of 'carwash sociologists'. Drawing from the many insights of W.E.B. Du Bois (1903), Glynn is wary of criminologists (in particular) who observe from car windows and then drive on or back to the security of their own neighbourhood. This is a kind of drive-by sociology that uses research as an invasive avenue into people's lives. Glynn's extensive and richly varied body of work demonstrates how boundaries can be broken and collective intellectual growth fostered. His appeal for more personal investment in 'storytelling, narratives, chronicles, biographies' and the arts of expression (Glynn, 2021) is consistent with the approaches we have tried to develop in the collection and that I strive towards in my own work in convict criminology and anti-racist collaborations with Alpa Parmar and Coretta Phillips (Phillips et al, 2019; Parmar et al, 2022; Earle et al, 2023).

Several contributors explore and use the salience of music in young people's lives and its connections to the on-road life. Young people's involvement with and creation of distinctive new music seems to be almost irrepressible and eternal but is probably a relatively specific feature emerging from post-war racial capitalism in 'the West' (Savage, 2008). While we have not gone down this analytical road very far, the experiences in common around music that foster its capacities to elicit narratives and stories, depth of feeling and points of connection are bound up with what is personal about this kind of academic work. It is a place where life interests meet work interests, and one flows into the other. My own 'coming of age' music, the music and musicians that bound me to friends, helped me make new friends or see sense in a senseless world spinning with threat and opportunity, was punk and reggae. It is a time (late 1970s to 1980s) best captured in Jon Savage's vibrant account *England's Dreaming* (Savage, 1991). While I cannot come close to Lambros Fatsis's encyclopaedic knowledge of musical genres and cultural contexts, I think we are both caught up in such music's capacity to challenge the racial logics of our time and offer a kind of affective moral compass by which we can navigate our paths, different and changing as they are.

The nickname thrown at me (mostly without malice) by the young men and women I worked with in Kennington was 'Beastie' because I wore a cap and (they said) looked a bit like one of the Beastie Boys, a White hip-hop group making waves in the charts. Hip-hop, rap, punk and reggae may have given way to grime, drill, trap, RnB and so much more but the countercultural politics, the resistance, they infer can also hook us back into the cultural politics of on-road life and the politics of race. Musical forms gripped the imagination of the young men I worked with in London in the 1980s and 1990s, much as it still does young people's aspirations now. Arguments raged over the relative strengths and possible futures of junglist, RnB or rap forms. One young White man's failure to engage effectively with his school work was tolerated because of his burgeoning talent and ambition as a rap artist. The road he was starting to inhabit took him far. Several years later a large tour bus parked around the corner from our youth centre and in he walked saying he had begged his fellow traveller, the American legend, Ice-T, to pull in so he could hop out and do 'two things'. He wanted to thank us and he wanted to give us the opportunity to meet his famous mentor.

Another young man I worked with in that centre, also White, fared less well on-road. Some 20 years later I saw him in HMP Maidstone as I was conducting research with Coretta Phillips on men's social relations in prison. He was a badly broken man and I was shaken up by our meeting. He told me: "It's been a bumpy ride, Rod, a bumpy ride." Although neither of the men used the term 'on-road', both had hit the road, and it had taken them to very different places.

One of the things we wanted to do as editors of this collection was to gather wider knowledge of the social world of life on-road and make it accessible and intelligible to more people. In doing so we hoped that the terminology and optics of 'the gang' as a dominant modality of thought about young people living on-road could be displaced, dislodged or unsettled. In its place we wanted to find new ideas and energy at the edges of the conventional groves of academic life. Bakkali and Chigbo's chapter is a powerful example (Chapter 3). It shows in form, method and practice what can be co-produced by co-production. Yusef Bakkali and Ezimma Chigbo open with Kahlil Gilbran's Prophet, Almustafa, musing on the powers of love. Moving on-road, say Bakkali and Chigbo, engages the gears of love, as does much else in life, yet love rarely features in the research academic's theoretical toolkit or conceptual horizons. Bakkali and Chigbo refuse such omissions by guiding their analysis through the desires and erotics of road life, seeing love's work where others have been blind to it. Their insistence on responding to the fullness of people is consistent with Gibran's reading of youth and the dangers they are put in by insensitive adults: 'Some of your youth seek pleasure as if it were all, and they are judged and rebuked. I would not judge nor rebuke them. I would have them seek', says Gibran (Gibran, 1970: 83). Bakkali and Chigbo trace this seeking and critically interrogate the trails and trials of the 'tainted love' they find on-road. In their concluding observation that '[t]he violent work of stripping marginalised people of their sense of self, history and value was crucial in the process of cultivating the most violent experiences of intimacy on the margins, our solutions must be generative for the psyche and the spirit' they simultaneously diagnose many of conventional criminology's failings and point to better futures, better work. They show there may be a road ahead where, to repeat a phrase used by another of our contributors, Esmorie Miller, in an interview with the British Society of Criminology, I can 'see myself working with youth in a context devoid of criminalisation' (British Society of Criminology, 2023). I hope readers can do the same and that this collection helps make this road wider.

Note

[1] Created by Julia Donaldson and illustrated by Axel Scheffler in 1999, a Gruffalo is a fictious monster imagined by a small mouse who believes that he would be swallowed up by it if he ever crossed its path. For the mouse, the Gruffalo is the ever-present, yet largely unseen, monster in his midst.

References

Alexander, C. (2008) *Re-Thinking 'Gangs'*. Report prepared for the Runnymede Trust, available at: 617be0268dcf89bf9cc45a73_RethinkingGangs-2008.pdf

Alleyne, E. and Wood, J.L. (2014) Gang involvement: Social and environmental factors. Crime and Delinquency, 60(4): 547–568.

Alleyne, R. (2008, May) Knife crime is epidemic, top judge claims. *The Telegraph*.

Amnesty International (2018) *Trapped in the Matrix: Secrecy, Stigma, and Bias in the Met's Gangs Database.* Available at: www.amnesty.org.uk/gangs

Bakkali, Y. (2022) Road capitals: Reconceptualising street capital, value production and exchange in the context of road life in the UK. *Current Sociology*, 70(3): 419–435.

Barron, L. (2013) The sound of street corner society: UK grime music as ethnography. *European Journal of Cultural Studies*, 16(5): 531–547.

Baudrillard, J. (1981) *Simulacra and Simulation.* Michigan: University of Michigan Press.

Billingham, L. and Irwin-Rogers, K. (2021) The terrifying abyss of insignificance: Marginalisation, mattering and violence between young people. *Onati Socio-Legal Series*, 11(5): 1222–1249.

Billingham, L. and Irwin-Rogers, K. (2022) *Against Youth Violence: A Social Harm Perspective.* Bristol: Policy Press.

British Society of Criminology (2023) Dr Esmorie Miller. *Criminologist Corner(ed)*, 5. Available at: https://www.britsoccrim.org/wp-content/uploads/2023/01/EM-interview-1.pdf

Cameron, D. (2011, August). Riots: David Cameron's Commons statement in full. *BBC UK Politics*. Available at: https://www.gov.uk/government/speeches/pms-speech-on-the-fightback-after-the-riots

Cohen, S. (2003) *Folk Devils and Moral Panics: The Creation of the Mods and Rockers.* Abingdon: Routledge.

Crenshaw, K.W. (1991) Mapping the margins: Intersectionality, identity politics, and violence against women of colour. *Stanford Law Review*, 43(6): 1241–1299.

Crewe, B., Hulley, S. and Wright, S. (2014) *Written Evidence Submitted to the House of Commons Justice Committee on Joint Enterprise.* HM Government Justice Committee. Available at: http://www.crim.cam.ac.uk/research/ltp_from_young_adulthood/evidence_to_justice_committee.pdf

Davis, J. (2022) *HM Inspectorate of Probation Adultification Bias within Child Protection and Safeguarding.* June. Available at: https://www.justiceinspectorates.gov.uk/hmiprobation/wp-content/uploads/sites/5/2022/06/Academic-Insights-Adultification-bias-within-child-protection-and-safeguarding.pdf

Du Bois, W.E.B. (1903) *The Souls of Black Folks.* Chicago: A.C. McClurg and Co.

Earle, R., Parmar, A. and Phillips, C. (2023) Criminal questions, colonial hinterlands, personal experience: A symptomatic reading. In H. Carvalho, A. Aliverti, A. Chamberlen and M. Sozzo (eds) *Decolonising the Criminal Question: Colonial Legacies, Contemporary Problems.* Oxford University Press.

Fatsis, L. (2019) Policing the beats: The criminalisation of UK drill and grime music by the London Metropolitan Police. *Sociological Review*, 58: 1–17.

Firmin, C. (2010) *Female Voice in Violence Project: A Study into the Impact of Serious Youth and Gang Violence on Women and Girls*. London: Race on the Agenda.

Firmin, C. (2011) *This is it. This is my life…Female Voice in Violence Final Report London*. London: Race on the Agenda.

Gabbidon, S.L. (2010) Race, ethnicity, crime, and justice: An international dilemma. *In-Spire Journal of Law, Politics and Societies*, 5(1): 93–94.

Garland, J., Gildart, K., Gough-Yates, A., Hodkinson, P., Osgerby, B., Robinson, L., Street, J., Webb, P. and Worley, M. (2015) Youth culture, popular music and the end of 'consensus' in post-war Britain. *Contemporary British History*, 26(3): 265–271.

Geertz, C. (1973) *The Interpretation of Cultures*. New York: Basic Books.

Gibran, K. (1970) *The Prophet*. London: Heinemann.

Glynn, M. (2021) *Reimagining Black Art and Criminology: A New Criminological Imagination*. Bristol: Bristol University Press.

Gunter, A. (2010) *Growing Up Bad: Black Youth, Road Culture and Badness in an East London Neighbourhood*. London: The Tufnell Press.

Hallsworth, S. and Young, T. (2004) Getting real about gangs. *Criminal Justice Matters*, 55: 12–13.

Hallsworth, S. and Young, T. (2008) Gang talk and gang talkers: A critique. *Crime, Media, Culture*, 4(2): 175–195.

Hallsworth, S. and Silverstone, D. (2009) 'That's life innit': A British perspective on guns, crime and social order. *Criminology and Criminal Justice*, 9(3): 359–377.

Hallsworth, S. and Young, T. (2010) Street collectives and group delinquency: Social disorganisation, subcultures, and beyond. In E. McLaughlin and T. Newburn (eds) *The SAGE Handbook of Criminological Theory*. London: SAGE, pp 72–96.

Harding, S. (2012) *Unleashed: The Phenomenon of Status Dogs and Weapon Dogs*. Bristol: Polity Press.

Helm, S. (2000, November) It's lawless out there. *The Guardian*. Available at: https://www.theguardian.com/society/2000/nov/29/socialcare.crime

Home Office (2008) *Tackling Gangs: A Practical Guide for Local Authorities, CDRPS and Other Local Partners*. Available at: http://www.safecolleges.org.uk/sites/default/files/local_authorities.pdf

Home Office (2015) *Preventing Gang and Youth Violence: Spotting Signals of Risk and Supporting Children and Young People: An Overview*. Available at: http://cdn.basw.co.uk/upload/basw_23304-10.pdf

Home Office UK (2018) *Serious Violence Strategy*. April. Available at: https://www.gov.uk/government/publications/serious-violence-strategy

hooks, b. (2018) To love again: The heart of feminism. In *Feminism Is for Everybody*. Abingdon: Routledge, pp 100–104.

hooks, b. (2012) The practice of love. In *Writing Beyond Race: Living Theory and Practice*. London: Taylor & Francis, pp 191–199.

Hulley, S. and Young, T. (2022) Silence, joint enterprise and the legal trap. *Criminology and Criminal Justice*, 22(5): 714–732.

Hulley, S., Crewe, B. and Wright, S. (2019) Making sense of joint enterprise for murder: Legal legitimacy or instrumental acquiesce? *British Journal of Criminology*, 59(6): 1328–1346.

Ilan, J. (2020) Digital street culture decoded: Why criminalizing drill music is street illiterate and counterproductive. *British Journal of Criminology*, 60(4): 994–1013.

Johnston, P. (2003) A day in the life of a yob culture Britain. *The Telegraph*, 15 October, p 6.

Lemos, G. (2004) *Fear and Fashion: The Use of Knives and Other Weapons by Young People*. London: Bridge House Trust.

Lynes, A., Kelly, C. and Kelly, E. (2020) Thug life: Drill music as a periscope into urban violence in the consumer age. *British Journal of Criminology*, 60: 1201–1219.

McRobbie, A. (1994) Different, youthful, subjectivities. In *Postmodernism and Popular Culture*. London: Taylor & Francis, pp 172–191.

Millett, K. (1970) *Sexual Politics*. Chicago: University of Illinois Press.

Murray, C. (1990) *The Emerging British Underclass*. London: IEA Health and Welfare Unit.

Parmar, A., Earle, R. and Phillips, C. (2022) Seeing is believing: How the layering of race is obscured by 'white epistemologies' in the criminal justice field. *Journal of Criminal Justice Education*, 33(2): 289–306.

Pease, B. (2019) *Facing Patriarchy: From a Violence Gender Order to a Culture of Peace*. London: Zed Books.

Phillips, C., Earle, R., Parmar, A. and Smith, D. (2019) Dear British criminology: Where has all the race and racism gone? *Theoretical Criminology*, 24(3): 427–446.

Pitts, J. (2008) *Reluctant Gangsters: The Changing Face of Youth Crime*. Cullompton: Willan Publishing.

Powell, A. (2011) Generation Y: Problematic representations of youth and sex. In *Sex, Power and Consent: Youth Culture and the Unwritten Rules*. Melbourne: Cambridge University Press, pp 10–28.

Richardson, F.C. and Woolfolk, R.L. (2013) Subjectivity and strong relationality. In R.W. Tafarodi (ed) *Subjectivity in the Twenty-First Century: Psychological, Sociological, and Political Perspectives*. Cambridge: Cambridge University Press, pp 9–40.

Rose, D. (2012, September) Inside Britain's terror cells: A chilling insight into how gangs of convicted terrorists recruit prisoners for Al Qaeda – and the courageous men and women sent in to 'turn' them. *The Mail on Sunday*. Available at: https://www.dailymail.co.uk/news/article-2210437/Britains-terror-cells-A-chilling-insight-gangs-convicted-terrorists-recruit-prisoners-Al-Qaeda.html

Sacks, J. (2002) *The Dignity of Difference: How to Avoid the Clash of Civilizations*. New York: Continuum.

Savage, J. (1991) *England's Dreaming: Sex Pistols and Punk Rock*. London: Faber & Faber.

Savage, J. (2008) *Teenage: The Creation of Youth 1875–1945*. London: Pimlico.

Shute, J. and Medina, J. (2014) Hunting gruffalo: 'Gangs', unreason and the big bad coalition: Jon Shute and Juanjo Medina point to the rhetoric and inaccuracies behind recent policy responses. *Criminal Justice Matters*, 96(1): 26–27.

Shute, J., Aldridge, J. and Medina, J. (2012) Loading the policy blunderbuss. *Criminal Justice Matters*, 87(1): 40–41.

Smithson, H., Ralphs, R. and Williams, P. (2013) Used and abused: The problematic usage of gang terminology in the United Kingdom and its implications for ethnic minority youth. *The British Journal of Criminology*, 53(1): 113–128.

Stanley Hall, G. (1904) *Adolescence: Its Psychology and its Relations to Physiology, Anthropology, Sociology, Sex, Crime, Religion and Education*. New York: D Appleton & Company.

Stelfox, P. (1998) Policing lower levels of organised crime in England and Wales. *The Howard Journal*, 37(4): 393–406.

Stokes, M. (1997) Voices and places: History, repetition and the musical imagination. *Journal of the Royal Anthropological Institute*, 3(4): 673–691.

Townsend, M. (2006, September). Teens and guns: Britain's deadly new menace. *The Observer*. Available at: https://www.theguardian.com/society/2006/sep/03/youthjustice.gunviolence

Williams, P. (2015) Criminalising the other: Challenging the race-gang nexus. *Race and Class*, 56(3): 18–35.

Williams, P. (2018) *Being Matrixed: The (Over) Policing of Gang Suspects in London*. London: StopWatch.

Williams, P. and Clarke, B. (2016) *Dangerous Associations: Joint Enterprise, Gangs and Racism: An Analysis of the Processes of Criminalisation of Black, Asian and Minority Ethnic Individuals*. London: Centre for Crime and Justice Studies. Available at: https://www.bl.uk/collection-items/dangerous-associations-joint-enterprise-gangs-and-racism

Wood, J. (2006) Gang activity in English prisons: The prisoners' perspectives. *Psychology Crime and Law*, 7: 605–617.

Wood, J. and Adler, J. (2001) Gang activity in English prisons: The staff perspective. *Psychology, Crime and Law*, 7(2): 167–192.

Young, J. (1971) The role of the police as amplifiers of deviance. In S. Cohen (ed) *Images of Deviance*. Harmondsworth: Penguin.

Index

References to endnotes show both the page
number and the note number (231n3).

A

academia xiii, 184, 194
　attitudes to on-road researchers 172, 173, 174, 184
　carwash sociologists 171–172
　citation practices xi–xii
adultification ix, 139, 193
adverse childhood experiences 6, 142, 149
　see also child sexual abuse
African American street-oriented community 42
agape 43
Albania, translocal on-road hustle 13–14, 134–154
　adverse childhood experiences 142, 149
　attitudes to women and girls 144
　besa 145, 146
　code of the street 144–146, 148–149
　external negative perceptions of 141, 142
　gendered solidarity 135, 143–144
　haram 144
　kanun 145, 146
　marginalisation experiences 136, 142, 149
　methodology 140–141
　neighbourhood solidarity 141–142
　patriarchy 135
　poverty 136
　rap and gangs 136–138
　rurban migrants 135
　violence 143–144, 146
　youth migration 5, 138–140, 144, 147, 148
　　moral panics and myth construction 136–138
　　stereotyping 138, 145, 148
　　'taking the road' 147, 148
　　UK government discourse on 138–139
Anderson, E. xi, 11, 42, 59, 65, 88, 142, 145, 149, 158, 166
Appadurai, A. 135
Aristotle 62, 63
Ashcraft, C. 156

Asian youths 15
associates, friends and 70–72
authenticity 128–130, 131

B

'bad' boys 48, 142, 143–144
'bad character' 107–108
Bada$$, Joey 122
'badness' 43, 65, 66, 71, 77n3, 77n4, 93
Baier, A. 44
Bakkali, Y. 6, 11, 40, 42, 43, 45, 47, 50, 53, 65, 101, 192
Batsleer, J. 157
Baudrillard, J. 190
BBC Radio 4 139
Becker, H. 27, 173
Beier, A. 8
Bergner, G. 47
Bernard, C. viii, ix, x, xi, 23, 24, 26
Bernard, J. 111
besa 145, 146
Billingham, L. 6, 115, 127, 138, 190, 193
Black Atlantic 119, 120
Black feminism 21, 81, 83, 84
Black masculinities 84, 117–118, 127–128, 178
Black women
　academic citations xii
　oppression of 84
　vulnerability of young 23–24, 25, 29, 34, 52–53
Black young women on-road
　contemporary positioning 23–26
　hypervisibility paradox 23, 34
　interpersonal violence 25–26
　intersections of historic gendered, racial marginality 21, 26–29, 34
　over-policed and under-protected 25, 28, 33
　paucity of research on 24, 34
　race and gender in interwar British youth penal reform 22, 30–33

racialised, gendered exclusion 21, 29–30, 32
underclass status 28
blood feuding 146
Blue Story 3, 158
Blunkett, D. 191
Bourdieu, P. 158
Bourgois, P. 11, 42
Boyle, K. 85
boys, sexual exploitation of 90–91
British Society of Criminology 196
Burt, C. 31

C

capitalism 7, 20, 41
carceral state
  encroachment of 117–119
  music and 116, 119–123
Carlile, A. viii, x, 23, 24, 26
carwash sociologists vs. on-road researchers 171–172
Centre for Social Justice 3
Chesney-Lind, M. xi, xii
child sexual abuse 89–90
  sexual exploitation of boys 90–91
Cicero, M.T. 62, 63
citation practices xi–xii
code of the street 65, 88, 144–146, 148–149
Cohen, S. 22, 25, 27, 28, 136, 191
Connell, R.W. 8, 43, 82, 84, 85, 90, 135, 136
correctionalism 24–25
'county lines' 4, 116, 139–140, 192
COVID-19 pandemic xii
Crenshaw, K. xi, 4, 21, 23, 26, 27, 34, 81, 83, 188
Crewe, B. 124, 192
crime
  act of resistance against narratives of criminality 187–188
  attributed to 'underclass' 191
  delinquency, credible friendships and 59–61, 65, 66
  racialisation of punishment and 24–25
  retrieving a sense of 'mattering' through 15, 127
  stereotypical connections between Black youth and 41, 108–109, 110
  'urban bias' 100–101
Criminal Justice Act 2003 107
criminal justice system
  adultification in 139
  CPS guidelines 104, 106, 108, 110
  and criminalisation of road culture 101–103, 109–111
  drill music as 'evidence' in 101, 102, 103–109, 128, 189, 192
  'gang talk' in 192
  overrepresentation of Black people in 116, 118
  punitive approach 4, 116, 117, 176, 177

racial bias in 108–109
references to gangs 3–4
critical race theory (CRT) 21, 27, 28–29
Crown Prosecution Service (CPS) 104, 106, 108, 110
cultural capital 158

D

Dave 3
Davis, J. 5, 139, 192–193
De Sousa, R. 43, 44
Delgado, R. xi
Dennis, A.L. 103, 104, 108, 109, 110
desire
  fixity, heterosexist eroticism and 46–51, 55
  racialisation in relationship to 41–42
  risks taken in pursuit of love and 45, 49, 50
discipline and punishment 29–30, 31
disequilibrium 30, 33
double consciousness 176
drill music 121
  see also UK drill music
drug dealing 4, 87, 121, 162
  Albanian gangs 136
  county lines 4, 116, 139–140, 192
  'trappers' 118, 129–130
Du Bois, W.E.B. 176, 194

E

Earle, R. 1, 41, 42, 141, 194
Easton, M. 139
Eddo-Lodge, R. 83
'End Times' 7
Ending Gang and Youth Violence initiative 191
entrapment 115, 117–119, 120, 131
eros 43–44
eugenics 32–33
Eugenics Review 22
evidence
  CPS guidelines 104, 106, 108, 110
  drill music as 'evidence' of criminal wrongdoing 101, 102, 103–109, 128, 192
exclusion 4
  government policy in response to entrenched social 25
  interwar youth penal reform and 32–33
  music and resisting 116
  racialised, gendered 21, 29–30, 32
  as spatial confinement 118
  of those with insecure immigration status 5
  using violence to overcome 7, 26

F

families
  adverse childhood experiences 6, 142, 149
  fracturing of Albanian 142, 147, 148, 149
  histories of sexual violence 92–94
  normative discourse of nuclear 157

INDEX

prison and displacement of 121, 122
relationships with families of sexual partners 88–89
on-road 51–52, 54
role in irregular migration 147
fatherhood 94, 157, 179
fathers
  absent 143, 157, 163, 165
  violent 92, 93
Fatsis, L. 12, 100, 101, 102, 103, 105, 106, 108, 109, 110, 111, 116, 121, 122, 192
faux friendships 73–75, 76
feminism
  Black 21, 81, 83, 84
  failures of White 83–84
  personal is political 81, 187–188
  'turn to culture' 187
feminist praxis xii–xiii, 190
Firestone, S. 44, 51, 52
Fletcher Report (1930) 10, 22–23, 30–31, 32
forensic linguists 109
Foucault, M. 29
Freire, P. 173
Freud, S. 44
friendships 59–67, 188
  delinquency, crime and credible 59–61, 65, 66
  of pleasure and utility 62–64
  understanding 62
  of virtue 62
friendships, on-road 11, 61, 64–67
  biblical references 68, 69
  data collection and analysis 67–68
  faux friendships 73–75, 76
  friends and associates 70–72
  imprisonment and end of friendships 75
  loyalty 72–73, 76
  methodology 67
  participants 67
  reflecting on misplaced loyalties 73–75
  researching 67–77
  'street love' 66, 69, 75
  supporting friends in need 69
  utility friendships 71–72, 75
  virtuous and good friendships 66, 68–69, 71, 76
Fromm, E. 44

G

Galton, F. 32
gangs 3–4
  Albanian 5, 136–138
  assumption of link between drill music and membership of 106, 107, 109
  contrasting past and present 86
  CPS charging guidance on gang-related offences 106
  a critical view of gang violence 191–192
  databases 192
  exploitation of women 43
  'gang talk' 192
  gay 82
  government initiatives to eliminate violence 6, 191–192
  media portrayals 136–137, 191
  mentoring interventions 157
  moral panics and myth constructions 136–138
  peer distinction between being on-road and in 86
  Policing and Crime Act 2009 definition 107
  sexual violence perpetrated in 82–83
  stereotypes 83
  violence 60, 94, 191–192
    in prison 123
gangsta rap 120–121
  see also UK drill music
Garland, J. 186, 187
Garner-Perkis, Z. 137
'Gate keeper' (Glynn) 180–184
gay gangs 82
Geertz, C. 140, 187
gender
  intersections of race, class and 81–82, 95
  intersections of race, youth and 21, 23, 26–29, 33–34
  and race in interwar penal reform 22, 30–33
  racialised, gendered exclusion 21, 29–30, 32
  road life, patriarchy and 42–43
  trauma 95–96
gendered solidarity 135, 143–144
gendered violence 25–26
  on-road 43, 52–54, 55
gentrification 115, 118
geography
  and likelihood of imprisonment 117, 118, 121
  neighbourhood solidarity 141–142
  in prison 123–124, 127
  significance in Black expressive culture 116, 120
Gibran, K. 39, 196
Gilroy, P. 5, 41, 103, 119
global regime, new 7
Glynn, M. 41, 42, 171, 180–184, 194
Grandmaster Flash 120
grime 4, 119, 120, 137
The Guardian 105
Gunter, A. 2, 3, 6, 41, 43, 45, 64, 71, 93, 101, 158, 187

H

Hall, S. 24, 25, 41, 42, 83, 159
Hallsworth, S. 1, 4, 5, 20, 24, 41, 42, 60, 61, 64, 66, 101, 187, 191, 192
Hamdi, H.A. 66, 69, 75
Han, C.S. 88
haram 144

203

Harré, R. 159
Harris, P. viii, 157, 158
Headie One 122
hegemonic masculinity 65, 82, 90, 136
  heterosexism and 82
  male teachers performing 156
  rape and 85
  on-road masculinities and 142
  as sites of failure 42
  young women on-road adopting 43
Hellbanianz 136, 137
heteronormative
  identities 43
  space, on-road 76, 87–89
heterosexism 82
heterosexist-eroticism 40, 48, 55
hip-hop culture 117–118, 120
  media focus on 137
  see also grime; rap music; rap music as a site of carceral convergence; 'rap on trial'; UK drill music
historical antecedents of being on-road 10, 20–38
  intersections of gendered, racial marginality 26–29
  methodology 22–23
  race and gender in interwar youth penal reform 30–33
  racialised, gendered exclusion 21, 29–30, 32
  racialised young women's contemporary experiences 22, 23–26
homophobia 88
homosexuality, Black 88
Honneth, A. 20, 24
'hood rich' lifestyles 48–49
hooks, b. 40, 41, 44–45, 47, 48, 82, 188
Hulley, S. 67, 73, 74, 192
hyperincarceration 117, 120, 121
hypermasculinity
  male body and 117
  male teachers 156
  on-road 40, 42, 118, 126, 159
hypervisibility 3
  paradox 23, 34

I

identity
  ascribed 159–160
  formation 158–159, 160, 165, 167–168
Ilan, J. 2, 3, 4, 41, 102, 105, 108, 115, 116, 120, 125, 128, 129, 192
immigration status, insecure 5, 139
institutional racism viii, 111
intersectionality 4–5, 188
  blind spots 83–84
  of gender, race and class 81–82, 95
  of historic, gendered racial marginality for Black young women 21, 26–29, 33–34

  of interwar penal reform 30–33
intimate relationships, on-road *see* tainted love
Irwin-Rogers, K. 6, 115, 126, 127, 138, 190, 193

J

Jade LB 53–54
Jamaican Patois 2
Jefferson, T. 90, 158
Joey Bada$$ 122
joint enterprise 77n6, 111, 192
Jones, N. 21, 24, 25, 26

K

kanun 145, 146
Keisha the Sket (Jade LB) 53–54
knife crime 60, 157, 191

L

Lamb, M. vi, 101, 111
Lammy, D. 157
law and order as a social service 23, 24, 25, 28
Levell, J. 1, 6, 9, 11, 26, 65, 82, 83, 85, 126, 134, 136, 140, 142, 143, 149
Liebow, E. 42
limerence 43–44
love
  'street love' 66, 69, 75
  theorising 43–45, 188, 196
  see also tainted love
loyalty on-road 72–73, 76, 126, 127, 177
  reflecting on misplaced 73–75

M

male teachers as role models 156, 162
male victimisation 84–85, 95
  blind spot 90–91
  gender trauma 95–96
  sexual exploitation of boys 7, 90–91
Marsh, N. 5, 139
masculine pride 143–144
masculinities
  articulating masculinities through violence 65, 144, 146, 176, 177, 178
  Black 84, 117–118, 127–128, 178
  caring 94
  hierarchy of 82, 84–85, 95, 135–136
  outlaw 49
  patriarchy and 7–8
  prison 127, 128
  protest 82, 90, 136
  on-road 42, 48, 49, 65, 88, 142, 146, 158, 176, 178
  role models and modelling of 163, 165–166, 168
  virile 88
women's valuing of provider 48–49

INDEX

see also hegemonic masculinity; hypermasculinity
Maslow, A. 91
McGuffey, C.S. 95
McRobbie, A. 187
Medina, J. 191, 192
Mele Mel 120
mentality, on-road 66, 87, 130, 144
mentoring 157
  see also role models and roadmen
Mercer, K. 47
Merton, R. 20, 22, 27, 28, 30
'The Message' (Grandmaster Flash) 120
#MeToo movement 83–84
  male victims and 85, 95
migrants
  Albanian youth 5, 138–140, 144, 147, 148
    moral panics and myth construction 136–138
    stereotyping 138, 145, 148
    UK government discourse on 138–139
    undocumented child 5, 139
Miller, E. 21, 22, 23, 25, 31, 32, 196
Millet, K. 12, 81, 187
mixed-race
  identity 92–93
  racist attitudes to people of 32
mobility 8
Modern Slavery Act 2015 139–140
moral panics 27, 28, 136–137, 191–192
'munpain' 6, 50
music 3, 4, 189, 190, 194–195
  see also grime; rap music; rap music as a site of carceral convergence; 'rap on trial'; UK drill music
music elicitation 13, 14, 85–86, 134, 140–141

N

Nas 121–122
Ness, C.D. 25, 26
New York Senate State Bill S7527 110
Newham, North London 118
Nietzsche, F. 63, 64

O

O'Doherty, D. 137
on-road 1–6
  Albania, translocal on-road hustle 13–14, 134–154
  defining 1–2, 5, 20, 64–65
  families 51–52, 54
  friendships 11, 61, 64–67, 67–77
  gangs and groups 3–4
  heteronormative space 76, 87–89
  historical antecedents of being 10, 20–38
  hypermasculinity 40, 42, 118, 126, 159
  intimate relationships and gendered violence 10–11, 39–58, 196
  masculinities 42, 48, 49, 65, 88, 142, 146, 158, 176, 178
  mentality 66, 87, 130, 144
  mundane struggles of life 5–6
  parallels between medieval and contemporary 8
  patriarchy, gender and life on 42–43
  peer distinction between gang membership and 86
  rap music as a continuum between prison and 13, 115–133
  sexual politics 11–12, 65, 81–99
  street social capital 53, 65, 125, 158, 168
  subculture incorporated into mainstream culture 3
  see also road culture; women on-road
on-road researchers 14–15, 171–185, 189–190, 194
  accountability to community 172–173
  Blackness 173–174
  breaking the fourth wall 180–184
  vs. carwash sociologists 171–172
  case example 174–180
  marginalisation in academia 172, 173, 174, 184
  and need for change 184–185
  role as 173–174
The One (Headie One) 122
'One Love' (Nas) 121–122
Onwubolu, A. 3

P

Pahl, R.E. 62, 70
Palmer, L. 45
Panfil, V.R. 82
patriarchy 7–8, 189
  in Albania 135
  love in context of 44, 47
  reproduction of 157, 160, 166
  values on street 42–43, 51–52, 53–54
Payne, Y.A. 66, 69, 75
Pearson, G. 60, 100, 137
Pease, B. 189
penal reform, early youth 10, 22, 30–33
philia 43
Phillips, A. 142
Phillips, C. 22, 83, 103, 109, 127, 194
'Piece of Mind' (Joey Bada$$) 122
police
  as rap music experts for prosecution 109
  roadmen and struggles with 40, 46, 47
  stereotyping of Black youth 41
policing
  of disadvantage 25, 26, 28, 29, 116, 118
  gangsta rap as a response to 120–121
  over- 4, 24, 25, 28, 33
  of road culture 101, 102
  of young Black men 116, 118, 119, 122
Policing and Crime Act 2009 107

policy
  correctionalism 24–25
  focusing on gangs and violence 6, 191–192
  interwar youth penal reform 10, 22, 30–33
  law and order as a social service 23, 24, 25, 28
  on role models and roadmen 155–158, 167–168
  shift from welfarist to punitive 117, 122, 176
  of surveillance and penalty 24, 25, 26, 29–30, 73, 192
  towards most vulnerable and marginalised in society 24, 115–116
  weaknesses with regard to young Black men 178, 179, 180
positioning theory 159
  and psychosocial theory 158–161, 168
  role model and roadman case study through lens of 164–167
prison
  in Black Atlantic cultures 120
  geography and likelihood of going to 117, 118, 121
  listening to radio shows 125
  masculinities 127, 128
  outside friendships that continue 75
  overrepresentation of Black people in 4, 116, 118
  rap music as a site of carceral convergence 13, 115–133
    authenticity 128–130, 131
    entrapment 117–119
    music and carceral state 119–123
    urban geography and rap in prison 123–128
  references in UK drill music 116, 121, 122
  'reputational networks' 124–125
  systems of status 124–125, 126
  in US 117, 121
prison freestyle 122
'prison letters' 121–122
The Prophet (Gibran) 39
protection strategies, personal 90
protest masculinity 82, 90, 136
Psychodrama (Dave) 3
psychosocial and positioning theory 158–161, 168
  role model and roadman case study through lens of 164–167
punishment
  discipline and 29–30, 31
  racialisation of 24–25

Q
Quinn, K. 88

R
race
  and gender in interwar penal reform 22, 30–33
  intersections of class, gender and 81–82, 95

intersections of youth, gender and 21, 23, 26–29, 33–34
racial ambiguity and road culture 41–42
racial bias in criminal justice process 108–109
racism viii–ix, 4, 121, 183–184
  collective consciousness of 41
  in criminalisation of road culture 102, 110–111
  institutional viii, 111
  internalised 188
  of interwar reform efforts 32–33
  as a material phenomenon 95
  structural 42, 83
  White feminism and 83–84
racist stereotypes 4, 102, 103, 107
  of Albanians 138, 145, 148
radio shows, listening to 125
rap music
  Albanian gangs and 136–138
  'bad boy' content 48
  gangsta rap 120–121
  geographical references 120
  moral panics 136–137
  'positive' 130
  prison as a theme 116, 121, 122
  significance 120
  see also UK drill music
rap music as a site of carceral convergence 13, 115–133
  authenticity 128–130, 131
  entrapment 117–119
  music and carceral state 119–123
  urban geography and rap in prison 123–128
'rap on trial' 104–105
  and criminalisation of road culture 110–111
  expertise in court 108–109
  nature of lyrics and videos 105
  procedural injustice in handling of 'evidence' 106–108
  in US 110
rape
  family histories of 92–94
  male victims of 85
  within marriage 93
rehabilitation account of youth justice 31
Reid, E. 41, 67, 115, 118, 119, 123, 126, 130, 131
relational ontology 188
relationality 188, 190
'reputational networks' 124–125
researchers, on-road *see* on-road researchers
respectable fears 100, 137
Rich, J. 171–172
'road capital' 53, 65, 125, 158, 168
road culture 41, 87, 101
  code of the street 65, 88, 144–146, 148–149
  criminalisation of 101–103, 109–111
  moral code 76

INDEX

music and convergence of prison and 116–117, 119–123, 125
racial ambiguity and 41–42
significance to mainstream culture 3
road rap *see* UK drill music
roadmen 2–3, 158
racial stereotypes of 41
and role models *see* role models and roadmen
similarities with medieval men on edge of society 8
role models and roadmen 14, 155–169
case study 161–164
analysis 164–167
maximising transformative potential 167–168
policy and positioning 155–158
roadmen 158
role models 155–157
psychosocial and positioning theory 158–161, 168
rurbanity 135

S

Savage, J. 195
Schwander-Sievers, S. 137, 138, 145, 148
Sernhede, O. 41
Sevier, B. 156
sexual politics, on-road 11–12, 65, 81–99
child sexual abuse 89–90
gender trauma 95–96
heritage of sexual violence 92–94
heteronormative space 87–89
intersectional blind spots 83–84
methodology 85–86
on-road space, place and mentality 86–87
sexual exploitation of boys 90–91
sexual prowess and gang stereotypes 82–83
sexual victimisation as anti-masculine 84–85
sexual risk behaviours 88
sexual violence 53–54, 82–83
family histories of 92–94
gender trauma and 95–96
intersectional blind spots 83–84
#MeToo movement and 83–84, 85, 95
Shabazz, R. 116, 117, 118, 120, 123, 127
Shepard, A. 8
Shute, J. 191, 192
Silverstone, D. 20, 41, 42, 101, 192
Small, L. 62, 65, 66, 73
social capital, street 53, 65, 125, 158, 168
space of street 20, 86–87, 100–101, 115
patriarchal 42–43, 51–52, 53–54
a social space 64–65
unsafe for young women 43
Spencer, L. 70
storge 43
Stormzy 3, 130
strain theory 27, 28

street culture 41, 87, 101, 121
see also road culture
'street love' 66, 69, 75
street performativity 40, 48, 50
street social capital 53, 65, 125, 158, 168
'street supernovae' 40, 50
structural violence 6, 40, 45, 54, 191
subjectivity 158–159, 187, 188, 189
surveillance
continuity between ghetto and prison 117
of girls' lives 26
policy of 24, 25, 26, 29–30, 73, 192
'symbolic locations' 100–101

T

Tack, A.M.C. 62, 65, 66, 73
tainted love 10–11, 39–58, 196
attractions of dating men on-road 48–49
defining 39–40, 45
ephemeral nature of life at margins 46–47, 50
fixity, desire and hetrosexist-eroticism 46–51, 55
and hope for future 55, 196
implosion and gendered violence 43, 51–54, 55
men's need for love, compassion and care 50–51
methodology 45–46
risks taken in pursuit of love and desire 45, 49, 50
road and racial ambiguity 41–42
road life, patriarchy and gender 42–43
roadmen's views of women on-road 46–47, 47–48, 50
'street supernovae' 40, 50
theorising love 43–45
television dramas 3, 158
Thatcher, M. 23, 24, 25, 29
translocal on-road hustle *see* Albania, translocal on-road hustle
translocality 135
'trap' (drug economies) 118, 121
Trap music 121
'trappers' 119, 129–130
Trickett, L. 9, 11, 25, 43
trust 69, 72, 76, 177–178

U

Ugoala, O. 84
UK drill music 12, 100–114
assumption of link between gang membership and 106, 107, 109
authenticity 128–130, 131
commercial aspects 103, 105
criminalisation of 101–103, 109–111, 116, 122
defining 103–104

as 'evidence' of criminal wrongdoing 101, 102, 103–109, 128, 192
  artistic nature of lyrics and videos 105, 108, 109, 111
  lack of rap expertise in court 108–109
  legal guidance on use as evidence in court 106
  procedural injustice 106–108
geographic references in 116, 120
as 'negative' 121, 130
prison as a theme 116, 121, 122
racist attitudes to 110–111
'self-snitching' 128
spatialising 101
violence as a theme 103, 105, 127, 130
underclass 28, 29, 191
undocumented children in UK 5, 139
United States (US)
  imprisonment 117
  New York prison inmates 121
  origins of gangsta rap 120–121
  'rap on trial' 110
utility, friendships of 62–64, 71–72, 75

V

verstehen 68
vertigo thesis 28, 30, 33
victimisation, male 84–85, 95
  sexual exploitation of boys 7, 90–91
violence
  Albanian translocal street life 143–144, 146
  articulating masculinity through 65, 144, 146, 176, 177, 178
  blood feuding 146
  a critical view of youth 191–192
  gang-related 60, 94, 191–192
  gendered 25–26, 43, 52–54, 55
  girls' experiences of interpersonal 25–26
  government initiatives to end gang and youth 6, 191–192
  loyalty and 72–73, 76, 126, 127, 177
  to overcome exclusion and alienation 7, 26
  in prison 123
  to protect masculine pride 143–144
  a reaction to feelings of vulnerability 143–144
  to retrieve a sense of 'mattering' 6, 115, 127
  structural 6, 40, 45, 54, 191
  a theme of UK drill music 103, 105, 127, 130
  see also sexual violence
virtue, friendships of 62, 66, 68, 69, 71, 76

vulnerability
  adverse childhood experiences and 6, 90, 91, 142, 149
  male identity formation and 158–159, 160, 165, 167–168
  men's need for compassion and care 50–51
  violence as a reaction to 143–144
  of young Black women 23–24, 25, 29, 34, 52–53

W

Wacquant, L. 115, 117, 119, 120, 121, 123
Waller, C. 116, 123
wealth 7, 28
White, J. 115, 116, 118, 119, 120
Whiteness, politics of 83, 137
Wilson, A. 179
women on-road 9
  adopting hegemonic masculinity 43
  attractions of dating men on-road 48–49
  capacity to care 51, 52
  contemporary positioning 23–26
  heteronormative identities 43, 47
  hypervisibility paradox 23, 34
  interpersonal violence 25–26
  intersections of historic gendered, racial marginality 21, 26–29, 34
  Jeta e Rrugës attitudes to 144
  over-policed and under-protected 25, 28, 33
  paucity of research on 24, 34
  race and gender in interwar British youth penal reform 22, 30–33
  racialised, gendered exclusion 21, 29–30, 32
  roadmen's views of intimate relationships with 46–47, 47–48, 50
  safety 43
  underclass status 28
  violence towards 43, 52–54, 55
words, appropriation and invention of 2

Y

Young, T. 1, 4, 5, 9, 11, 20, 21, 22, 24, 25, 30, 43, 60, 61, 64, 65, 66, 67, 73, 187, 191, 192
youth
  concept of 186–187
  excesses of 8
  intersections of gender, race and 21, 23, 26–29, 33–34
  penal reform, interwar 10, 22, 30–33
  representing future 6–7
youth workers, male *see* role models and roadmen

www.ingramcontent.com/pod-product-compliance
Lightning Source LLC
Chambersburg PA
CBHW051541020426
42333CB00016B/2044